Essex Within Living Memory

Compiled by the Federation of
Essex Women's Institutes from notes sent by
Institutes in the County

First Published 1995

COUNTRYSIDE BOOKS
3 Catherine Road
Newbury, Berkshire

ISBN 1 85306 337 1

The cover photograph shows a day out at Clacton in 1905,
supplied by Berechurch WI

Designed by Mon Mohan
Produced through MRM Associates Ltd., Reading
Typeset by Paragon Typesetters, Queensferry, Clwyd
Printed by J.W. Arrowsmith Ltd., Bristol

Contents

Foreword

Few counties can have changed more than Essex since 1900. Great areas have become urbanised, and the industry and commerce of the twentieth century are evident side by side with the enduring rural and agricultural heritage. This book is the witness of those who remember the county between 1900 and 1960. They share with us their memories of 'how it was' from the days of Queen Victoria, through two great wars, good times and bad, storms and sunshine. Not an historian's history, it is the story of ordinary lives. I hope you will enjoy it.

Dwin Hendry
Federation Chairman

Acknowledgements

The Federation of Essex Women's Institutes sincerely thanks all those members and friends, men and women, who have contributed with such obvious enjoyment their personal recollections. They regret that through lack of space it has not been possible to reproduce in full all the contributions that have been received.

They would also like to thank Sheila Gunson of Tolleshunt Knights WI for her map of the county; Joan Bill for her charming illustrations; and Ken Neale of the Sampfords Society for permission to print an article from the Sampford Notes.

And finally a special word of thanks to all those members who diligently typed the hand-written entries.

Introduction

Essex, although so close to London, is one of England's less well known counties. It has no high hills to attract the tourist, no rolling moorlands, no spectacular coastline. But it is not without natural advantages; the heavy Essex clay has always supported a prosperous agriculture and, with its deeply indented shore, it has a long history of close connections with the Continent. Indeed, when London was little more than a riverside village, Colchester was a capital city minting its own coinage and importing wine from abroad.

The period covered by this book saw sweeping changes in every part of the county. In the west, the growth of London meant a rapid development throughout the suburban fringe, so much so that in 1965 a large slice of Essex was amputated to form part of the newly-created Greater London Council. Recollections from these districts are included in this book, for when the events recorded took place, the scene of action was still part of Essex. Towards the south of the county, there was a steady growth of industry along the banks of the Thames, for example at Dagenham, Thurrock and Tilbury. But these developments left much, indeed most, of the county pretty well untouched until the 1939-45 war. In rural Essex, away from the western and southern fringes, the pace of change was slow, and modern times often seemed far away in the many quiet, old-fashioned villages – the 'sweet, uneventful countryside' of Betjeman's poem.

All this and more, the changing face of life in Essex over the first 60 years of this century, is told in this book, in the words of those who lived through the changes. The contributors come from all parts of the county. The majority of them are women, but many men have also helped to make the book what it is, and indeed the tale would not be complete without their side of the story. Looking back to this period has proved an exercise of immeasurable value in that it has opened the floodgates of memories hitherto locked away and almost forgotten – with sighs going up from time to time from older residents for the good old days. Perhaps it has made us all a little more aware that we need to relive our past in order to understand our present a little better and also to help us accept the future as it unfolds.

Margaret Gracey
Co-ordinator

THE COUNTY OF ESSEX

ESSEX

'The vagrant visitor erstwhile,'
  My colour-plate book says to me,
'Could wend by hedgrow-side and stile,
  From Benfleet down to Leigh-on-Sea.'

And as I turn the colour-plates
  Edwardian Essex opens wide,
Mirrored in ponds and seen through gates,
  Sweet uneventful countryside.

Like streams the little by-roads run
  Through oats and barley round a hill
To where blue willows catch the sun
  By some white weather-boarded mill.

'A Summer Idyll Matching Tye'
  'At Havering-atte-Bower, the Stocks'
And cobbled pathways lead the eye
  To cottage doors and hollyhocks.

Far Essex, – fifty miles away
  The level wastes of sucking mud
Where distant barges high with hay
  Come sailing in upon the flood.

Near Essex of the River Lea
  And anglers out with hook and worm
And Epping Forest glades where we
  Had beanfeasts with my father's firm.

At huge and convoluted pubs
  They used to set us down from brakes
In that half-land of football clubs
  Which London near the Forest makes.

The deepest Essex few explore
  Where steepest thatch is sunk in flowers
And out of elm and sycamore
  Rise flinty fifteenth-century towers.

I see the little branch line go
  By white farms roofed in red and brown,
The old Great Eastern winding slow
  To some forgotten country town.

Now yarrow chokes the railway track,
  Brambles obliterate the stile,
No motor coach can take me back
  To that Edwardian 'erstwhile'.

John Betjeman

TOWN & COUNTRY LIFE

SOME TOWNS AND VILLAGES REMEMBERED

Lamplighters on the streets at dusk, the sound of the blacksmith's hammer ringing out, horse-drawn fire engines and roads which had hardly seen a car – not so long ago and well within living memory in Essex. Here are just a few memories of times past in our towns and villages, and of characters and events that made their mark on our lives.

'DOWN THE NORTH' AT COLCHESTER

'I was born in 1921 and have lived in Colchester all my life. My childhood was spent "down the North". Our front door was in Northgate Street, and the back door and garden opened on to St Peter Street, with an alleyway between the two streets on one side of our house. This alleyway led on to West Stockwell Street. I think the area was called "down" the North because we were at the bottom of four hills, North Hill, West Stockwell Street, East Stockwell Street, and Maidenburgh Street – all of which led up to Colchester High Street. At the top of West Stockwell Street was the town hall, a tall impressive building which housed the law courts and police station. The public library was next to it in West Stockwell Street.

Although we were living so near to the town centre, the set up in our neighbourhood was more like a village. We had our hierarchy – our traders, our engineering firm, Trusloves, our medium stratum of society as we knew it, and our very poor, who lived at the bottom end of the street in hovels, one up, one down, with a communal lavatory and washhouse.

Life seemed very peaceful and unchanging. We started school at the age of four. The street (St Peter Street) was our playground. We had our seasons for different games like hopscotch, whip and top, skipping and ball games; sevensy was one of these played up against the outside wall of somebody's house. Cars were almost unheard of on our street. Deliveries were made by horse and cart, milk and bread daily, coal once a week. Rubbish was collected by dustmen, again with horse and cart.

Most people had the coal stored in a cupboard in the living room. It had the advantage that you did not have to go outside in the cold weather to get in the coal. We had our own coal yard in Northgate

Street belonging to Hardwicke the coal merchant. He kept his own stables there, and one of my earliest memories is of waking up in the night and hearing the clip-clop of hooves as one of the horses was walked round the two streets – sometimes for hours on end – to get rid of an attack of colic. If the horse had been allowed to lie down it could have died.

We were not well off. My mother took in "home" work, when she could get it, from one of the clothing factories, as well as coping with the family. My father had a job as tailor's presser at a clothing factory. There were five or six clothing factories in all and they were flourishing at that time. We could not afford butter, but rather than feed the family on bread and margarine we had to go to Sainsbury's in the High Street to buy their own blend called Crelos. I can remember my mother standing cutting up bread and spreading it with Crelos while we children had races to see who could eat fastest and most.

Of course, we had our fears too. There was an old man who lived alone and talked to himself. He frightened us so much that if he was on the street we would run indoors. The older children taunted him and he used to give chase. Then there was the mortuary at the eastern end of the block of two streets and opposite the lower end of the Castle Park. Anyone who died other than from natural causes was taken there, and word would get round when there was a body lying in there. We imagined that ghosts came out on certain nights to haunt us. The cattle market was at Middleboro opposite the western end, and on Saturdays – market day – it was quite common for a herd of sheep or cows to be driven along St Peter Street to the cattle market. We were not afraid of the sheep, but the cows were another matter. They would much rather have been in a field munching grass, and sometimes they were stubborn and refused to obey the orders of the herdsmen, and would run amok. The children would run indoors like lightning and the cry would go up "Mad Bull" as they invaded gardens, and we escaped to the shelter of our homes. I can still feel the sheer terror of it.

The Castle Park opposite the mortuary held the traditional skipping on Good Friday morning. There was a general holiday, and the factories were closed. Colchester being a military town, some soldiers would come, huge skipping ropes were produced, two people would turn the ropes, and five or six would run in. The fun would be endless. I suppose it was a release from winter and from work, and many a romance sprang from the Good Friday skipping. But it only took place in the morning; the rest of the day was spent in a more sober manner. It was a tradition which ended like so many other things with the onset of the Second World War. Another tradition was that of the steam trains sounding all their whistles to welcome in the New Year.

In Northgate Street there was a fishmonger's with grounds down to St Peter Street. He always had a good selection of fish. We were customers for sprats, herrings and bloaters, which he smoked in a shed in the garden. I can still smell that special aroma and the resultant bloaters cooking. Another family were in the rag and bone trade, again carried on in the backyard. We would take our accumulated rags (woollens separate as these fetched more), they were weighed, and we were paid a few pence. We also could take rabbit skins, for which we were given tuppence. The sons used to go round the district with an old horse and cart collecting rags, and an aunt of mine worked for them in their yard, sorting and bagging the rags, ready to be picked up when they had enough. There must have been money in it because it kept five or six men in full-time employment.

Adjoining the local butcher's shop and situated in St Peter Street was a slaughterhouse where the awful squeal of pigs could be heard as they were killed. At the other end of the street next door to the mortuary was a bakery. It supplied a shop in the town with freshly baked bread and cakes. For a small sum of money they would bake cakes for people round about. The housewives made the cakes and took them covered in a cloth to the bakery. The smell of the bread baking was tantalising if you were hungry. Another mouth-watering item was the meat pies baked and sold by the two Misses Rose, who ran a small teashop, catering especially for the farmers and herdsmen on market day. They also specialised in home-made chocolates, which were on display in a glass cabinet. They worked hard, but I should not think they made a fortune out of it.

Such a wealth of memories, good and bad, contained in those two streets, all my childhood. The terraced houses in Northgate Street and our row of houses are still standing, but the rest of them have been replaced by modern flats and offices. The council flats are tasteful and built in the style of the old Dutch quarter, but the character has gone. I feel privileged to have known it as it was.'

SILVER END – A UNIQUE VILLAGE

'I was born in the village of Silver End in 1932. The village is situated midway between Witham and Braintree. It is a unique village as it was built by the Crittall family in 1926 especially for their employees. The school followed in 1929.

At first it was a self contained village as the roads were privately owned and no other traders were allowed in. There was a large store and in the beginning Crittalls had their own piggeries, herd of cattle and slaughterhouse. The products of these were sold in the store.

The store sold everything and the cashier sat high up in a little office. When a purchase was made they put the money for our goods into a metal cup, screwed it into the lid and pulled a lever which sent the cup along a wire to the cash department. The change was put into the cup and sent back to the sales assistant. She looked after several departments at one time, so she was kept quite busy.

There was a local bus service under the name of Hicks in the Crittall colours of dark blue and gold. The seats were not padded like today's but were wooden benches. The return fare to Witham or Braintree was sevenpence or fourpence for a child.

The factory generated the electricity for the entire village and the rent for the flat I lived in with my parents was ten shillings in the summer and eleven shillings in the winter, the extra shilling to cover electricity used during the winter. The house was very strongly built but only the more expensive ones had plastered walls and then only in the lounge.

The village was a very pleasant place to live. Everyone knew everyone else and no one ever bothered to lock their doors. How times have changed.'

'I moved to Silver End in 1929. The bank in those days was just a wooden hut with a fried fish shop next door. One day the fat in the pan boiled over and the shop went up in flames. The fire engine then was simply a large barrel on a barrow, pushed by hand, with hose pipes.

Buses ran to Braintree from Witham every 20 minutes but everything in Silver End village belonged to Crittalls – the village shop, the pig farm which made sausages, the milk round, the bread round, everything until they sold out to the Co-op. Crittall built a large hotel and the local inn and ruled village life. You were not allowed to build a shed or even hang out washing at weekends. This continued until 1939.'

SHEERING IN THE 1920s

'The road through the Street was tarred, but the Back Lane and Church Lane were gravelled and very dusty in summer. Water was laid on, but most of us had only one tap which was outside the house. We had open fires with an oven at the side and used paraffin lamps at night in our living rooms, and a candle to go to bed. In the winter our bedrooms were freezing cold and we would take a brick which had been warmed in the oven and wrapped in a piece of flannel and put it in our beds. We children had our bath in front of the fire with water heated in the clothes copper. There was great rejoicing when gas came through the village.

There were meadows along the Street, which are now filled with houses, and there were several ponds stretching from Chambers Farm to the Cock Inn. We had great fun sliding on the ice in winter.

There was no council estate and Primley Lane really was "Primrose" Lane – just a cart track with primroses growing either side in spring and continuing as a footpath which led to Quick Wood where there were masses of blackberries in late summer. All the trees have been grubbed out now and it is a field.

Next to the Crown Inn was a blacksmith's shop. The blacksmith was Basil Hutley, who wore a goatskin apron. He would mend our iron hoops for us if they were broken, and would sometimes let the boys use his bellows when he was making horseshoes.

It was usual to play in the road as there was very little traffic. We used to bowl hoops, skip, play hopscotch and spin tops, which were kept going with a whip. Sometimes haycarts would come through on their way to London and the boys would hang on the back for a ride. One of our local haycarters was fined for falling asleep in charge of a haycart, and after that his wife would cycle up to Epping, put the cycle on the cart and drive the horse home herself.

There were three shops in the village. Polly Peacock's, my mother's and Mrs Uncle's Post Office Stores. The butcher and baker came in their carts and the milkman on his milk float. He used to measure out pints of milk from his can straight into our jug.

There were no buses, of course. You either walked or biked or hired Mr Uncle's waggonette. It was usual for the ladies to go to Bishop's Stortford on market day (Thursday) when they would walk across the fields to Quickbury Farm and down the Hatfield Heath Road to Sawbridgeworth station.

If we were ill we had to go to Harlow to Dr Tommy Day's who lived on Mulberry Green. But of course if you were really ill he would come out to see you. One of my earliest memories is walking to Harlow at the age of five with the mumps!

The front of Sheering school looks almost the same now as it did when it was built apart from the fact that the school house has been removed. There used to be a small room for infants and the rest of the children were all together in one long room heated by two fires. It was very cold in winter and we envied our schoolmaster who nearly always stood with his back to the fire.

There was quite a lot of caning, mostly of the boys. One boy, Willy Whitbread, was caned on the hand most days, but we all admired him because he would never cry. We girls were made to stand out in front of the class, or sit with our hands clasped on top of our heads. Sometimes we were made to stand on our forms and very silly we felt, too, although there was the advantage of seeing out of the window!

On Empire Day we would stand by the flag in the playground and sing patriotic songs.'

LEYTONSTONE – A QUIET SUBURB

'Before the First World War Leytonstone was a quiet Essex suburb. I lived in Church Lane from January 1909, over my uncle's shop.

At the bend in the lane was the railway station, on the old Great Eastern and then the London and North Eastern line. Waggons full of coal arrived there and were shunted into a large coalyard from where men with small carts shovelled it into sacks, loaded their carts, and carried it off to their customers. I cannot remember any motors or motor-driven vans. Horses were used. The North Pole Ice Company had mules. At the road next to the station approach there were horse-drawn cabs, with the cab drivers sitting up on their seats, ready for customers. When wet they wore large waterproof capes.

Motor cars and vans became usual after the 1914-18 war. Charabancs became *the* mode of transport for organisations' days out. All the shops were privately owned and each had its own trade. They kept to it and didn't encroach on neighbours' trades. The butcher and fishmonger had no refrigerators. The North Pole Ice Company came and the driver cut a huge block of ice, lifted it on to a sack on his shoulder and carried this into the shop.

Most of the traders, or managers, lived over their shops. The assistants at Evans and Davis, the draper's shop selling women's and children's clothes, underwear and millinery, lived in. Sometimes on summer evenings, when the windows were open, we could hear them talking and laughing.

In the main road there were tramcars and open-top buses. At the appropriate season hay could be seen on horse-drawn carts led by drivers taking their load to Stratford market.

During the summer men's outings travelled in brakes. The men would buy flowers in the country to take home to their wives and these would be hung and sway backwards and forwards in the brake. Often a man with a cornet would play standing on the steps.

At Bearmans, the biggest store, customers sat on chairs at the counter while the assistants set out their goods for the customer to see and choose.

In the Home and Colonial Stores there were large, moulded pieces of butter and lard on the counter, barrel-shaped, and the small pieces for the customer were cut off and patted into shape before wrapping. Snippets of cheese were sometimes offered to taste before buying. Tea, coffee and sugar had to be weighed and put into paper bags, blue ones I think, twisted paper made into cone-shaped bags. These were wrapped with brown paper and string into neat parcels. In other shops biscuits were loose in large tins with glass tops, and weighed out as needed. Bars of chocolate were not wrapped. Some chocolates were in boxes, but many were weighed out.

The baker called with bread. The milkman had a churn filled with

Mr Randall outside the forge at Collier Row. The blacksmith was one of the most important village craftsmen.

milk on a cart and each house had its zinc can with brass handle and bands which was filled with a dipper. Milk was delivered early morning and again later in the day (no refrigeration to keep it good and sweet in warm weather).

A man with a pole lit the gas standard lamps in the side roads in the evenings.

If families had pets these were often fed from pieces from the family meal supplemented with dog-biscuit or cats' meat. A woman used to come along with the latter in a basket – little pieces of meat on a wooden skewer for a halfpenny or penny each. Dog biscuits were sold at the cornchandler's.'

LIFE ON FOULNESS ISLAND

'I was born on Foulness Island in 1907. Foulness is a unique area of Essex situated at the extreme south-east corner of the county. It is the largest of a group of islands formed by the creeks and saltings between the estuaries of the river Crouch and the river Thames. When I was a child, bridges and roads between the islands and the mainland were non-existent. Southend was our nearest town and although not very far away by today's standards, it was a major expedition to get there.

In those days there were two ways of leaving the islands: either by sailing boat which took us along the river to Burnham on Crouch; or more usually by horse and cart along the Maplin Sands to Great Wakering. It is the latter journey that I remember as though it were yesterday.

The only way across the Maplin Sands was via "The Broomway" at low tide. This was a track across the hard sand, running parallel to the shore, marked out by bundles of broom bushes which were buried deeply in the sand leaving a portion above ground. These were only visible at low tide. These bushes had to be renewed periodically. The reserves were kept in a shed at the back of the village shop where I worked.

We always had a very healthy respect for the sea. Nonetheless it could still be treacherous at night or should the tide or a fog roll in unexpectedly. Fatalities have been known to occur in such circumstances. I well remember one such incident. A man was returning to Foulness on foot, when the fog descended. People on the land could hear him in the water, but despite shouting and firing guns the fog was so disorientating that he did not make the shore and was never seen again.

Whatever the time of the year, the tide governed our excursions. When we wanted to go shopping in Southend, we would first check the tide times then we would find out if there was a horse and cart available. It could be anybody who might be going, my uncle or even the postman. The carts could only take four passengers. We would make for the Broomway and join it by one of the six access places known as "Heads". I usually used the Fisherman's Head, which was the most distant one from Great Wakering. Our journey would be some six or seven miles at trotting pace across the sand and would take approximately one hour. I am not a good traveller now and it was no better then. The motion of the cart (no springs!) often made me travel-sick. Many is the time I have crossed the sands lying on the floor of the cart because I have felt so ill. We would join the mainland at Great Wakering. Then the horses would be stabled in the yard of the Lion public house in the High Street. This was a purpose built stable yard for the benefit of Foulness Islanders and their visitors.

After leaving the yard we would make our way on foot across the fields, either to Bournes Green to catch a tram, or to Shoebury railway station to catch the train, finally arriving at Southend.

Most of the girls on Foulness belonged to the Girls' Friendly Society. This was run by the church and was for single women. Meetings were always held in the rectory. When the girls married they were presented with a beautiful leather covered Bible. But it was never given until at least twelve months later. If a girl was pregnant at her wedding she did not get her Bible!'

The old mill on Foulness Island, which eventually became a family home and business.

'I was born in 1923 on Foulness – an island that has always been in the hands of the Government (at present the Ministry of Defence). To gain access a Government Pass has always been necessary, and permits are only issued to those who work and live there and to those who wish to visit relatives, or have business connections. There is a police box at the entrance to the island, which is manned at all times to keep a close watch! No cameras are allowed, and anyone caught taking photographs will have the film confiscated.

Farming is about the only activity, and the community these days is getting smaller as younger generations are moving away. There are only the usual village facilities – a pub, a post office and shop, and a church, visited once each Sunday by a neighbouring vicar. The small school closed several years back. This little island suffered greatly during the floods of 1953 when sadly lives of people and animals were lost.

Back in 1923 things were so different and so much happier. My grandfather and grandmother lived in what was called the Old Mill (which years before it was, complete with sails). It consisted of a five bedroom house and a general shop, and when I say "general" I mean it. One could buy everything from bacon to buttons, fancy goods to flypapers, and butter and biscuits to blotting paper! This was not all. Within the shop was a built-in telephone kiosk, complete with a hand and bracket phone, and a post office. The building also included a bakery where the islanders frequently found the huge ovens useful to cook their large weekend joints, and turkeys at Christmas. Grandfather kept pigs – he cured bacon and ham, besides making pork sausages and brawn. He also ran a coal business – you could say those living on the island depended on him for a great many things. Just as well he had three sons and two daughters to help him!

My father and mother lived in a small bungalow at the bottom of the Mill garden. Father was the baker in the family. He also did the bread deliveries, with a horse and cart – no motorised transport then, in fact no made-up roads, just cart tracks. Deliveries to the two neighbouring villages, Great and Little Wakering, were made by following tracks along the sands at low tide, and had to be done in double quick time in order to get back before the next high tide!'

SOUTHEND IN THE 1930s

'I was born and raised in Southend on Sea where my parents ran a small boarding house. In the 1930s I well remember the stream of Londoners and their families who would arrive on packed trains, eager to spend their week's summer holiday in Southend. Our visitors used to insist on having the same rooms each year, and woe betide my mother if she had not reserved them.

My childhood memories in the 1930s are of long, hot summers – it was not uncommon for some visitors who could not find accommodation, or could not afford it, to sleep out overnight on the beaches. The cost of bed and breakfast varied between 2s 6d and 3s 6d per night. The men would arrive in their Sunday best suits, usually navy serge, complete with stiff collar and tie and highly polished boots – and not forgetting the braces. They would roll their trousers up to the knees, the ladies would hitch up their dresses and the little girls would have their dresses tucked in their knickers – all to enjoy a good paddle.

Many local children would regularly take part in the weekly talent competitions (against our parents' wishes) which the concert party called "The Jolly Boys" put on daily on the beach opposite Pier Hill. Needless to say one of the locals usually won – my younger sister was particularly good at capturing the audience with her rendition of Shirley Temple singing and tap-dancing. The prizes were usually boxes of soft, sticky toffees. Another attraction was the Kursaal – in those days it was always crowded with trippers enjoying the Scenic Railway, the Water Chute, the Wall of Death, and sideshows. We could spend all day in there – residents had free passes into the Kursaal. One year the most enormous dead whale called "Mickey" was brought in, in a huge glass container, and put on display. Thousands of people filed past to view Mickey – however, after about a week the most awful stench arose. Sadly, Mickey had to be transported out of the Kursaal, which proved to be a mammoth task because of his size!

In the early 1930s the famous steam engine called the *Flying Scotsman* was on show at the station. I feel particularly privileged to have seen this magnificent train in all its glory; how the boys of today would have loved to see it.

On Sundays we would gather on the promenade opposite the Kursaal to listen to "Happy Harry" as everyone called him. He was a well known preacher who was conspicuous in winter and summer in his long black overcoat and black Homburg hat. The crowds would jeer and ridicule him, but Harry would just smile and carry on – he was one of Southend's best loved characters, and carried on preaching right up until the beginning of the war.

In 1938 Rochford aerodrome was in its infancy, and my father used to fly regularly to Kent at weekends on business, for the princely sum of 7s 6d return.

I must also mention what the locals called "Southend-on-a-Monday". This was the day in every week when coach loads of East End ladies would descend on the town in their droves – hell bent on enjoying themselves. They would don large paper bonnets, usually inscribed with slogans such as "Kiss Me Quick". At the end of a fun filled day they would return to their coaches armed with their giant sticks of Southend rock, singing at the tops of their voices and dancing to "Knees up Mother Brown".

Sadly the heart seemed to go out of Southend with the onset of the war; many foreigners who had settled in Southend and had built up thriving businesses were interned as aliens for the duration. Among them were the parents of children we had gone to school with. There was the Rossi family of ice cream fame. The happy times I spent in the basement of the Rossi house in Whitegate Road watching (and sampling) the very first batches of the famous ice cream!

In conclusion, this account would not be complete without my saddest memory of Southend, and my proudest. This was the day when local fishermen and small boat owners went over to Dunkirk to help rescue the survivors stranded on the beaches. Many lives were saved by these brave fishermen in their small craft. Some of the soldiers were brought to York Road (where we lived), and laid all along the pavements. Our house was commandeered by the police to house some of the more sick and wounded until they could be moved to hospital. All in all I am very proud of my Essex roots.'

ALDHAM VILLAGE

'Changes are so gradual that we are not really aware of them until people start to look back and recall their memories of past times. One lady's clear recollections went back almost to the beginning of the century, when she was born on Boxing Day over 90 years ago. Immediately after her fifth birthday she started school; fortunately it was only half a mile away. Some children had to walk three miles to get there, coming along very rough unmade roads, full of pot holes and very muddy in wet weather. Many of these children had to go to work before they went to school, doing housework, pea picking or picking up stones from the fields which were used to fill the pot holes. The girls all wore white pinafores – stiffly starched to keep them fresh and clean longer – and black boots. These were often reinforced with metal toes and heels, or hob nails, to make them last longer. Boots were costly and in large families were handed down from one child to the next.

All the children had to go to school on Sunday and then walk from the school to church in a crocodile and were not allowed to speak during the walk. The school at this time was very important as there was no village hall. Dancing classes were held there, at threepence an evening, and also dances.

This part of Aldham, known as Poplar Town, was quite remote and everyone had to walk wherever they wanted to go. Many of the women were outworkers, making shirts and other garments for shops in Colchester. These had to be carefully pressed, buttons sewn on, parcelled up and taken into Colchester usually by children on Saturday morning, walking the five miles there and if the work was not up to standard bringing it home again.

Children made their own fun. Girls and boys played with whips and tops, hoops, knuckle stones, and marbles. Boys also practised pole jumping across ditches and high jumping over a long stick stuck horizontally into a hedge. So many things happened that children found exciting and fun. They swam in the river on hot summer days or watched their fathers catch eels. These were brought home in a bucket and were skinned alive but when cut up and cooked were delicious and very sweet!

Otter hounds hunted along the river Colne and the fox hounds met at various farms in the area.

The A604 to Cambridge, as it is now, was just a quiet rough track going between the houses, shops and pubs in Ford Street. It is hard to believe that children could play football in the road, only occasionally having to get out of the way of a cart. In the 1920s the river Colne burst its banks and Ford Street was flooded and people were rescued by rowing boat. A fire broke out in the stackyard at Aldham Hall in 1921 and 21 stacks of corn were destroyed. Everyone came to witness this horrifying sight. Soon after that they all turned out to see a house in the rectory grounds jacked up and rolled across the fields and lanes, for two miles, to its present site.

Although parts of the village were so remote and transport was non-existent people were not short of supplies as tradesmen called every day. A fish man came twice a week by donkey and cart. When he got to Aldham Hall you could hear him shout, "Yarmouth bloaters twelve for a shilling". He had all sorts of fish all the year round. You could rely on him. Little Old Toby walked round the villages with a basket on his head, full of pots and pans. A Mr Creswell came from Bures with cottons and elastic and things like that and he had a bottle of sweets and we children bought a halfpenny worth from him. Mr Smith came from Coggeshall with curtains, materials and clothes. He brought whatever was ordered. Also the butcher, baker, coalman and oilman called and, on Saturday, the carrier passed through the village on his way to Colchester at 8 am taking people's orders and delivering the goods that night.

On one of the wide verges in the village people remembered a small thatched building covering a saw pit. Great timber waggons came up from Earls Colne to have tree trunks sawn up and children would run up to see the "Timber Jims" coming. They thought it was fun to see them but it was not much fun for the boy, not much older than they were, who worked in the pit getting sawdust in his eyes as he pulled on the saw while his grandfather worked up above.

Every farm had a horse pond where the horses were taken to drink before being turned out into the meadows for the night. The horses literally charged down into the ponds at the end of the day, their thundering hooves frightening the children. In the winter time these ponds froze over and the children all slid and had fun on the ice while older people went down to the large pond on the village green and skated. Winters must have been much colder then as these ponds seem to have frozen every year.

When the First World War broke out women all worked on the land as husbands and sons had volunteered for the army. They were very sad times. In fact 17 of these men did not return. As they walked through the village on their way to Marks Tey station, and so to France, it did not occur to their friends that they would never see them again.

After the war changes began to take place. Council houses were built and people left their tied cottages and were able to leave the land, several of them going to work on the railway. The little line that now runs to Sudbury was very busy, employing a full time crossing keeper who lived in the isolated cottage by the line. He and his family used to walk up the line to get to Marks Tey as that was the quickest route. Later on, in the 1950s, boxes of carnations grown in Aldham were taken to Marks Tey station en route to Cambridge and then the north of England.

The depression hit Aldham badly. Cottages fell into disrepair and farms stood empty. People remember some fields being so neglected and overgrown that hedges almost met in the middle. Soon new farmers arrived. My father-in-law, a Scottish farmer, brought everything – lock, stock and barrel – by train.

Many people remember the off-licence, now an attractive house on the green. It was a place where children went to buy sweets – raspberry drops that stuck to the paper bag – and they were often sent to get a jug of beer, but beer was also brewed on farms for the workmen to take to the fields. Most people made their own wine from every kind of flower or vegetable. I was told of one man who made a very potent drink called "All Nations Wine" which was quite dangerous as it was so strong.'

LIFE AT THE BLACK BULL

'It was on a hot summer's day in 1913 that my family (father, mother, my two brothers and I) left our house in Leyton to move to Great Sampford. We caught the train from Liverpool Street travelling through beautiful countryside (no Harlow New Town) to Elsenham station where we changed to a local connection to Thaxted station, now long since closed. From Thaxted, we journeyed to Sampford by pony and trap, our belongings piled high.

When we moved to the Black Bull, as it was then called, it was owned by Watney Combe and Reid. The ale we sold was brewed in Saffron Walden on a site opposite the Saffron Hotel.

The Black Bull seemed enormous after our house in Leyton. There were four doors in the front and inside there were six bedrooms, a sitting room, kitchen, bar parlour, club room and the tap room. The only entertainment was in the bar and that was an old fashioned gramophone with a large horn.

Outside there was a large yard and beyond that an enormous garden. Along the Finchingfield Road was the stable block incorporating room for five horses, some piggeries and large hay lofts above. Another building was the Scout hut where Mr Beale from Tindon Manor instructed all the village youths once a week. The last outside item was a good solid water pump to which a lot of local folk came to get their water.

Ale used to be twopence a pint. Cigarettes we sold were, I seem to recall, Woodbines and Players. Tobacco available was Sam Slick and Nut Brown, the latter being a penny three farthings an ounce.

Our neighbours were, on one side, Mr and Mrs Farmer and their two daughters who ran the village shop. On the Finchingfield side was the police house. PC Pearson was village policeman at that time. Closing time was 10 pm *prompt* and PC Pearson enforced it rigidly. We had a terrier which absolutely loathed anyone in uniform. So at 10 pm each night my father used to let him out and he would rush across the road barking madly to where PC Pearson would be standing by the trees in the churchyard.

Each season the Essex Foxhounds came by train to Thaxted and would then hack to Sampford where we put them up at the Black

Bull, horses in the stables and hounds in Mr Beale's Scout hut on a generous covering of straw. The huntsman slept at the back of the pub and if any of the hounds made a noise in the night, he would open his window, call out its name and all was quiet again.

There was a tunnel under the pub running towards the church but I never went far down it as it was dark and eerie.

I started a newspaper delivery in 1915 and from then until the end of the war cycled to Thaxted every day to get the papers, together with any medicines for people in the village.

After the war, the pub was sold to Benskins and became just the Bull. We moved from the Bull in 1922 to Flint Cottage. Great Sampford in the second decade of this century was a beautiful village; quiet and peaceful and unknown to outsiders as it was not on a main route to anywhere. There were very few cars and lots of grass meadows to walk in.'

FROM STANFORD LE HOPE TO HOLE HAVEN

In 1958 an old Essex countryman wrote of his life around Stanford le Hope. W.G. Styles was born in 1882 and these reminiscences take us back to the Victorian age.

'Looking back to the time when I was a boy of ten years of age in the year of 1892, I had just left school in Stanford le Hope. In memory I walk by the river Thames from Stanford le Hope to Hole Haven, which is to the south of Fobbing creek.

Starting from Stanford le Hope church one proceeded down Wharf Road and across the Warren. I have watched many a cricket match

Harlow High Street in 1910, a scene typical of many Essex towns at the time.

being played there. To my recollection, this was called "glebe land". There was an old manor house near to the railway and hundreds of rabbits made the Warren their home.

We wend our way to Stanford Wharf and the seawall. The wharf was owned by a Mr Ambrose Ellis who had several barges, some of which brought corn for the Stanford mill whilst others brought stones for the various councils. These stones were called Kentish ragstone, and were used for making roads. The barges loaded with hay or straw bound for London were a sight to be seen as they glided out of the creek; but they could only do this on the high tide.

Further on we come to what was called Mr Smith's Crossing. This was a footpath to Hope Farm, Stanford or Corringham. Then, across the saltings, was the Curry Marsh Explosive Factory, which manufactured blasting ammunition. The manager's name was Mr Walter Levitt who later became JP for Grays, the local market town. The chemicals used in this ammunition turned the employees' hair yellow and this made them quite distinguishable as to the type of work they did.

I would here like to relate an incident when the seawall gave way. This was in the year of 1895. At that time I was a shepherd's boy living in lodgings on the marshes over the railway lines opposite Curry Marshes. I think it must have been in March of that year because of the very high tide. This was up to the seawall, with strong winds blowing across the marshes.

The shepherd told me to go quickly to my own home as his house would soon be under water. Following his directions I started off and, on the way, saw several girls on their way home from Curry Marsh. So, all together, we made our way to Stanford, along an old county-wall to Great Garlands Farm. There was water all around us so we kept to the high ground into the Stanford Road at Oak Farm. The next morning there were "sleepers" everywhere which had been washed up from railway lines. The flood did a lot of damage, with salt water everywhere and people having to vacate their homes, as well as the loss of sheep and poultry.

Leaving this rather sad tale behind I go back, in memory, to the walk to Mucking lighthouse. This boasted of two light-keepers and a pier, which one had to cross in order to reach the lighthouse. The keepers would sometimes invite a party of us boys to see the lantern inside the lighthouse, but whether this was such a splendid gesture is left to the imagination, as we always had to carry a bottle of paraffin for them. However, they used to allow us to watch a yacht or barge race from the pier.

Proceeding with our walk we come to the European Oil Works, the one and only oil works at that time in this area. To my knowledge no petrol was ever brought into this oil wharf, but I have seen plenty of paraffin and naphtha, in barrels, brought in by ships from America.

The wharf manager's name was Mr Dick Easterbrook, and the foreman's name was Mr Jim Braydon. At a later date I was employed at this works for ninepence a day. It was whilst I was working there that a tragedy occurred. A full-rigged ship was unloading its cargo of naphtha, which amounted to several thousand barrels. The hold was open and the fumes from the naphtha were almost overpowering. Suddenly, a violent storm broke and lightning struck the ship. The inflammable cargo quickly caught fire and it became impossible to extinguish the flames. The only possible course was to batten down the hold; and although there were men down below it had to be done. Four German sailors perished but the fire was brought under control, and these unfortunate men were buried in Stanford le Hope churchyard, where a stone was placed in their memory.

The effect of the naphtha was alarming. When men were working in a confined space, unloading the barrels, they were only able to stay below about half an hour and on coming up into the fresh air would roll about as if drunk. But the effects soon wore off. Eventually this oil company works was sold to a firm called The Asiatic Oil Company which started the first oil refinery in this area, about 1897.

Our walk takes us next to a place of interest, the old Pig and Whistle. This was a very old pub, opening every day and night when the ships were unloading merchandise at Thames Haven. The landlord was Mr Sauch who would supply callers with a large piece of beef or half a round of cheese for one shilling. The pub was built only about six feet away from the seawall but, in view of the danger of the wall being washed away, a new wall was built behind it and the old Pig and Whistle was pulled down and a new one was erected close to the London Tilbury and Southend Railway.

Further along the seawall was the Thames Haven pier, railway station and several houses for customs officers and the pier master, who was also the station master. There were one or two railway carriages for officials and dock labourers. The railway lines ran onto the pier in order that goods could be loaded from the ships on to the trucks direct. About two ships per week unloaded their cargoes of live bullocks, sheep, horses, apples in barrels and cheeses sometimes weighing a ton each. The cattle were put into very large yards and sheds. They would then be loaded into trucks and sent to London.

At times I would take food to my father, who worked on the unloading, and I remember on occasions the crane driver would manage to drop a tub of apples onto the pier; and I have an idea the Customs officer would look the other way until our baskets were full and then would shout for us to "be off". However, we always got away with the goods.

We had fun too, when the horses were being unloaded. When

they were led down the gangways, as soon as they saw the open fields they almost went mad with excitement and the men had quite a harassing time trying to keep clear of their hooves.

We carry on with our walk to the last place of interest, Hole Haven and the creek to Fobbing Wharf. This creek divided Hole Haven from Canvey Island and was, at that time, marshes and arable land. In 1894 I worked at what was then known as Borley House as a plough-boy and this was the first time I had lodged away from home. I remember when the horseman and I went down to Borley House. What a journey this was – to Corringham down the Manorway, in a tumbril cart with two horses. The mud was up to the horses' bellies and the bottom of the cart was drawn along like a sleigh, with the horses almost unable to get their legs out of the mud.

Borley House was later sold to the Government and Kynocks factory was built in its place. Ammunition for the Boer War was made there.'

HIGH EASTER

'In the 1930s a village was still an independent unit with many tradesmen to be found within its community. Such was the village of High Easter when I moved there in 1934, when my parents bought one of the village shops. Our shop was locally called "The Top Shop" to distinguish it from another at the bottom of the street in a building called "Penvites". Our shop carried a large range of grocery, drapery, footwear and hardware.

Some items stocked have long since vanished from the scene such as bath brick (a powder used for cleaning steel knives), balls of whitening (used to brighten doorsteps) and block salt (used for preserving). The main line of footwear stocked was a very heavy leather boot called a "Norfolk Champion", many pairs of which hung from the beams at the lower end of the shop. These boots were designed for heavy service on the farms. Also available were wellington boots and low shoes for men and ladies.

Behind the shop was a bakehouse where bread was baked. This was let to a baker at Good Easter, Mr Coates, who supplied bread to our shop. The baker was one Will Shed, who lived in the village. Each evening Will would come to the bakehouse to make up the dough by hand for there was no mechanical mixer. In the winter this had to be carried out in the faint light of an old oil lamp which hung on the wall. Hygiene was less of a concern then, and Will would often smoke a Woodbine as he mixed the dough – doubtless a little ash falling into the mixture from time to time. Early next morning Will returned to bake the bread. He would first fire the oven with faggots (bundles of small wood as cut from the hedgerow) before placing some lump coal in. Once the oven was heated, he would get a long pole on the top of which a large piece of rag was fixed. The rag was dipped into a pail of water and then Will would clean the floor of the oven with this. Next, he would fetch down a long wooden item called a "peel". On to this he would put some huffers (or pads) and then put them into the oven to test that the heat was correct. If these came out satisfactorily he would then put in his first batch of bread. Despite the rather primitive production methods, local people always said, "I like ol' Will's bread, it al'us tastes so sweet"!

Much of the economy of the village was based on agriculture and certain seasons of the year saw a great influx of the unemployed with no Social Security, a great number of people travelled the country looking for casual work such as pea picking, sugarbeet hoeing and pulling and potato picking. Most of these travellers arrived pushing a pram in which they transported their few possessions. Some would find an old cart shed or outbuilding where they could sleep, but many would lie under the hedgerows on a bed of straw or sacks. A few had tents. They came in great numbers at pea picking time – possibly 100 to 150. Naturally their arrival in the village brought with it a lot of business for the local shops and pubs.

Many of the travellers spent their evening down at one of the local pubs – The Punchbowl or The Cock and Bell. The latter was more popular with them since it contained a barrel organ so they could have music at a penny a time. Perhaps the most remarkable aspect of this invasion of the village was that very little lawlessness occurred and seldom was anything stolen.

Across the road from the shop stood the village smithy where Mr Coe the blacksmith still plied his trade. While a few farmers had a tractor, the horse was still the main power on every farm. Horses came regularly to the smithy to be shod and waggon and cart wheels were brought to have new iron bands fitted on them, so the smithy was still a great hive of industry.

Down the road, to deal with the sadder side of life, lived Hugh Franklin the village undertaker. Hugh made his coffins in a workshop adjoining his cottage. For most funerals he used a hand bier, and his bearers were all men from the village who took time off from work to participate. Joe Little was then the local grave digger and he would also toll the church bell which was customary then – one sombre boom to mark each year of the age of the deceased. Franklin headed the sad procession, with the bearers following pushing the hand bier and the mourners following on foot. Such a funeral cost but a few pounds – probably £10 at the most. A woman living in the village known as a "layer out" would usually, after a death, wash and lay the body out for burial. One of these ladies who used Lux toilet soap for this purpose, would never have that brand of soap for her personal use.

For the water supply the village still relied on pumps and most people in the main part of the village street collected their supply from the pump on the village green – but others used another pump situated near the roadside in front of Randler's Cottages. We were lucky and had a pump on our premises, as did several other properties in the village.'

CHINGFORD IN THE 1920s

'I was born in Chingford, then an Essex town, in 1917. Until the 1920s our road had not been tarmacked, so in winter it was a morass of mud and puddles. The milk-girl from Sopers Farm called twice a day. She had substituted for a man called up in 1914 and continued in the job at war's end. She drove a horse-drawn two-wheeled milkcart. The milk was kept in a large churn and she ladled it into the housewife's own milk jar with a leaden half-pint measure. A man from the local grocer would call once or twice a week and take the grocery order which would then be delivered by an errand boy. He had to pedal a very heavy bicycle with the groceries piled in a frame in front of the handlebars, through the rutted roads.

The street was lit by gas lamps. Each evening around dusk a lamplighter would come with a long pole to light the gas. He came again to put the lamps out at dawn.

A winter's delight was to sit in front of the open fire and toast a muffin or crumpet. A muffin man often came down the street. His wares were contained in a tray which was balanced on his head. He wore a special flat cap to keep the tray from slipping and rang a handbell for attention.

In the early 1920s there were few cars on the road. The horse was still widely used for most trade purposes. Besides the milk float, the baker, coalman, grocer, greengrocer, builder, all had horse-drawn vehicles. At Chingford station there were horse-drawn cabs for hire, four-wheel carriages – open in summer and with a cover for winter – driven by a cabby. The best known cabby was "Old Kemp". He stabled his horse and carriage at the King's Head. He passed along our road at night on his way to the stables, and we children would not sleep until we heard the clip-clop of the horse's hooves and the creaking of the carriage as Old Kemp urged it homewards.

Chingford, until the great house-building boom of the 1930s, was still a smallish Essex town. Indeed the shopping area was known as "the village". Some Essex weather-board buildings were still in use in Station Road in the 1920s. Butcher Law occupied an Essex-board building where the Roman Catholic church now stands. This old building had large meat hooks fixed to the fascia from which carcasses were hung. Another wooden building stood where the Co-op building now stands. It was the smithy. How exciting it was for children to look through the open door and watch the flames spurting from the forge and hear hammer on anvil as horses were shod!'

A MONOTONOUS LIFE?

'Being a farming community, village life at Horndon must have been monotonous. There were two pubs, the Bell, an old coaching inn where the tradesmen and farmers gathered, and the Swan, which was very much an alehouse where the workers gathered. The twain did not mix. The only relaxation for women was the Mothers' Union, but not many of the village wives belonged to it. As all needs were catered for in the way of shops people did not go beyond the village very much, except to the cinema in Stanford, which meant a four-mile walk or cycle ride, and on agricultural wages there was not much spare cash for the pictures.

For the old and housebound the one treat was on Wednesday afternoon, when the post office was shut and the postmistress Dorothy Allen, daughter of the undertaker, took the pensions round to those who were not able to get out. In the days before telephones, urgent messages were sent by telegram, and Miss Allen would stand at the door of the post office hoping to catch someone who would deliver the telegram, preferably with a cycle if there was any distance to go.'

STORMY WEATHER

'The telephone rang in the early hours of 1st February 1953 and a voice cried, "Guv'nor, the waters have come in!" At first my husband David was bewildered, but quickly realised the implications. Realising it was the caretaker at the Baltic Wharf, the centre of my husband's timber importing business, David quickly telephoned its nearest neighbour Colonel Basil Carey and alerted him.

We learned two days later that Colonel Carey went to Creeksea Ferry Inn beside the river, only to find it completely flooded and the licensee Ivy Taylor clinging to the top of a door, where she had been struggling to keep hold for eight hours. On the roof, it being only one storey, were two customers – a third had insisted on trying to swim for help. Unhappily he was later found drowned. All three were taken to the seawall together with our caretaker, where by now other helpers had gathered. All the buildings at the timber wharf were one storey high, so the two storey barn at least saved one life.

David then looked ahead – no road or fields, just water – such buildings as he expected to see were under six feet of water. What a sight to shock the eye! Then David realised that the whole wharf

Walton on the Naze in the grip of the 1953 floods. Mill Lane lies under water and caravans float on Bath House Meadow.

was under water – sawmills, workshops, sheds, lorries, cars, forklift trucks and of course the timber. All the structure of his timber importing business seemed to have disappeared. He then went back to Paglesham and down to the river Roach to give what help and advice he could offer. I did not see him again that night.

The following day he went again towards the river Crouch and Wallasea Island, at least to the place where the road still existed, only to find all his men there, tears streaming from their eyes. For them, their work was no more, the wharf seemed to have disappeared. They had worked there all their lives even before David took over. Their emotions almost unnerved my husband.

The sea wall had been breached in several places along the Roach and the water was as deep on the landward side as it was in the river itself. Two tides had come in and the wind had not allowed the tides to go out. The walls were breached all along the Roach and Crouch – and of course all along the East Coast.

Farmers and other friends called round to share notes and commiserate and to reassure that he would build again, but by now he was too ill with pneumonia to be heartened by their encouragement.

Gradually the waters went down but, as Wallasea Island was virtually uninhabited, the authorities did not attempt to drain the marshes as they did on Canvey Island, for instance, where there had been great suffering and loss of lives. Colonel Basil Carey did manage to cajole the army into building a wall across one of the fields, but it seemed of little benefit.

The waters did go down slowly and a week later David and his colleague took a boat and managed to get to what was left of the offices and with great difficulty climbed in through a window and extracted files, ledgers and money etc from the safe, wet as it all was. The house was used as a temporary office and whenever there was a clear day books were laid out of doors to dry. That smell stays in my nostrils forever. I smelt this again when visiting Canvey Island. I've been through the war, seen part of our London factory burning down and been involved in a severe air raid, but that particular smell is unforgettable. Somehow, stale water is more pungent, fire is acrid and does burn down, water stays and is inexorable.

As the water slowly receded rescue of the timber seemed possible; it was strewn along the banks of the Crouch and Roach and resting inland wherever the wind took it. Men with boats manhandled it back to the wharf – a backbreaking business in such bitter weather.

Years go by and things recover. We were never homeless, we were not personally flooded, we were not starving. Others were in a ghastly jobless, homeless plight, but for a sensitive caring employer the strain of those weeks of never knowing if Baltic Wharf would rise again told on his constitution and nervous system.

That night will live in my memory for ever, or perhaps the next days must. Canvey Island, the East Coast flooding, the loss of lives and the disaster. That night of such bitter cold, such biting wind, such relentless water. Even now, when there are any really high tides I go to bed uneasy.'

'On 5th September 1958 a severe storm started about 8 pm at Great Baddow. There was not much thunder, but continuous sheets of lightning and torrential rain. Suddenly there was a terrible roar as the force of the water broke the cellar windows, and in a matter of minutes the water had risen to the top of the cellar steps, just half an inch below our hall floor. Looking out of the window we could see that we were surrounded by a sea of water. By midnight the moon was shining but the roar of water continued. We were very fortunate that by 2 am the water in the cellar had dropped two feet. The next day we heard that the water was seven feet deep at the Blue Lion.'

RUSSIANS AT PURLEIGH

'During the first years of the century a small colony of Russian exiles from the Tsarist regime came to live in and about Purleigh. They were exiled for their political beliefs and spent a lot of their time printing pamphlets, books and other works considered seditious in their own country. Naturally their children seemed a little odd to us; they dressed queerly and couldn't always make us understand. One little boy and girl came to Purleigh school for a few months and we would try and tell them the names of things in the garden.

The first Russians, Mr and Mrs Chelov, came to live in Mill House in 1899. Later another family came and one of them, a Mr West, could talk to us. They installed printing machines in the downstairs rooms on which they printed Russian newspapers and Leo Tolstoy's books. My mother was asked to go and clean for them and it was my job to go early, fill the copper and get it going. I used quite a lot of waste paper from the printing machines. Paper was used to wipe the oil from the machines and it made grand kindling. We lived for some years in Chapel Lane and from there my mother could see when I had got the copper going. The Russian lady would pat me on the back and say, "Good, good." Another Russian family came to live in the Chelmsford Road and I was nursemaid to their little boy Leora, a dear child with lovely fair curly hair. His parents were always writing, typing or studying.'

SAMMY LAVENDER

'Like most villages, Hatfield Broad Oak has had its share of village characters – no one causing more interest and concern than Sammy Lavender. He strolled into the taproom of the Fox Inn one fine day during the 1920s, looking hot and dusty but not unduly dirty for a tramp. He ordered his pint and chatted to the regulars and before long he showed signs of being of a religious turn of mind. He mentioned angels and saw them frequently – also he heard mysterious whisperings from above and rumblings from below. He seemed a cut above the ordinary run of tramps – someone to be respected, so the kindly landlady, Mrs Patmore, allowed him to stay a night or two in the loft of the nearby stable.

Sammy approved of his quarters ten yards from the taproom and stayed for some years, becoming part of village life. He worked in the fields, earning enough to pay for his beer and tobacco.

One day he returned from work and startled his company by solemnly announcing, "I'm a-goin' a die – next Saturday night at midnight." This was met with roars of laughter but Sammy was not to be silenced. "When I was a-workin' in that field be'ind the pub," he persisted, "a angel came out of the clouds and stood afore me and said, 'Sammy Lavender, you'm a-goin' a die at twelve o'clock next Saturday night'."

The news spread like wildfire. Some believed it, others did not. Saturday night came and a crowd gathered at the Fox to witness events. Sammy drank his last drink on earth, emerged from the taproom and climbed the steps to his loft. His well wishers followed and gathered round him as he lay on his bed of straw. With 15 minutes to go Sammy clutched at his throat and emitted painful gurglings. He tossed and writhed. More gasping and the death throes intensified. "Two minutes to twelve," whispered the timekeeper. More choking noises and at last the clock struck the midnight hour. On the last stroke, Sammy lay still, his agony over. Someone held a lantern to his face. He still breathed – but only just. "Is he dead?" was the question on everyone's lips. All eyes turned to the expert on death rattles, who quickly decided to "test for it". Taking a pin from his waistcoat he administered several quick jabs to Sammy's leg, which brought forth loud cries of, "Oh! Oh! Stop it!"

The game was up. Sammy was dragged to his feet, punched, pushed and cursed and thrown back on his bed. He stayed in his loft all next day in disgrace but was soon forgiven – but never again did he mention anything supernatural!'

MARKET DAY

Market day brought the world and his wife to town, buying and selling, looking and gossiping.

ROMFORD – A SMALL COUNTRY TOWN

'Our family moved to Romford in 1927 when it was a small country, cattle market town. We lived near the railway line and cattle were regularly herded from the cattle trucks, down our road, to the abbatoir at the other end of the road. We lived in an end of terrace house and the cows often diverted and followed one another down our alleyway. They would get stuck between the two fences between our garden and next door and the herdsmen couldn't possibly turn them round. They had to drive them down to the end of the alleyway and do a sort of three-point turn. Once there were so many that they pushed our garden fence over and our garden was full of cows trampling all over it, ruining the flower beds. It was just something we took in our stride.'

'Most people nowadays think of Romford as part of London – indeed it is now part of the London Borough of Havering, but when I lived there from the 1930s to the 1950s it was a pleasant market town.

I loved Wednesdays and Fridays when the market would be in full swing when I walked home from school. In those days there was still a large cattle market at the top near the old Laurie Cinema, and I always lingered there, looking at the sheep, pigs and chickens, and balancing on the rails to watch the cattle being auctioned. Best of all there were puppies and kittens in cardboard boxes, and I would spend ages choosing which one I would buy – if only I had the money. In the winter time the stalls were lit with paraffin lamps, and on rainy days you had to be careful not to slip on the cobblestones. On Saturday mornings my best friend and I hurried through the market, buying an apple each on the way to the "tuppeny rush" at the Laurie Cinema which stood near where the subway is now.

During the war there weren't quite so many stalls, but I often went with my mother on Saturdays to see what bargains were to be had. "Lou's" stall was one of our favourites – he sold bomb-damaged goods from warehouses in London, and my mother often bought rolls of fabric, singed down the edges (no coupons required) which my older sister would patiently try to fit paper patterns on to make dresses for us.

Often on Saturday afternoons there would be a wedding at the church in the market (St Edward's) and we would always wait to see the bride and groom walk through the stalls to their cars. Our school was closely connected to the church, and we often walked two by two to church services through the market place – our teachers making sure we behaved ourselves.

When I left school my first job was in a solicitor's office which overlooked the market, and at lunchtimes I often hurried round the stalls to buy dress materials and later still always bought my fruit and vegetables there.'

'My grandfather, a builder, must have been one of the first to enjoy an aerial view of Romford market from his perch repairing the cockerel on St Edward's steeple in the early 1900s. But my memory of "Blareham" as the noisy market was called is of affronted bulls being prodded to the weighing machine, squealing pigs, bleating sheep and the cattle. Most of all I remember the man in the brown trilby selling puppies from a cosy baby cot. Next to him the day old chicks were sold – twelve pale yellow puff balls in a box for a shilling.

I don't think I shall ever forget the day when a nun from the local convent picked up her skirts, veil flying, and took to her heels in Laurie Square to escape the attention of a very inquisitive escaped cow.

My delight was Saturday night when Grandfather collected his old shopping bag and off we went to the now magical market with its hissing lamps and stallholders frantically trying to sell off their vegetables and meat (no fridges in those days). Then the long awaited stop at the home-made sweet stall – humbugs, bullseyes, coconut ice – how long it took me to choose. Time to go home, refusing Grandad's offering of chips in newspaper. Mother said "young ladies do not eat in the street".

In the middle of the crossroads at the end of the market stood the ever-patient policeman – what were his thoughts I wonder when my father appeared (this was in the 1920s) bearing in his wheelbarrow his crop of allotment-grown potatoes, cornered too quickly and sent the whole barrowload flying. With a raised hand all traffic was stopped and he, with the owners of carts, bicycles and old-fashioned lorries, picked every one up and sent Dad happily on his way.'

MARKET DAY IN WALTHAM ABBEY

'Tuesday was market day in Waltham Abbey in the 1920s, as it had been since the charter was first granted by Henry II, and still is today, though very much changed from the memories of my childhood.

Then, as well as the many stalls in The Square, there was a cattle market in The Romeland. This was a large cobbled area surrounded by picturesque old cottages, the Crown Inn, and on the corner a larger building known as Cranmer's House. Down either side were iron pens for the sheep, calves and pigs, and at the far end the bullocks were tethered. There was also a water fountain, and the weighbridge. At one side, behind the pens, was a crude corrugated iron construction which served as a men's lavatory – very unsanitary, and we hurried past holding our noses.

A visit to see the animals was a must for the younger children, who particularly loved the sheep and calves, but were a bit wary of the larger cattle. The animals began to arrive early in the morning, mostly on the hoof, herded in from farms in the surrounding villages and hamlets. Others from farther afield came in carts and waggons, and many arrived in cattle trucks at Waltham Cross railway station, and had to be driven a mile along the road to the market. These last were the great excitement for the older children, who had to walk that road to school. The cattle were the "enemy" and had to be avoided by nipping on to the marsh which ran alongside the road at one point, or hiding behind somebody's hedge and waiting for them to pass. Then we could penetrate behind enemy lines – much more fun than just walking to school. I remember the consternation caused by a bullock straying into our shop. A very large creature to turn round in a restricted area, and it did not seem to have a reverse gear!

Of course, with the influx of animals came the farmers and butchers to buy and sell, dressed in their tweeds, boots and leather gaiters, caps or bowler hats, carrying a variety of sticks and crooks, leaning on the pens, prodding the animals, talking business, and surrounding the auctioneer, who seemed to us to be speaking a foreign language. All this was thirsty work, but they were well catered for. As well as the nearby Crown, the extraordinary number of public houses in this small town were open all day.

In the afternoon the movement was in the opposite direction. Butchers from far afield loaded their purchases into carts and lorries, while the local ones just drove them to their slaughterhouses, usually adjoining their shops. Once the animals were driven away and the great wooden gates had closed behind them, the girls gave them not another thought; the boys of course had to try to scale the gates and peer over the top to see what happened next, but the animals just disappeared into the buildings.

When the auctioneer's task had been completed, and the money had changed hands, the men drifted away, some no doubt satisfied, others disappointed, but either way the hostelries were still open. It was then that the men with great hoses came on the scene. All had to be swilled down until not a straw or a cowpat was in sight.

I imagine the cottagers breathed a sigh of relief, as all was quiet and serene – until next Tuesday.'

BRAINTREE MARKET

'I drove my father to Braintree market on Wednesdays. He would leave me on arrival and watch the animals being sold. If we sent animals they would be collected by a cattle truck. If we sent chickens I would take them in crates on the car. I would also help to put them into pens to be sold by auction (woe betide you if one escaped). Certain old men used to walk up and down where the hens were in the hope of finding an egg. They would then take it and crack it and swallow the contents whole.

In season I took the wild rabbits that were caught on the farm. I would also take apples, to be auctioned when we had more than we could use. At one time eggs were graded there, but they were later collected from the farm. Sometimes there were all kinds of mysterious goods. I was able to buy a ship's bell, to be hung in the bell chamber on Greenstead village school, as theirs was missing.

The market was held on a site that had once held houses. There were wonderful examples of walls of old straw and mud plaster, with hazel sticks between, and little pins of twisted hazel holding sticks in place. If I had a visitor with me I regularly showed off this old building skill to them.'

EPPING MARKET

'Every Monday there was a market held in Epping, as there is to this day. In the 1930s there were great pens set up to hold all the cattle and sheep which were up for auction. these were in the High Street itself. The cattle were driven to market past our house, and our little spaniel used to love to join in the herding as they went by.

There were also small animals and birds such as rabbits, turkeys, ducks and so on, sold in Sworder's yard which is now the George and Dragon car park. There was great bustle and excitement with the noise of the animals and the bidding and auctioneers calling.

On the corner of this yard was the blacksmith's shop, Clark's, and I used to love to watch the smiths at work from the doorway, with the pungent smell of the hooves as the irons were pressed on, red hot from the forge which glowed and flamed at the back, the noise of the hammers (always two blows, one heavy and then a little tap, perhaps to arrest the vibration before the next blow?). The horseshoes had to be made from pieces cut from long bars of iron, heated and shaped on the anvil, offered to the hoof of the tethered horse, altered to the right contour and trimmed to fit. It seemed amazing that the horse never objected to the heat or the nails in his foot.'

HOPING FOR A BARGAIN AT GREAT YELDHAM

'Monday was market day at Great Yeldham – a real auction market, selling absolutely everything from old books and furniture, through to fat beasts for the butcher. It was situated in the High Street, between the Waggon and Horses pub and Whitlocks foundry.

People converged from all the villages around, by car, by horse, on bicycles and many on foot, bringing with them such a variety of items for sale and hoping against hope to find a bargain, and not only that but to take back to their villages the latest gossip and opinions. On the opposite side of the road, a small corrugated iron building housed a branch of Barclays Bank, open just on Mondays. An elderly gentleman stood on the customer side of the counter, vetting all those who came in, mostly on first name terms anyway. I have often thought since, whatever good would he have been if determined robbers appeared? Times were hard for the farming community in the 1930s and there would be many anxious faces watching to see how much their stock made, wondering how many creditors they would be able to pay. In our orchard now, at Belchamp St Paul, there is an apple tree – an early dessert – still known as the Yeldham tree, bought all those years ago when a new tree was a luxury.'

CHURCH AND CHAPEL

Sunday was a special day, quiet and set aside from the toil of the week. Most families went to church or chapel at least once and the children attended Sunday school regularly. Those Sunday school outings are still fondly remembered, often the only time in the year children saw the sea or travelled out of the village.

GRANDMOTHER'S SUNDAYS

'My paternal grandmother exerted a very strong influence on our family life as she lived so close to us at Hutton. She was strongly religious and no work except that dealing with the farm stock was ever done on Sundays. Reading was allowed but no knitting or sewing. I often rebelled against this but made sure I was never caught out! Carrying her prayer books in a purpose-made black velvet dolly bag, I would accompany her to church on Sunday mornings. She always wore a lace front to her dress and a band of narrow velvet ribbon round her neck. In the evening the whole family, headed by my father wearing his best suit, trilby hat and carrying a walking stick, attended evensong. Sunday school at a little mission hut nearby came in between. From there we had an annual outing to Walton on the Naze, travelling by train – the edge of the world to us.'

SUNDAYS

'A knock on the door one Sunday afternoon. A local woman reports to our mother: "Your daughters were jumping on and off a log in the meadow!" "Yes?" queries Mother. "But they were laughing!" answered the straight-laced officious woman, in a shocked voice. It is supposed merriment on Sunday was not in her book of rules!

Sunday at Great Bardfield in the 1920s was a day of dressing in our best and attending Sunday school in the building now called the church room. Almost every child from four to 14 was on the register, and Miss Fuller, the superintendent, would call the full names of every pupil for attendance. Some would have three or four forenames. Boys were sometimes called after battles, or leaders in the First World War, be it Fritz, Foch, Mons or Kitchener.

There were four or five teachers and pupils sat in groups on backless forms. We were taught to memorise the catechism from the age of five. In Miss Fuller's class, for the oldest, the collect for the day had to be learned so it could be recited in turn. The "babies" had to learn texts, and listen to Bible stories. After three quarters of an hour tuition we all processed, wearing hats or caps, from Sunday school to church, and sat in pews near the belfry, (dark and eerie in winter). There we remained throughout the service, on our best behaviour, throughout the matins, litany and sermon. We knew the Book of Common Prayer as we perused it, reading all the offices of marriage, burials etc to while away the time when we did not understand the sermon. It was a treat when young Rev Tristram Mears of Little Bardfield preached; he had such a pleasant voice!

In Sunday school there were rarely any visual aids, and in church we were bored during the long morning service, for there was no "going out during the sermon", however young. In boredom, if not old enough to read the Prayer Book, we would turn our knitted gloves inside out or exchange texts, kept in our personal prayer books. We were hidden from view, kneeling most of the time.

The Primitive Methodist chapel was the other place of worship, and we sat in the gallery for the Harvest Festival. This was a novelty, and there was a certain amount of muffled giggling.

There was a Gift Day, when there was a "silver tree". Gifts of silver coins were hung in envelopes on a fir tree. A text was usually written by the donor, and was read out by the pastor as each gift was cut from the tree by a little girl. I remember one text stated "Practise what you preach". "One for you, Mr Dodds," remarked one of the Elders.'

SUNDAY SCHOOL

'Every Sunday we went to Sunday school in the morning and afternoon at St Andrew's church, Shoeburyness. We were each given one halfpenny for collection. I remember the odd occasion of running into a little local corner shop, and buying a halfpenny ice cream. These were made of custard powder. Whether I spent my collection or not, I cannot be sure. I do know we were very poor, and only got one halfpenny each week for pocket money.

Every Sunday evening, when we got a little older, we used to beg my mother to let us go to church in the evening. This was only for an ulterior motive. Firstly we were not allowed out in the evening, and secondly, we girls used to like to sit in church making eyes at the choirboys, and trying to make them giggle. Indeed, sometimes we even dared to take a walk down to the beach afterwards, and sit in the shelters on the promenade, talking to the boys. We felt very daring.

One year, 1935, we were all greatly excited. We had a Sunday school outing from Shoeburyness (Cambridge Beach) to Canvey

Shoeburyness Sunday school outing to Canvey Island in 1935, a memorable day out.

Island by boat. That was a magical day, and I still have a treasured photograph of our entire family (with the exception of my father) sailing from Shoebury Common beach.'

THE OUTING

'I was a child living at Purleigh in the early years of the century and once I was allowed to go to a tea and social at Maldon Congregational chapel. I remember we travelled in waggons from Mosklyns Farm. Such events were highlights in our simple lives.'

'Most children at Tolleshunt D'Arcy in about 1910 attended church or chapel Sunday school and looked forward to the annual outing to Mersea Island. My father used a horse-drawn waggon fitted with straw bales for seats as transport. Also provided was a picnic tea. No one had a bathing costume but we tucked our dresses and underclothes in our drawers so we could paddle in the water, often getting very wet.'

'We attended Sunday school regularly and apart from Christmas parties in the hall at Leyton, there was the summer outing to various retreats in Epping Forest. The one I remember particularly was at Theydon Bois where there were some "amusements" consisting of a coconut shy, a small roundabout (hand operated) and an aerial runway. As we only had coppers for pocket money we could not have many goes on these things, but I believe I spent all my money on the aerial runway, which was a pulley running on a slanting wire with two side struts to hold and a wooden seat. You were launched from one end down the wire, and I seem to remember there was another wire to return.'

'Sundays between the wars were special. Most of my friends at Shenfield went to Sunday school, and some to the afternoon children's service at church. We always had an outing during July, and usually went to Walton on the Naze, Dovercourt or Felixstowe by train specially hired for the day. We took picnic lunches for the beach and then at about 3.30 pm we assembled at a local restaurant for a special tea – shrimps, bread and butter, assorted sandwiches, fancy cakes and drinks. Sometimes during the afternoon we went to a local funfair and had rides on the dodgems.

We also had a Christmas party in early January, held in the parish hall from 2.30 pm to about 6 pm, when our parents came for us. We were usually entertained by a conjuror or an impersonator and played party games. After tea, prizes for "Good Attendance" were awarded, usually books of the classics.'

'For many years during the 1930s I attended Sunday school in the morning and the children's service in the afternoon. Our superintendent at Writtle, Mrs Upson, was a lovely lady, very humorous and a real character. We always looked forward to our summer treat when we had an exciting bus ride to Oaklands Park, Chelmsford. Our mother packed our picnic tea of jam or paste sandwiches and lemonade. We always went to the museum and felt we knew every stuffed bird and animal on display. The park was ideal for playing hide and seek and it was a lovely afternoon.'

GETTING ABOUT

The little travelling we did was by horse-drawn transport, by bicycle or by Shanks's pony in the first decades of the 20th century. Gradually the bus and the car replaced the carrier's cart, but there was still a sense of adventure about transport, whether it was steam trains or paddle steamers.

FROM THE CARRIER TO BUSES

'The roads in Little Baddow village were all gravel and consisted of two tracks (ruts). After heavy rain, the tracks looked like rivers. The centre of the road was higher because of material squashed out of the ruts and an accumulation of horse manure. Occasionally the centre ridge would be thrown back into the ruts by the village roadman who also kept the verges cut and the drainage channels to the ditches in good order. I remember well when Little Baddow hill was first metalled. Several steamrollers attacked the existing gravel surface with heavy spikes which tore it all up. Then gangs of men spread a liberal layer of granite lumps over it. The whole lot was flooded with water and the granite rolled into the gravel. After a few months the road settled to a rough granite surface and was tarred and shingled. Several years later, tarmacadam was laid.

Twice a week the village carrier went to Chelmsford and back with his horse and cart. He would blow a whistle as he approached a house or would stop if a card was hanging in the window or on the gate. He took his instructions and money to make purchases in Chelmsford and brought them back in the afternoon. One of his main duties was to call at the railway station to collect any parcels or goods addressed to the village.'

Open-topped buses could be a pleasure in good weather, but overhanging branches were a problem!

'Our local carrier, Mr Stracey, lived at the bottom of the hill in Little Baddow and used to run in to Chelmsford three times or so a week. If you put an "S" in your window he would call and take your order; so convenient.'

'Most people walked or cycled anywhere they wanted to go. There was a service offered by carrier's cart, an open cart with seats either side and a hood to pull up if it rained. It was lighted by a candle in a sort of lamp on the sides and was drawn by one horse. It operated from Tollesbury to Colchester on a Saturday. This was superseded by a charabanc operated by Osbornes.'

'There were two private bus companies in Maylandsea in the 1930s, Quest and Pride of the Marshes which ran services to Maldon. On Saturdays, for the sum of one shilling and sixpence each, a van would take us to Maldon to the shops, which were open until 9 pm, and then we could go to the pictures. Afterwards some of us used to go to Wheelers, the fish and chip shop, where fish, chips, bread and butter were served at one big table in Mrs Wheeler's front room for sixpence. Back home then, by van.'

'When we first came to Horndon on the Hill in 1925 the only means of transport was a bicycle, with the exception of two buses a week.

On Wednesday the bus went to Romford for market day and on Friday to Chelmsford. They were open-topped double decker buses and at intervals along the route the conductor would stand on the stairs and shout "Duck!" Then everyone on the top deck ducked down below the level of the seats as the overhanging branches of the trees swept across the top. We were told there had been some nasty mishaps when people did not duck in time.'

'In the 1920s open-topped buses ran hourly between Ipswich and Colchester. The driver sat in front, of course, and beside him were two passenger seats. These were nearly always occupied by two grammar school boys and none of us would ever dare to climb up to these. The buses always had a conductor who collected the fares. He stood on the back platform in the open air and the stairs to the upper deck went up behind him. The seats on the top deck were of wooden slats (no padding) so that they would dry out quickly if they got wet. Each seat had a mackintosh sheet fixed to the back, so these could be pulled over one's knees in case of a sudden rainstorm! The bus fare for us was twopence. I had a younger sister and brother, so there were three of us and we were only allowed to get the bus if the weather was bad, as it cost too much!'

'I was born in Walthamstow in 1911 and during my childhood people walked as the only form of transport for most of us was bus or tram. The trams were not comfortable. The seats were wooden and there was no heating. The drivers were forced to stand all day, without protection from the elements, until a glass front was introduced. Buses at first were without roofs, very pleasant for travelling in summer. Private firms ran what were known as "pirate buses", which would slow up when requested for you to jump on as it moved, a way of shortening the length of time on the journey.'

'When I was young there were trams to Liverpool Street station, then electric trolley buses (which survived until the 1950s). Omnibuses were introduced by 1926. In the 1950s the double decker buses could still not reach the top of Chingford Mount with a full load. Passengers had to get off and walk up the hill.

Special excursions were made by charabanc. This was an open-topped single decker which cost ninepence from Whipps Cross to High Beech.'

BUSES AND BIKES

'A bus ran from Gestingthorpe into Halstead on Tuesdays and into Sudbury on Thursdays and Saturdays. On Tuesday and Saturday nights we went by bus to the pictures. On Saturdays it got packed from the four villages it called at and sometimes the men had to help push the bus up Sudbury Hill. The fare was a shilling. Some Sundays we would walk a mile to the main road to get the bus to go to the pictures but that didn't happen very often. There were also the two factory buses called "Bluffy's Buses".

Bicycles were used a lot as there were few cars then. My friend and I used to cycle into Halstead to work. It was hard going in the winter but the worst was thunderstorms, especially if it was dark. Our feet would go round so fast you'd have thought we were training for a race! The policeman also used to do his rounds by bicycle to the different villages. Many a lad had a clip round the ear from him!'

THE EARLY CARS

'Dad bought our first car in the 1920s, an old 1910 Humberette with two front seats and a dicky at the back, a hood, side screens, and a horn that you squeezed! She still had good leather upholstery though. Alas, she got many punctures and would break down two or three miles from home at Ramsden Heath. It was a long walk back, but we loved her just the same.'

'When the car was got out we children liked to ride on the running board – no nonsense about having to sit inside or locking the doors. The running board was the place, or in the dicky.'

'In the mid 1920s when I must have been about four years old, Father, after much persuasion from my brother, bought our first car. This was a Trojan, and had a belt drive. The belt hung down underneath and my brother went to collect it from Wickford, and drove it home with very little tuition. It was not with us for very long as his friends all laughed at the belt! The car was exchanged for a later model, and that in turn for a Rover Tourer. It had gleaming paintwork, real leather upholstery and a walnut fascia. The spare wheel was on the back and a petrol can was firmly fastened to the running board. The hood when not in use was in a smart canvas cover. No test was necessary to drive a car and my father was not a good driver. When coming up Market Hill one day with my aunt as a passenger he had occasion to stop. On starting he had difficulty with the clutch and the car started to roll back down the hill. With one bound Aunt leapt straight out of the car and landed on the pavement.'

IN CARE OF THE GUARD

'My mother was left motherless when she was six years old, not uncommon in the early part of this century. She attended, as a weekly boarder, a local private school in Thetford. The holidays presented her father with a problem so she spent them with various aunts living in and around Romford. She was despatched as "a parcel", being collected from her home, taken to the railway station in Bury St Edmunds and put in the care of the guard on the train. Any transfers from train to train were his responsibility. Finally she arrived at Romford station where she was collected by a housemaid and taken off to the relevant aunt!

During the Second World War, when I was an evacuee in various parts of rural England, occasionally I was allowed to visit my mother who was living and teaching in Grays. I too always travelled by train in the care of the guard. If the train was not too full, I was locked in a carriage on my own and the guard would look in on me each time the train stopped – his attention secured, no doubt, by the strategic handing-over of half a crown in advance.

Both in my mother's time and over 30 years later in mine, there were no fears for our safety travelling alone in this way. The disappearance of guards, porters and other railway staff precludes it entirely nowadays. What a pity!'

A SENSE OF ADVENTURE

'Our hill at Laindon to the summit at the Crown Hotel was notorious in thwarting the efforts of some vehicles. We children would have bets on whether the Eastern National bus bound for Tilbury would make it to the top. More often than not it would have to run backwards down again and make another attempt. Passengers sometimes had to disembark and walk to the top, there to reboard and continue their journey. Which reminds me of another form of transport – the steam trains.

There seemed to be more sense of adventure when these snorting beasts hissed their way into the station. I didn't mind being enveloped in a cloud of steam and noise. It was fun just to stand on the road bridge peering through the railings to watch its departure, especially on Sunday evenings. The train would sometimes be so crowded with day trippers from Southend returning to London that it would give a series of rapid chug-chug-chugs as the wheels spun, struggling to get a grip on the rails. It was the practice also for someone from a wedding party to tip off the driver that there was a bride on board, when for a long way up the track, to much laughter and blushes, he would "cock-a-doodle-do" on the whistle.'

'The fare to Southend from Rochford by train was fourpence halfpenny in the 1920s. There also used to be a paddle steamer from the pier to Margate and to London up the Thames. You could go down below and watch all the workings of the boat.'

'In the days of the steam trains I used to see a man cleaning the signals at Epping. He would climb a ladder attached to the post carrying a lamp and cleaning materials. When he reached a small platform he then proceeded to clean the red and green glass. He opened a box and removed the lamp, and after cleaning the reflector inside he would put in the new lamp. This was a most important job as there was no electricity until the advent of the Central Line, when the old signals were removed. There were no hold ups from signal failures in those days.'

ON THE WATER

'I was born in 1916 in Leytonstone, which at that time was on the border of Essex. Sometimes summer Sundays were spent at Southend. Usually we travelled by steam train from Leytonstone LMS station, but on special occasions we went to Tower Pier in London where we boarded a paddle steamer, the *Royal Daffodil* or *Royal Eagle*, and sailed down to Southend Pier. We could go below to watch the huge polished pistons working the paddle wheels on each side. The steamer went on to Herne Bay, Ramsgate and Margate, but Dad and I got seasick so we stayed in Southend until it returned!'

'I well remember the big ships bringing grain to the flour mills and timber to Sadd's Wharf right up to Fullbridge. A dredger was at work until a dispute arose when Maldon Council increased the price of gravel sold to London for road making. London refused to pay, so the dredger was removed from the river. Hence the silting and so Maldon Port ended. No longer did we see the Customs officers and foreign sailors shopping in the town.'

HOUSE & HOME

THE WAY WE LIVED THEN

From tiny country cottages to manor houses, the way we live has changed so much within living memory. Household routine often followed a rigid pattern and there were no labour saving devices – and usually no electricity. There may have been roses round the door, but inside our homes were often cramped for space, cold and draughty!

HOUSE PRICES

'Our house in Chingford, built in 1914, was part of the large outward growth of suburbia which took place before the First World War. Few people then purchased their homes. In 1914 the rent for our house, a typical three bedroomed home of the time, was £52 a year. This included rates, water rates, and the landlord to be responsible for all outside repairs and decoration of rooms. My father, working in London for Westminster Bank, earned £185 a year.

The house had open coal fires in the downstairs rooms and the two main bedrooms. The lighting was by gas; a gas mantle covered a jet to give a diffused light. The mantles were most fragile and needed constant renewal. In the scullery and toilet there was only a naked gas jet. My father, for preference, continued to use an oil lamp for reading.'

'We moved to Essex from London in 1928. Our new three bedroomed house in Harold Park cost £675, and my mother paid £3 12s 10d into the bank each month for the mortgage.'

IT HAD ITS PECULIARITIES

'Woodrow is a small hamlet adjacent to Hatfield Forest. Its 21 houses, which are almost unaltered today, were up to the outbreak of the Second World War occupied by my relations who were agricultural workers.

Living in a 300 year old farm cottage in the 1920s had its own peculiarities. The walls were lath and plaster allowing ample ventilation. On a windy evening the bulging wallpaper, caught in the rays of a dim oil lamp, created untold fantasy to the young mind. The kitchen cum living room with its uneven brick floor covered in coconut matting called for accurate placing of the kitchen table, over which hung the oil lamp.

The centre of the household was the fireplace around which the family huddled on a winter's evening. The stove itself had long passed its maximum efficiency, an open range with a burnt out oven, and the flames percolating through could only be made usable by the insertion of used ploughshares. Nevertheless the front was cleaned regularly with blacklead, the hearth whitened and the fender buffed with emery paper. Father kept the large chimney clean by dragging brushes through attached to poles.

The scullery contained no sink but washing was done in a bowl on an old table. By the window was a mirror before which Father had a twice weekly shave with a cut-throat razor which had been previously honed on a belt he wore around his waist. On the window sill stood my toothbrush in a mug. I used salt to clean my teeth!

Water was carried from a pump 100 yards away. Eight families depended on this supply and during the summer there was a general agreement to use only two pails per household. Normally washing water was caught from the roof or from drainage ponds in the garden. During dry spells a horse and water cart was borrowed from a farm and a mile journey made to Pincey Brook. This was then eked out, usually on a Sunday, for the weekly wash on Monday.

Bedrooms were always draughty, the leaded light windows saw to this. When climbing the "wooden hill" it was not unknown for the candle to be blown out, a measure of wind velocity which was a talking point next day! In winter the bed was warmed with a housebrick, previously heated in the oven, and wrapped in an old piece of blanket. Bed covers were supplemented by old coats. I was fortunate not to have to sleep head to tail!'

EACH DAY SET ASIDE

'If the house had a flight of steps up to the front door they needed to be cleaned with hearthstone. My mother used to wear a rubber-backed apron for this chore, and over it a "coarse apron" which was like sacking and was worn for dirty outside jobs.

Inside the house fireplaces were swept every morning, the ashes emptied and the fire laid with scrunched up newspaper (*The Times* didn't burn well!), sticks of kindling and small knobs of coal. The kitchen range needed to be blackleaded to keep it shining. Zebo was the brand we used.

The carpets were swept with stiff brushes. It was customary to sprinkle water or even tea leaves on the carpet prior to sweeping to "lay the dust". At spring cleaning time the carpets were rolled up, carried to the garden and hung over the washing line to be beaten thoroughly with a cane carpet beater.

Suburban houses that were built before 1920 often had two

gates. The front gate had a porcelain or enamel label saying "No hawkers or circulars" screwed to it, and the other one was labelled "Tradesmen's entrance" and led to the side way and the kitchen door.'

STONE FLAGS AND BARE EARTH

'My aunt's cottage at Pebmarsh had the front door split in half like a stable door and she only opened the top to callers. The floors were mostly stone flags, though the kitchen had brick laid floors and the one little sitting room had floorboards placed across bare earth. My feet were always freezing as the floors were covered only by home-made rugs. My aunt worked so hard on her knees scrubbing those floors.'

NO ROAD PROVIDED

'We moved from London to Thundersley in 1934. In those days it was not the custom to provide a road before building houses, so our brand new bungalow, bought for the grand sum of £500, was with several others on an unmade road, originally farmland. My mother used to say how worried she was by the sight of the removal van coming up the road swaying from side to side in the ruts.'

A BRAND NEW HOUSE

'My mother was delighted when we moved to a brand new house at Shoeburyness in 1936 as the house had electric lights and a coal-fired copper built into the kitchen. The dining room possessed a blackleaded kitchener that had a coal-fired oven. The front room had a tiled surround open fireplace.

The electricity was on the "flicker" system. If more than three lights were switched on at once, the lights flickered up and down until one light was switched off. I think my parents used to be scared to death as to how much it would cost to run, as hitherto we had only had gas lighting. Indeed, I think we still had gas lighting in the kitchen.

Even though we had electric light, we used to go to bed by candlelight, and were never allowed to turn on the upstairs lights. Neither were we allowed to play in the bedrooms or read in bed.

My dad bought a new dining room suite when we moved to Shoebury, of which he was very proud. He gave a special prize to whoever kept their chair free of scratches every year. I can still hear myself loudly complaining when my brother put his feet on my chair, and I won a lovely stuffed toy rabbit for keeping my chair the best.

I think we were lucky compared with a lot of kids. Some friends of mine didn't even have blankets on their beds – only old coats. At least we all had a bed to sleep in, with sheets and blankets. My mother was a wonderful manager of money. She got paid on a Friday, and didn't do her weekly shop until the following Thursday. She had saved her money all that time, and we never had anything on "tick" as lots of people did. I don't know about "good old days". I think I prefer the present age.'

HOUSEHOLD ROUTINE

'Household routine made a very full day in our house at Woodham Ferrers in the 1920s. Basic tools were brooms, brushes and dustpans. Floors covered with lino were scrubbed and shaking those awful coconut mats, as we called them, would never yield all the dust. When lifted next day they showed a dust pattern underneath. We had an open fire in the living room and one in the kitchen with an oven at the side; both had to be blackleaded and the hearths whitened with step powder. Kindling wood, small twiggy sticks, was brought in each day and put in the hearth to dry for the next morning's fire lighting. This wood was collected in the summer evenings and logs sawn up to store in the lean-to shed behind the washhouse. We washed the crockery in an enamel bowl with hot water from the black, sooty kettle kept on the side of the fire to soften the water. One knob of soda was added to help move that awful line of grease that collected round the sides.'

AN INCONVENIENT HOUSE

'As a young child in the 1930s I lived in a villa at Loughton directly facing Epping Forest. It had two floors above a basement kitchen, and a spooky cellar, dark and mysterious, where my father had a work bench and kept his carpentry tools. The household coal was kept there and my father's bicycle. Scarcely any one owned a motor car then.

It was an inconvenient house with its two flights of stairs, but the rooms were large and there was plenty of space for my sister and me to play. There was no electricity or hot water system. Each room was lit by gas, which cast a gloomy yellow glow. I remember the glass light-shades, and delicate white gas mantles making a popping sound as the gas came hissing through when they were lit. Mother made tapers from twisted newspaper in the belief they were safer than matches, and kept them on the mantelpiece in a pewter jug. In the bedrooms there were very small gas lights but I do not remember these being lit. We went to bed by candlelight.

Unlike many kitchens of the 1930s there was no kitchen range, to be cleaned with blacklead. My grandmother who lived nearby, had such a stove with a hearthrug in front, hand-made with knotted pieces of coloured cloth, but Mother used a gas cooker. Our open fireplace was surmounted by a long mantelpiece, and surrounded by a high fireguard. On the hearth reposed the essential requirements for a coal fire – a poker, fire-tongs and a small brush to sweep the fallen ashes.

Upstairs were two grander rooms – a dining room and sitting room. In the latter was a three piece suite, a china cabinet with a glass front, a carpet (the only one in the house), and an aspidistra on a polished stand. In spite of the better quality furnishings, it was a cheerless room, seldom used.

We spent more time in the living room, which we children called "the top kitchen". The wireless was here, working on a battery and accumulator, which had to be recharged at frequent intervals at the local cycle shop. There were two accumulators, one always ready to replace the other when the power ran out – generally during a particularly exciting programme!

At the top of the house the bedrooms had washstands, complete with china washing bowls, soap dishes and large jugs to hold hot water. There were built-in cupboards, chairs made of wickerwork and feather-filled eiderdowns.

There was no bathroom and only an outside toilet. Nevertheless, of its type, it was well furnished compared to many homes in the village, for there were countless old cottages with four small rooms and a scullery – and much higher up the social scale, some very grand establishments where the owners employed a cook and maidservant.'

A COUNTRY RECTORY

'In 1928, when I was eight years old, the father of my best friend was appointed rector of a country parish in south-east Essex. During the next 15 years or so I was a regular visitor to the rectory and village and got to know the area and people very well.

The rectory was a Victorian house of 1850 standing in something like three acres of grounds, including a spacious drive, flower gardens and shrubberies which surrounded the house, and a field with two small coppices beyond the gardens. There were extensive outbuildings comprising stables and a coach-house across a cobbled yard from the house, pigsties and a cowhouse and henhouse. There was a large kitchen garden, partly walled for espalier fruit trees and equipped with cucumber frames and glass houses.

At the time this was considered an appropriate residence for the rector, who was quite high in the village hierarchy. All has changed now; a modern rectory has been built to replace the old house and most of the grounds are under a modern housing development. But on a recent visit I noticed a remnant of the old coppice with a hollow in the ground where we used to find traces of the fires left by the tramps who, in those days, preferred to camp out rather than spend the night in the local workhouse.

The rectory had a domestic staff of cook, housemaid and gardener. The latter was a man of great character. He was a native of the village, the chief bell ringer and a sidesman at the church. Looking after the gardens and supplying the house with vegetables and fruit was a full time job. There was no hose-pipe system and watering was done with cans replenished from a small water cart mounted on two wheels and filled from a tap in the yard.

The rectory was a large house by present day standards. On the ground floor was a sizable entrance hall from which ran the main staircase. There was a dining room, a drawing room, a study, a cloakroom and sundry small storage rooms. At the rear of the house was a large kitchen, a scullery and a wash room equipped with a boiler. The kitchen contained a large coal-burning range and a gas stove and was the social centre of the house for the domestic staff and junior family. Tea seemed to be available there at any time of day. On the first floor there were five or six bedrooms, opening off a long corridor. There were servants' rooms on the second floor and a back staircase.

The house was lighted by gas – there was no electrical supply. Candles were often used in the bedrooms and candlesticks and matches were set out ready for collection in the hall. There was, of course, no central heating and the house could be exceedingly cold in the winter. I remember vividly, during the intensely cold winter of 1939/40, sitting close to the banked-up fire in the drawing room and then moving back as the coal burnt through only to move forward again when the fire was made up. This performance went on throughout the evening until one retired to a freezing cold bed equipped with a hot brick wrapped in a duster.

Life in a country rectory had its unusual features. I must be one of the few people of my generation to have attended family prayers in the dining room after breakfast – at least I think it was *after* breakfast. It may have been before with breakfast as a reward for good behaviour. Sunday meant attendance at morning service and evensong. The morning service seemed very long, particularly on those dreaded occasions when the litany was read. The organ in the church had to be pumped by hand and this was a task allocated to the rector's sons, who had time for a cigarette outside the vestry door during the sermon.

There was a lingering feudal atmosphere in the village at that time. At the head of the hierarchy was the squire who lived in the big house and who was one-time Lord Lieutenant of the county. After

Cottages round the village green at Ridgewell – an idyllic picture but our homes were often cold and draughty without today's mod cons.

him came the rector and the doctor and some of the more well-to-do farmers. Then came the local tradesmen and the village people. There seemed to be a clear division between church people and chapel goers.'

AS VILLAGERS HAD FOR CENTURIES

'I came to live in a village in the north of the county in 1940 as a London evacuee, and it was my lot to be billeted with an elderly couple in a tiny cottage which backed onto woodland. The experience proved to be a cultural shock for this city-dweller, who grew to love the countryside and its ways.

The cottage had a thick thatch and cream washed walls. There was a roofed well close by the front door from which all water had to be drawn in a bucket lowered on a rope and hand cranked. Every drop, summer and winter, had to be wound up: not much fun on a freezing December morning. We were lucky. Some in the village had to rely on the village pump which stood on a small green in the centre of the community. It was not unknown for the pump to seize up in the worst of the winter weather. On the other hand, rumour had it that those living in the newly built council houses could actually draw water from modern taps that were fitted over their kitchen sinks – such luxury! However, my foster mother was very proud of our water, arguably the best in the county as pronounced by the local doctor, who insisted on a glassful whenever he called.

We lived as villagers had for centuries. My foster parents were over 65 years old, so they qualified for the Old Age Pension of ten shillings per week; an early 20th century innovation. However, this was hardly enough to live on, and the garden was the mainstay as a provider. It was worked on by the man of the house to yield food the year round. Potatoes and green vegetables of every variety were grown to cover all seasons. Salad plants flourished abundantly. Freshly harvested, washed and taken straight to the table, they were delicious. On summer nights nothing could surpass a supper of newly pulled spring onions, a heap of home-made curd cheese spooned from its muslin bag hanging in the larder and a chunk of crusty cottage loaf hot from the oven, with a mug of creamy milk, delivered that morning by the local farmer. He kept a herd of cows at the nearby farm and made a round each day with his churn-like milk container on wheels, ladling out one's requirements with a stainless steel measuring scoop into our largest milk jug. At calving time he also offered the first milk of the mother cows, known as beestings. It was thick and rich and when baked was like the best egg custard ever tasted. It was good served alone or with fruit.

Possibly the worst aspect of simple village life was the sanitary arrangements for such outlying residents. The best on offer was a small shed at the end of the back garden, well away from the cottage. The lavatory seat was a wide plank with a hole cut in the centre, and one perched over a deep pit, which by the "enlightened" days of 1940 was emptied once or twice a year in the dead of night by a council tanker with a suction device. In previous times, no doubt, the shed would just have been moved to a new site nearby when necessary, and the pit filled in.

There was no such thing as a super soft toilet roll. Stiff newspaper cut up and threaded on to a loop of twine was the only attempt at refinement. In winter the wind whistled up from below, in summer the stench was sickening and the accompaniment of flies and bluebottles made one's visit to the shed quite unpleasant.

Despite being rudimentary, cottage life could be very comfortable. The thick walls and thatch ensured that inside the temperature was cold in summer and very snug in winter. Winter evenings were particularly cosy. The light was soft, being a central large oil lamp with a dark green shade. This was known as the reading lamp and was the only light available apart from candles which were used to show one to bed. The lamp was complemented by the glow of the range fire, and we clustered around the main piece of furniture in the living room, a big scrubbed wooden table, sporting a deep red chenille cloth, which was the pride of my foster mother.

One was never idle. There was much to do, and only when all jobs were completed could one resort to reading the weekly local newspaper or a book borrowed from the mobile library. In my case there was usually homework to be done. However, a task I well remember was rug making. All discarded clothing and such was saved, and during winter evenings it was my duty to cut all the saved materials up into short strips for my guardian to hook through oblongs of hessian. She would co-ordinate the colours and devise patterns just as one would with patchwork, and some of the finished rugs were very fine. Of course, they had a limited life, and new ones would be made each winter. The finished works of art needed thousands of strips and my young fingers would become quite bruised by the overuse of the scissors.

We also needed a constant supply of spills to take lights from the fire. Using a match would be far too extravagant. Therefore, squares of waste paper were cut out and rolled from one corner, then given a twist at one end for easy lighting. They were bunched and stood in an old copper pot down by the hearth to be ever ready for use.

Most of the cooking was done on the range. Its fire never went out. It had to be carefully riddled to keep it unclogged, but at the same time not to make the ash fly, as all the washing had to be dried and aired on a cord strung from each end of the mantelshelf. I was warned, "We don't want the clothes covered with ash, thank you." The top of the range was very hot, and so a kettle was usually singing away ready for the next brew-up of tea, and the flat irons were heated up on it on Tuesdays, which was religiously Ironing Day. Great pride was taken in the range's appearance. It was polished regularly with blacklead and brushed until it shone. The brass fire-irons, brush, shovel, poker and tongs, which rested on the brass topped fender were also burnished until they gleamed.

It was quite amazing how the women of that time managed every form of cooking on these ranges; anything from frying and stewing to simmering, and the two ovens at the side were used with equal skill for fast or slow baking. We did have a small oil stove kept by the larder as an auxiliary help, but this was an exception.

Almost all the meat we ever tasted was when the master of the house went poaching in the woods, about which I was cautioned to say nothing. Rabbits would mysteriously appear hanging in the larder and were quickly turned into mouth-watering stews. Sometimes on Sundays roast rabbit would be on the menu, stuffed with breadcrumbs, onions and herbs. Very occasionally one of our hens would succumb to the master's neck-wringing prowess, but could never compare with rabbit stew.

By and large we lived very well on very little. Life was busy and rewarding. Everything we had was from our own efforts. An air of deep contentment pervaded our little world and we were happy.'

FURNISHING WAS A PROBLEM

'We moved to Chingford soon after my husband Ken was demobbed from the Navy in 1946. After walking around North Chingford every day for about three weeks in search of a house to buy (they were not easy to find) he had found a little house in Epping Glade, facing the forest, which rose up ahead of us to the top of Pole Hill: the cost was £1,985, an absolute fortune to us at that time.

Although the house was small, furnishing it was quite a problem; everything was in short supply and as well as money, coupons were needed to buy even the basic necessities such as a bed, mattress, cooker, floor covering, blankets or sheets and then only very plain utility designs were available. We had bought some heavy antique dining furniture during the war, so the dining room we did not have to worry about. We also had a cot for our baby son, and Ken had made the rest of the nursery furniture. Our bedroom was the biggest problem, because after buying bed, blankets, pillows, sheets and floor covering we had no coupons left for wardrobes and dressing table, and wood was also in short supply so Ken could not make them. Our bedroom became festooned with our clothes hanging from the picture rail, and piles of underwear stacked on the floor where the dressing table should be. However, one day we saw a wonderful notice in the local paper. It was an advert put in by the borough council, announcing a sale of furniture for which no coupons were needed.

This furniture had been kept by the council for people whose homes had been destroyed by bombing and it was no longer required for this purpose. This was the only time in his life that Ken was first in a queue. Only one of each article was available to each customer so Ken got one single wardrobe, of unstained deal, a small chest of drawers with a mirror fixed on top, and a small rug. I was much further back in the queue, with the baby in the pram, and all the furniture had gone by the time I got in, but I also got a rug.

The single wardrobe became two when Ken dismantled it, using the wood to fill in the recesses beside the chimney breast, thus producing two double wardrobes. The chest of drawers with mirror became our dressing table. Painted a delicate green to match the door and picture rail, our bedroom suite filled us with pride and a great sense of achievement.'

LIVING WITH GRANDMA

'During my childhood I lived with my parents and my widowed Grandma in a two up, two down cottage, the like of which many were built. The living room one step up from the kitchen was the hub of the cottage. It was dominated by the fireplace (a fire and oven combined), made of steel which frequently had to be cleaned with emery cloth to keep it shining, as Grandma was houseproud. The high shelf above the fireplace was dressed in a velvet cover, edged with bobbles which swung in the heat from the fire. An open fire makes plenty of cinders and some were used to make a path along the side of the house, as this pathway was used every day. I fell over on this path and even now I still carry the marks of black ash in the scars on my knees.

The downstairs rooms were lit by gaslight which hissed and wavered under its pretty glass globe. When the fragile gas mantle broke, one of my parents would stand on a chair to remove the useless mantle and carefully put on a new one. The ring and chain attached to the piping would be pulled to release the gas and a match applied and the mantle would start to glow and be adjusted.

We needed a candle to light us to bed. There were fireplaces in the bedrooms but I cannot remember there ever being a fire lit in them. Probably too expensive. My parents' room had a set of cream china with a rose pattern on it on a side table; this consisted of a large bowl for washing in and a large jug to carry water, a soap dish with a lid and a vase for toothbrushes and two useful round potties with handles to go under the bed.

The toilet facilities meant a walk from the kitchen door in all weathers to the small brick extension at the rear of the kitchen. There was no lighting, no hand-basin or toilet paper as we have today, but a wooden seat the width of the brick building with a hole in the centre over the pan and an elementary cistern that worked when a metal chain was pulled. It had a wooden door and an iron latch. It could be creepy as spiders and other insects lurked inside and a Virginia creeper grew over the walls and roof wherever the tendrils could take hold, pretty in the autumn when the leaves turned red and gold. At the rear hung the tin bath. Friday night was convenient to carry the bath into the kitchen or living room (in winter near the fire). Several kettles full of water needed boiling to fill the full size bath. I had a smaller version, which could be used for washing some smaller items of clothing, or I could paddle in it during hot summers.

In 1896 the South Essex Water Company were sinking bore holes to provide water for new housing. This was a boon to all homes, as new mains and pipes were installed and kitchens had water piped into sinks with taps.

During the First World War there was practically no building but the ammunition factories and the like continued to take water from reservoirs. After the war London County Council built an estate at Becontree to take the overspill from London and much more work was done by the waterworks company to bring water to the increasing population. My father worked for the Waterworks Company. This meant shift work around the clock, so housework had to be fitted in according to when Father required a meal or slept during the day. We lived a short walk from the town and visited the market which was very varied with a cattle market on Wednesdays. On other days stalls sold food and clothing. It was a colourful scene.

When Grandma was a young wife milk was sold from a barrow, ladled out by cans from huge churns. In later life milk was delivered by a horse-drawn float and the coal came in a cart piled high with hundredweight sacks and pulled by an even larger shire horse. Once a year a chimney sweep would be ordered, usually in the spring or as soon as we no longer needed a fire. I would run up the garden to see the sweep's brush emerge from the top of the chimney.'

WE ALL HAD TO HELP

'I was born in 1904, the tenth child out of eleven. My father was very strict with us. He was a master builder and we lived in a three up and three down house in Ilford. We all had our jobs to do. The boys did the heavy jobs like chopping firewood, and as they got older and went to work as apprentices to my father, so the girls took over their jobs at home, including blackleading the kitchen range till you could see your face in it. The brass fender and tongs had to shine, and there were all the beds to make and all the slops to empty.

Monday mornings we were up at about 6 am to get the copper going for a wash that lasted about four days. As each one of us got older and went to work it got harder for those who were left, like me and my younger sister. Obviously there was no fridge, but we had a big galvanised tin which was dug deep into the ground and held butter, cheese, bacon and milk. We had to have a large amount of food each week with such a large family.'

WHAT A HARD LIFE

'Next time you put your washing in the machine, think of living in the 1930s. Some houses at Brentwood had one cold tap between them. On washday the copper was kept boiling, burning anything one could find to keep it going. Mother would be all hot because it was a day's work, and there were big families in those days. When the eldest girl came in from school she had to put the clothes through the mangle. Mother would have to iron on the kitchen table with flat irons, heated on the kitchen fire. There was no electricity.

We had to sleep two or three top and bottom in bed. When one turned we all turned. The houses were not very big, two up and two down, with a small kitchen or outhouse where the copper was kept. There were no warm bedrooms and there was often ice on the windows in winter.

No hoovers, no washing machines, no electrical gadgets, no carpets and only lino on the floors so Mum had to clean them on her hands and knees. What a hard life she had.'

CLEANING THE STEP

'My grandmother used to pay a woman sixpence to clean her step. This had nothing to do with the desire for a clean entrance. The idea was that the neighbours would assume that she had somebody to do all the housework. As several other neighbours employed the same woman it would not seem to have been a very successful idea.'

A GRUESOME FIND

'My father was a farmer who came to Boxted in 1925. We lived in a big, timber framed and lath and plaster farmhouse. It must have been one of the coldest houses in East Anglia. Some of the rooms, including bedrooms, were heated by coal fires in cast iron grates. The main rooms downstairs burned enormous wood fires; the heat went straight up the cavernous chimney without warming the room at all and the east wind howled through numerous gaps and cracks and ill-fitting windows.

When my father moved in, the builders (Deaves of Nayland) discovered and opened up an ancient powder closet which had been bricked up. In the ceiling was a trapdoor leading into the roof space. When this was opened the skeleton, uniform and armour of a long dead Cromwellian soldier fell out. History relates that a brief skirmish took place in the area of the nearby Cross Inn during the Civil War and no doubt the grisly discovery was a casualty who had crawled away to hide and die.'

THE MANOR

'The Manor at Boxted is mentioned in the Domesday Book. We came here in 1922. Our father and uncle had recently left the army, and it was the only property for sale at the time, offering two biggish farmhouses and sufficient land – some 700 acres.

The sale was in the hands of Stanfords of Colchester. The brochure read: "Boxted Hall Estate, near Colchester, Essex being sold. A sporting old fashioned country residence, with second convenient residence know as Pond House. This is admirably situated on the southern portion of the estate. It is near the garrison and market town of Colchester, the scene of many stirring events, and provides a market for the produce of the estate and social attractions so often wanting in the country. Noted Essex and Suffolk Foxhounds kennelled within three miles and hunting the district five days a fortnight. Other packs of foxhounds are easily available by road or train. Two postal deliveries a day and a telegraph exchange in the village."

When we bought Boxted Hall all the main rooms faced north

because previous owners were, it was rumoured, afraid of fevers from the south wind – those rooms all have pretty friezes.

Our mother changed the main rooms to the south to have sunshine. The old dining room became the kitchen. She installed one of the very first refrigerators – it was in fact a Frigidaire – and also an Esse (like an Aga and guaranteed to burn no more than £5 of fuel a year – it burnt anthracite). When she came to cook on this Esse herself during the war she realised this vast kitchen had no water. If you wanted water you had to come out of the kitchen and into the scullery, and there was the sink. The fridge was down a long corridor, so the first thing that had to be done was to move them.

Before the house was altered in 1930 there was one bathroom upstairs and one almost out of doors through the servants' hall. Water was hand pumped from the well up to tanks in the roof. I have a memory of the carpenter's son, who came to us as a very young man to be chauffeur and then handyman and gardener, pumping the 150 strokes a day before the electric pump was installed.'

WATER AND WASHDAY

Every drop of water was precious when it had to be carried from the well or pumped up into the bucket. Bathnight meant a tin bath in front of the fire, and washday was a whole day of very hard work using copper and mangle. No running water meant, of course, no indoor sanitation and we all suffered the indignities of the little house at the bottom of the garden.

FETCHING THE WATER

'In the 1920s Prior Cottage in Lee Chapel Lane at Langdon Hills was a single storey wooden building of black ship lapboards with a large pink tiled roof that sagged in the middle.

We had to fetch our water from a spring which was up a hill about a quarter of a mile away, and to get to it we had to cross fields and climb through a fence. How ever my mother got enough water to do all the cooking and washing I cannot recall. We survived through some very severe winters and anyway, melted snow was nearer than the spring and made lovely light Yorkshire puds.'

A hoop was sometimes used to steady the full pails of water brought from pump or well.

'We lived in a farmhouse on the Blake Hall estate near Ongar in the 1930s. The well had been filled in at an earlier date and we had to cross two fields to the road to the standpipe for our drinking water. Whenever we went out we always had to take a water pail to leave at the standpipe until our return. After filling the pail and opening and closing the field gate the fun would start as there were cows in the field. From wherever they were browsing they would spot us coming and make a beeline for our water pails. It was quite a performance trying to prevent them from getting a quick slurp.'

'At Great Maplestead in the late 1940s we carted water from a communal pump some 300 yards away. My father built my sister and me a trolley on which was placed a tin bath and bucket which were filled and then dragged home.'

'I was born in Coggeshall and in the early years my father had the job of selling water to the people of the town. Water was drawn up from St Peter's Well in Stoneham Street and put into a tank on a horse-drawn cart and sold at one penny a bucket.'

'In the 1920s our water supply came from a pump in the shopkeeper's backyard at Wimbish. In summer it invariably dried up and in winter it froze, and water was brought round in a tank pulled by a sturdy horse.'

'We lived in East Tilbury village in the 1920s and most folk obtained their water from wells. Granny had one in her back garden which just had a wooden lid to it – a hazard indeed for youngsters.

Our water supply at Gravel Pit Farm was from a pump down the lane. In severe winter weather we had to take a kettle of hot water to pour over the pump and then pump hard to get the water up. The water was carried in two buckets on a yoke.'

PIPED WATER

'Houses that had bathrooms and WCs required some means of getting water into the cold tanks. There was no main water supply in Abbess Roding in the 1930s, but there were plenty of wells in the area.

It was possible to pump water by hand from a pump in the scullery of our house to covered tanks on a small area of roof above the airing cupboard where the hot tank was (but it was very hard work). We had a petrol engine in a shed by the back door which drove an electrically operated pump at another well a short way down the road. Water was piped to the three tanks on the roof and when they were full the water would overflow into the scullery sink.

Drinking water was obtained from another well in the cellar and collected in an enamelled pail.

When the tanks were full, one switched over the engine from pumping to operating the generator which charged the batteries for electric light, being careful not to get one's clothing caught in the belt while doing this.

The batteries were three rows of large glass cells on shelves at one end of the engine which provided a direct current of 50 volts to the house. It did not provide power for any appliances other than a specially adapted Hoover (50 volts) which could only be used when the batteries were being charged.

The engine took several hours to accomplish its tasks – but petrol was cheap!'

BEFORE THE MAINS

'Having the water cut off one day reminded me of the time when we had no mains water in Great Sampford. It had to be fetched from springs or the river (there were a few private pumps). When I married in 1934, we lived up Johnson's Hill and every drop of water had to be fetched in pails from either a pump at the house down the road, or more often from a spring across the fields. Two pails of water had to last me all day for drinking, cooking and washing up. There was no using of water to wash our hands and then tipping it out, it had to be left in the bowl to use again.

On washday it meant several trips the night before to fill the copper and baths. We had a butt to catch the rainwater and when it was full it lasted some time. but often it had to be strained as it was full of whirtigigs (little wriggly insects). I did not even have a sink, all the water had to be poured down the ditch to soak away. I often wonder how I managed with two small children but we all had to.

When mains water came we had a standpipe in the garden for us and the family next door. Then what bliss when we moved to Moor End in 1949; not just taps with hot and cold water but a bathroom as well. Now we just turn taps on without thinking anything about it.'

TAPS AND KEYS

'Mains water did not come to Hadstock until the late 1920s. Before that the main water supply was from the well in the churchyard, and there were a number of wells at the farms and several ponds in the village. Every house had a water butt to catch the rainwater from the roof. When piped water came to the village only the larger houses had taps inside and there were five standpipes in the village for which each house had a key. The water rate was three shillings and threepence a quarter and if you didn't pay, the key was taken away.'

BATHNIGHT

'We moved to Rettendon in the 1920s. On bathnight, once a week, a very large galvanised bath was brought in front of the coal fire and the family were bathed, one at a time. My sister and I thought this was wonderful and the first time one of my aunts came to visit, we fetched our little stools and sat down to watch her having her bath, much to the amusement of the adults, before we were packed off to bed.'

'I remember being on holiday at my grandparents' farm at White Colne, where bath water was heated in the kitchen copper. Trying to bath in one inch of tepid rainwater, with drowned spiders floating, in what had been the dairy and was the coldest room in the house – we didn't linger!'

'Saturday evenings in the late 1940s the copper which stood in the corner of our scullery was filled and the fire was lit beneath it. When the water was hot my father brought in the tin bath which hung on a nail on the shed wall. He stood this in front of the kitchen range and the hot water was ladled into the bath; our pyjamas and nightdresses hung on the fireguard to warm. My mother and my eldest sister then proceeded to bath my younger sister, myself and my four elder brothers. My sister and I went in first; we soon learnt to keep our elbows and knees in as the side of the bath became very hot from the fire. I can still smell the carbolic soap which was used! When we were scrubbed thoroughly we were taken out and dried by our mother while my sister ladled more hot water into the bath for the next two.

When all six of us were bathed my father then proceeded to empty the water. This had to be baled out into buckets, taken outside and poured into the ditch. Hot water bottles were filled from the remaining water in the copper and placed into our beds. The boys shared a double bed – two at the top and two at the bottom – and we girls had a three-quarter bed – two at the top and one at the bottom. When I recall those evenings I remember the love and care we received from our hard-working parents who took great pride in their large family.'

'In the 1930s my father, a policeman, was moved to Stapleford Abbotts. Here, we were told, the house would have a bathroom. This turned out to be a bath with two taps – but no water laid on and furthermore no plug hole! The pump servicing six houses was two doors along. All water had to be brought in by the pailful and heated in a copper. After baling the bath out, the water was put down the outside loo. "Waste not, want not" was a way of life.'

'By 1949 we had our second son, and at the time we were living in Walton on the Naze. As we did not have a bathroom it meant that when the boys were too big to bath in the sink we used to walk to my parents' home in Kirby Cross pushing two prams, bath the boys (and of course ourselves), then put the boys, ready for bed, back in the prams and walk home. In those days there was no street lighting on the main road from Kirby to Walton and the pathway was not paved.

NO INDOOR SANITATION

'It was usually down the garden. Just imagine a cold wet night, and of course that was when you always needed to go, so off you went with a hurricane lamp or a torch. Sometimes you were allowed to have a candle and a box of matches. I remember we usually went in pairs – and it was a good place to escape to when it was time to wash up!'

'As a child I remember the horse-drawn cart which travelled around the cottages in Maldon collecting the sewage. It always came after dark and was lit with one flickering oil lamp. Everyone referred to this as "Aladdin's Lamp" and the house windows were hastily closed when the cart went by. It only came once a week.'

'There were two lavatories across the yard at our farmhouse near Southend in the 1920s. These had to be emptied on a dunghill, the waste being carried right across the farmyard to a corner of the field where the dunghill was situated.'

'One job we hated was a call of: "Whose turn to dig the hole?" I might say that digging a hole in a frosty winter was no joke, and often a pickaxe was necessary. Then two of us in turn had to carry an often overfull bucket down the garden to the hole, empty the bucket and fill in the hole. After so many holes had been made, the chicken run would be moved over that area and later on it would be a vegetable patch. Nobody, but nobody, had better vegetables than ours in the village.'

WASHDAY

'Women did not have much time for leisure activities in the 1930s and the occasional visit to a friend was the most my mother could expect. Every chore had to be carried out by hand and in the winter, especially, life was very hard.

The washing was done in a small scullery where a copper stood in the corner. This was bricked in and a fire had to be lit underneath to heat the water. If all else failed an old pair of shoes was put on the fire, which soon made the copper boil. Washing took all day on Monday. We always had bubble and squeak and cold meat for dinner that day.'

'I would like to place on record how hard the mother of an average family had to work on washing day (which was usually a Monday) over 50 years ago.

Early on Monday morning before breakfast the copper had to be filled from the cold tap either by a large bowl or a hose fitted to the tap. Next the copper fire had to be lit. The copper was sometimes made of brick and later iron.

While the copper was heating the gallons of water, the children were given breakfast and dressed ready for school. After we departed, washday started in earnest. All the garments to be washed had to be sorted, the whites that needed boiling such as bedlinen, tablecloths, tray cloths, cotton underwear etc from the coloured hand wash.

My mother used to line the copper with an old sheet before placing in the white washing as the Hudson's washing powder which was added to the clothes to be boiled used to form a scum and it dried on the garments as copper grease stain. This boil would be stirred at times by a thick wooden stick.

Next came all the underclothes which needed hand washing. We all wore many more garments of a much larger size than we do today. The average schoolgirl wore a vest (woollen) or combinations in winter, a liberty bodice, a pair of bloomers (either white or navy), a petticoat and a gym blouse, which amounted to a lot of garments to be washed for a family of four girls. Mother wore a vest, bloomers, a bra, corsets, a petticoat, a blouse and a large apron and skirt. Dad had a thick vest with half sleeves, long pants, a thick shirt, also a pair of very dirty overalls which had to be washed each week (he was a marine engineer).

Mother fought bravely on with this heap till we all arrived home at 12.30 for lunch. Monday lunch was usually cold meat and pickles or "bubble and squeak" with fruit pie left over from Sunday lunch.

The big action really began when we arrived home from school. Large baths were brought in which had to be filled with clear rinsing water and another with "blue" water. It was my privilege, or duty being the eldest, to turn the handle of the large wooden mangle. The clothes had to be folded so as not to put in too many creases making the ironing more difficult. Clothes with buttons had to be thinned out at the button edges so as not to cut the garment or rip the buttons off. Everything went through the mangle two or three times. The whites, sheets etc went into the bath of blue water (made with a block of blue contained in a cloth bag). This ensured the whites were kept a nice bright white.

The last job of all was the socks and stockings – a job my mother hated. We all wore long black gym stockings. When we lived in Walton mine were hand knitted to save the sand cutting the backs of my knees as I had to cross the shore road four times a day.

When the washing was finished the copper water had to be emptied and the copper dried out. The fire had to be shovelled out and the outside of the copper whitened.

After that my mother used to scrub the kitchen floor. About 6 pm we would have our tea. Mother often had an egg or sandwiches made from raw steak which was scraped and spread like potted meat, as she said she felt tired out.'

'At Sheering one family had a giant mangle which used heavy stones in drums to press the water out of wet clothes. Villagers were charged a penny or twopence for this service. Some people used mangles with large wooden rollers to feed the clothes through, a chore children could help with. Later came the lightweight rubber adjustable Acme wringer – wonderful!

FOOD AND SHOPPING

Our food may have been plainer, but it was fresh and filling and many women produced tasty meals from home-grown vegetables and, perhaps, a harvest rabbit. When we did go shopping it was usually to local shops, or a once a week trip to the nearest town. Most commodities were delivered to our doors and much of the traffic on our then quiet streets would have been the various delivery vans and bicycles we relied on. There were other treats too, such as fresh muffins.

ROASTING THE JOINT

'At the beginning of the century we had a bakery at Colchester where the local women would bring their joints of meat on a Sunday morning to be cooked in the bread ovens for a small charge. The meat would be collected when the women were on their way home from church.'

MAKEWEIGHT

'My mother as a little girl was sent to collect the bread for her mother. Bakers used to put a piece of "makeweight" in with the bread, which she ate on the way home.'

MOTHER WAS A GOOD COOK

'Our mother was a good cook and made meals out of more or less anything. We kept chickens for eggs and our father caught wild rabbits from which we had delicious meals, with vegetables grown on the allotments nearby at High Easter. Father also made wine from potatoes, rhubarb, wheat and parsnips. We had an old black cooking range to heat and cook by.'

'Our diet consisted chiefly of suet puddings boiled in a cloth, and vegetables plus various soups and broths. Beef tea was taken if you were ill and caraway seed cake was a must for Sunday tea. Porridge was our regular breakfast and a large kettle was always singing on the hob.'

'The thing I remember most about food is my grandmother's lovely boiled suet pudding which she served with thick gravy, before eating the meat and vegetables.'

SLOW COOKING

'We used to grow our own vegetables. There was a constant battle to outwit the pheasants, pigeons and rabbits as they enjoyed the fruits of our labours. If there was nothing in the garden, we didn't eat. At harvest time we looked forward to meat for the pot. As the reaper and binder circled the cornfield cutting and binding up the sheaves, rabbits would move into the ever-decreasing centre until at the last circuit they would rush to escape the terrible approaching monster. All round the perimeter men and boys were waiting with sticks to catch them. One needed a good eye to do this efficiently and humanely. I remember one day my brother aged about ten came home triumphantly with seven rabbits he had caught. We were a large family, seven children, and my mother had nightmares trying to feed us all in those very hard times. This brother later became a valued member of the village cricket team, having such a good "eye".

We had no refrigerator, so in summer milk would quickly go off. This was not wasted but put into a muslin bag and hung up to drain to be seasoned and used as tasty cottage cheese. In those days our milk was not pasteurised so even sour milk was still palatable.

Some of our older residents at Sheering remember neighbours clubbing together to buy meat scraps; they would pool their pennies so that each family would get a taste of meat for the stew.

Slow cooking on the back of the stove or in the oven was the order of the day. Stews, creamy rice puddings, boiled and steamed puds, dishes of haricot beans with canned tomatoes and a small piece of bacon. When the wind was in the right direction and the fire bright, baking was at its best, often one special day in the week, and disaster if the fire wouldn't draw on that day. The oven-readiness was tested by the state of the fire and a knowledgeable hand inside to judge the temperature and temperament too.

As children we knew what we could eat off the hedgerows. Bread-and-cheese was the tender shoot of the hawthorn leaf buds. Cheeses were the round flat packs of seeds of the field mallow, sweetbriar the new wild rose shoots as thick as a finger and delicious when peeled. We knew which berries could be eaten, how to find hazel nuts, wild plums and harvest apples, not to be confused with crab apples. Secretly we knew where and when to find mushrooms, the best blackberries and how to enjoy wheat grains rubbed of their chaff to fill a hungry gap when far from home and ever-hungry.

Water was the main drink, tasting fresh and cold even in summer. Home-made lemonade too, carried across the fields at harvest time. We children helped put up the stooks, playing hide-and-seek too but woe betide if the sheaves were disturbed and fell over. Tizer was a rare treat saved up for, and gingerpop with the ball-stopper to keep the bubbles in.

The baker, butcher, fishmonger and paraffin/accumulator roundsman came to the village but we used to bake our own bread. Flour was obtained from Burton's Mill in 14 pound bags (a stone) and for large families bigger sacks which became weevil infested if not properly stored or left too long before use. In our cottage, attached to the washhouse was a large brick oven which would be fired with wood in the long fire chamber underneath. It had been in use before our time there. Neighbours would bring food to be cooked in it, bread, pies, roasts. It would be loaded up with flat long-handled tools and was the only one in the area. Above the oven was a flat area for storing the wood fuel. Sometimes the children would be sent off to get yeast if it had not been got from the baker's roundsman. I adored eating it and remember my mother complaining that it didn't look like four ounces to her so I had to own up in case she took her complaint back to the baker's shop. This was before the days of dried yeast.

From the maltings we used to get great glass jars of cod liver oil and malt and we all enjoyed our daily spoonful in the winter. Although the maltings were over a mile away as the crow flies the wind would carry the smell of the malt right up to us. This part of Essex prospered on the mills, maltings and breweries. To make malt, barley was spread all over the large areas of floor. The men would have to turn it at different times in the process as the barley sprouted in the warmth. There was a special cone-shaped kiln fired with bundles of faggots which were kept in great stacks in the yard. This malt was sent up to Scotland for special whiskies.

We used to wait after school in summer for the "Stop-Me-and-Buy-One" Walls ice cream man on his tricycle with the big blue ice box containing ice cream for wafers, cornets and the long triangular "Snowfruit" and "Snowcream" water ices. He must have pedalled a long way either from Harlow (three miles) or Sawbridgeworth, a very uphill three miles.'

PIGS AND SPARROWS

'Lots of people at Langley kept a pig in the back garden which was killed for eating. Neighbours killed at different times, sharing the salted or smoked meat which hung from the cottage beams. Other meat was obtained by poaching rabbits. Little boys had catapults and killed sparrows in thatched roofs at night. The birds were skinned and put into puddings with vegetables which had been grown in the garden.'

GOING SHOPPING

'We had two bakers at Great Yeldham – Baker Hardy came from Toppesfield and had a green van with two round windows just behind the cab. My mother always had a cottage loaf from him each Monday, and her washing powder – how that came about I don't know. It was always late when he arrived – after tea. The other baker was Greg Rice, whose bakehouse was at the back of the Three Bottles pub. He was a kindly old man, and on a Saturday there would be a free "pat" (small bread roll) for each child on his round. How we looked forward to that, no bread ever tasted so good, sometimes it would still be warm enough for the butter to melt and we were always allowed to eat it straight away.

There were two grocers in the village, Mr Carter and Mr Mortimer. We patronized Mr Carter because he was one of my father's customers, whereas Mr Mortimer, who had another shop in Castle Hedingham, wasn't. They were both real general stores, the layout the same in both; to the right the groceries and to the left the drapery, with hardware at the back in the middle. The weekly shop was a real social occasion; my mother would sit on a chair by the groceries and then it would begin. Almost everything was weighed and packed to order, though usually sugar would have been put up in the thick blue paper bags that were used then. I never could fathom how they could be filled so full and the top folded in such a way that the contents remained intact. There was usually a taste of the cheese before purchase, and the bacon side shown before the rashers were cut. If Mother needed anything from the drapery side, Mrs Carter would be summoned to serve her.'

'In 1930 there was a blacksmith's shop and a bakery at Jaspers Green. Mr J. Cheek was the blacksmith and his wife and her aunt were the bakers. There were three other bakers, one from Finchingfield, one from Wethersfield and Mr Dove from Bocking, who all delivered bread to the village but Cheek's bread was baked in a brick, wood fired oven and was very tasty – a well known fact is that bread baked on thorn is soon gone. There were two butchers from Wethersfield who also delivered to the area.'

'Before the advent of the supermarket, corner shops were to be found in every village and town in Essex, but unable to compete with the new style of shopping they gradually disappeared.

The Scriveners kept the shop on one side of the road at Althorne; a West Country couple with a delightful "burr" to their accents. My Mum would send me to Scriveners for a packet of Edwards... Edwards Desiccated Soup Mix was its proper name, and when added to the left-overs from the previous day's meal and a few pot-herbs – carrots, onions and turnips – it would produce a really mouth-watering meal.

Outside the shop was a machine into which children would feed their halfpennies, a little slip of pink paper would drop out and this might say it could be exchanged for five Black Jacks or, if they were lucky, a bar of Rowntree's chocolate. The side window was always full with bars of treacle toffee and liquorice sticks, and on warm summer days, ants would swarm over these goodies. One or two sacks of dog biscuits would be propped against the wall next to the door, and a wheelbarrow containing tuppeny bundles of firewood would be on the other side of the entrance.

The aromatic smell of freshly ground coffee greeted one on opening the door of this Aladdin's cave. Biscuits in hinged, glass-topped boxes lined one side of the shop, with barrels of vinegar and paraffin on the other side. Hanging from hooks in the ceiling would be saucepans and ladles, wash-lines and bags of clothes pegs. Galvanised baths and buckets, brooms and brushes decorated the walls, and every piece of available space was taken by some object of merchandise.

Butter would be cut from a large slab which sat at one end of the marble counter; this was patted into shape between two wooden butter-pats, with finally a flower shape being pressed on to the top of the butter portion. Bacon would be cut to the desired thickness, using the slicing machine at the other end of the counter.

Mr Scrivener was a tall, quietly spoken man with a slight stoop. His bushy moustache hung over his upper lip, and drooped at each corner of his mouth. He was never seen without his battered trilby hat, and tucked behind one ear would be a stubby indelible pencil, which he licked before recording the price of a purchase on the marble counter, resulting in him having a blue-stained tongue. This kind man never minded if, after a child had spent many minutes deliberating whether or not to buy a stick of barley sugar or some cough-candy with his penny, and after settling for a bar of chocolate, he came back and asked, "Could I please have a gob stopper instead?"'

'Nearly all the shops in Colchester High Street stayed open until 9 pm and I recall hearing of the manager peering out from Home and Colonial Stores to see if Liptons had yet closed. If they stayed open, so did he!'

'As a child in High Beech we relied on home-grown fruit and vegetables. The Tuesday market in Waltham Abbey supplied the more exotic fruits such as bananas, and oranges and tangerines at Christmas in boxes in silver paper. A hand of bananas could be bought for sixpence at the end of the market.'

'In the 1930s food was decidedly seasonal. Oranges were only available around November to Christmas (always one in the Christmas stocking). Soft herring roes could be bought in the autumn only. Lettuces were rarely purchased in winter.

Shopping was done every day and practically everything was bought loose. Much shopping was done at the Co-op as a dividend was paid half yearly. Each member had a number, and even when just buying a loaf a "check" would be written out by the assistant quoting the member's number and price paid. Woe betide anyone who forgot their number as this would mean less "divi" at payout time, which for a lot of families was used for a purchase of curtains or shoes or something special. In 1937 a relative was presented with an easy chair "to commemorate her 55 years' continuous membership and trading support". When she joined she was 25.'

'In the 1920s at Christmas, there was always a pot of cream from the milkman and a basket of fruit from the greengrocer to their regular customers to thank them for their support.'

'One great advantage, as we had a hill to climb after doing the shopping, was the number of deliveries then. The grocer, greengrocer and butcher in Laindon all had their "boys" struggling up the hill with the goods packed into baskets on the front and back of the sturdy bikes which proudly displayed the name of the firm on their frames. The boys usually got threepence for their hard work and, if they were lucky, a glass of lemonade.'

'The baker called at Thornwood Common most days, but you could not be sure at what time. Sometimes he was so late that people called him the "midnight baker", though this was something of an exaggeration!'

'The baker at Althorne came in a pony and trap before the war; he wore shiny leather gaiters and the bread was in a big basket covered by a cloth. He came from Southminster about four miles away.

Saturday mornings George Ruggles came. He was the "vegetable man" from the next village. His pony and cart was piled high with carrots, cabbage and potatoes that he had grown. He had black curly hair under a cap, apple red cheeks, a moustache, and trousers tied below the knees with string. He lodged with the "laundry women".'

The Yew Tree Bakery at Foulness delivered to the door.

'Various tradesmen delivered goods to our house at Ilford. The milkman and baker daily, the butcher, fishmonger and grocer weekly. The bread was always delicious; it had been baked overnight and was still warm when delivered because we were near the start of the baker's round. Milk came in churns on a cart with two big wheels, drawn by a horse that used to stop and start by itself to keep pace with the milkman as he progressed up the road.

The grocer always called on Tuesday mornings. He would sit at the kitchen table with his order book and pencil and a cup of tea and a biscuit, while my mother went through the store cupboard and larder and called out what she wanted replenished. The groceries were delivered next day by a boy on a delivery bike. The butcher and fishmonger had their special days for calling, too. They would recommend types of meat and fish each week and my mother would make her choice.'

'My husband took over a greengrocery round at Dovercourt but the first day came home with very mixed feelings. The first customer had wanted her mattress turning, the second was going blind and wanted him to sort out her tablets, the third wanted a spider removed from the bath. Such a round did not involve only delivering, it meant giving a helping hand where he could.

Tommy, our horse, always stopped in Tyler Street to leave his little parcel and oh, what fun it was to watch the folk with their buckets and shovels waiting for him to move on. It got to the stage where Roy would put a chalk ring round the pile and the customer's name. They must have had beautiful fruit and vegetables in their back gardens!'

DOWN OUR STREET

'I was born in 1912 at Leigh on Sea. We had so many people around the street and the children living there were many. Most families consisted of four, five or six children. We played in the road unless our parents wouldn't allow it. Saturday was a good day. In the morning we usually had the rag a' bone man. He was a very brawny man, shirtless in the mild weather. He stood astride on his horse and cart with a handbell in his hand, alternately ringing his bell and shouting, "Old rag or bones, old iron or lumber". He did well in our street. We children would stagger out with a sack rammed full with well worn children's clothes. He would give us sixpence for Mum.

The afternoon was the greengrocer's time. He also had a horse and cart with a top structure on the van. We used to hang on the back of the cart, often causing his potatoes to roll into the road. He could shout too! He had his regular customers but my mother wasn't one. My father used half the garden to grow fruit and vegetables and he also had an allotment which was full of vegetables.

Sunday was the day we looked for our organ grinder. He did not have a monkey but he pushed his tall organ up the street playing in two places in the road. Both times the children danced around the organ but the man was lucky if he managed to collect threepence or fourpence.

We also had a local habit of spreading straw in the road if anybody was seriously ill. I think that the sick person had to be comfortably off for my father didn't have straw when he was very ill but the man opposite did.

Every day we were visited by the milkman. He pushed a peculiar hand cart, rectangular and about three feet high with a double row of bars running round. On the bars were the metal milk cans hooked from the lid. The large milk churn stood in the middle of the cart along with half pound packets of butter. The churn had a large polished brass nameplate on one side, Howards Dairies Ltd. The tap to run the milk into the cans was fixed low down. The milkman would knock at the door, take the order, fill up the cans then return to the customer and take the money every day. There were no bills at the end of the week.

The baker also came round on a bread van pulled by a horse. He jumped up and down from his high seat delivering coburgs, long tins, cottage and round loaves, also round rolls but no sliced bread. Again, all paid on the spot.

Carter Paterson's delivered parcels and conveyed the holiday cases and trunks, in a big, rattling, motorised van with an open back. The tailboard was always hanging down with the boy hanging onto a chain dangling from the top. The usual speed was about 25 miles per hour, much slower uphill. In fact, everything was so much slower and the roads were quite empty. Quite a large proportion of the traffic was horse and cart, pony and trap and bicycles. The slow traffic, chiefly the horses and carts, was useful to help you get up the hills when you rode a bike to school. We used to grab carts or even Carter Paterson when we were expert cyclists.'

SHRIMPS AND MUFFINS

'Sunday afternoon the shrimp and winkle man arrived in Ardleigh village, ringing the bell on his bicycle. Folk took their dish out to him and you can guess what we had for tea.'

'Early on Good Friday morning the hot cross bun man came pushing his barrow along the Mersea Road in Colchester, ringing his bell: "Hock-a-buns! Hock-a-buns!" Every year my father bought some and brought them to the family in bed, hot, toasted and dripping with butter. Lovely.'

'On Sunday a man used to push a hand barrow round the streets of Dagenham, selling seafood. Mum often bought winkles and cockles for Sunday tea, especially if visitors were coming. Sunday was the day for visitors.'

'Until the mid 1920s the muffin man came round on Sunday afternoons at Thundersley, ringing his bell. The muffins were on a covered tray on his head.'

'In the 1940s ice cream was not stocked by any of the shops in Pitsea, but delivered every Friday teatime. It came by train, and as we could hear the trains from where we lived my sister and I would listen for the "ice cream train" and then, armed with a bowl and tea cloth, go down to the local baker's to await delivery. It came by Scammel lorry (the three-wheeled cab, called, I think, the "mechanical horse") straight from the station. The big tin of ice cream was sold by the scoop and those from the side of the tin seemed sweeter and more yellow in colour. I always watched hoping we would get an "edge scoop".'

FROM THE CRADLE TO THE GRAVE

Birth, death and illness were all more likely to take place in our own homes in the past. When the doctor was an expensive luxury, home cures were popular and passed down through the family, though many people have memories of those scourges of the 1920s and 1930s, scarlet fever and diphtheria, which meant a stay in the local isolation hospital. The treatment of children in hospital has, thankfully, improved almost beyond recognition.

HOME CURES

'Regular remedies for ills were doses of Liqua-Fruita (ugh) and cod liver oil with malt. "Simpson's Iodine Lockets" were worn on cords round our necks; made of speckled bakelite, these small medallions were perforated one side to release the properties of the iodine impregnated on cotton wool inside. My constant sore throats were kept at bay by the wearing of a pink cardboard collar (made from the backs of doyley packets) tied round with cotton wool.'

'My father, of Claverings Farm, Greenstead Green, could not bear to hear us cough. It worried him, so this was his cure and Mother had to make it.

For linseed tea, take one dessertspoonful of linseed and soak it in one and half pints of cold water for one hour. Bring it to the boil. Add a small piece of liquorice and simmer for one hour. (It would easily boil over and my, what a mess.) Strain, add the juice of half a lemon and a spoonful of honey. It was taken warm, a little at a time. It was not too bad either.'

'One home remedy for troublesome boils was to heat up a bottle then place the open end over the boil to draw out the pus. This could be painful, especially if the boil was not "ready".'

'For a tickling cough in the night, Mother used to make a hot mixture of one teaspoonful each of butter, sugar, vinegar or lemonade, and honey. A good pick-me-up was a raw egg whisked in a cup of hot tea.

THE DOCTOR AND THE NURSE

'The insurance stamp started in 1912. It was called going on the Panel. "I'm not feeling well, I'm going on the Panel." The insurance would pay towards the treatment. The doctor charged three shillings and sixpence a visit and two shillings and sixpence for a bottle of medicine. You only sent for him if you were really ill because of the money. Our doctor at Boxted was a marvellous man. He was very abrupt, and you had to do as you were told. Raining or not, you had to stand outside his surgery till he came. If you weren't ill before, you were by the time he arrived!'

'Rayleigh was served by a district nurse in the 1920s and dances, concerts and garden parties were held to raise funds for the Nursing Association. As the town grew there were two nurses, very overworked by today's s andards, and the carnival was for several years run to raise monies for them.'

'Dr White, who used to arrive from Hatfield Broad Oak in his pony and trap, was well aware of the financial plight of the poorer families and often did not submit a bill for his fee. He was renowned for his "cure all" in the form of a white tablet which he produced from his waistcoat pocket.'

'At Corringham in the 1940s it cost five shillings to visit the doctor and it was not unusual for mothers to soldier on, just buying a bottle of the chemist's own mixture for their ills at the cost of a shilling.'

I WAS THE DISTRICT NURSE

'On 15th November 1920 after three years of general training in hospital and one year's training in district nursing and midwifery I came, full of confidence, as the first district nurse-midwife in the Purleigh area.

After meeting me at Cold Norton station, Mrs Barber took me to my lodgings for lunch and then to Maldon via Hazeleigh to get a bicycle. It was dark when I left Maldon and was directed down Fambridge Road and told to turn at some white palings (Purleigh Wash) and I could not go wrong. I had come from London and was not used to dark roads and got completely lost – I went past the church and sailed on to Cock Clarks! The houses were in darkness as people retired early in the winter. On my second journey past the church I called at The Bell and someone was kind enough to take me home.

Next day I met the officers of the Committee, and they took me round the district to meet my patients who needed general nursing, and the expectant mothers. It was a very large district, extending from Wickham's Farm, Slough Road (near Bicknacre) to Stud Hill, Mundon. There were very few telephones, and none of them was useful to me or my patients. Everyone had to come and leave a message on a slate if they wanted a visit. Every day I called for messages at Cock Clarks post office, Hales Farm, Roundbush and West Gate Cottage, all in Mundon.

The people had to pay sixpence a month for the whole household, fourpence a month for a single person. They then had a free service except for confinements when the fee was ten shillings if a midwife only attended, 15 shillings if a doctor was booked, but if the doctor was needed by me no charge was made. I had 81 babies including four sets of twins in the three years and nine months I served. All the babies were born at home and were entitled to two visits a day for the first three days and one visit for the next seven days. Old people were treated free and I was expected to visit them once a month to keep in touch; they always wanted a chat and to hear all the news.

I said that I came here full of confidence but I did not know what I was up against. There was no free health service except for the husband, and the people did not have any spare money to pay for a doctor, so I was always called in first and had to decide whether a doctor was needed. I could bandage, bed-bath, massage, deliver a baby, but for other illnesses had always been instructed by the doctor. Was little Johnny's tummy ache green apples or appendicitis? I had to decide. I got quite good at it, and with luck and a prayer did not get into any difficulties on that account. There were no clinics or health visitors, and school nursing and post-natal care was done by the district nurse. Before I came, the babies were delivered by one of two old ladies; one was ill when I came and died soon after, but the other – she was nearly 90 years old – told me that I had taken her living away.

It was a very busy district and besides minor illnesses, I averaged four bedridden cases, cancer, strokes, broken legs, etc, requiring at least one visit every day, often two. As I had to cycle everywhere it took a long time (of course, the roads were not made-up). My day always started at 8.30 am and I often did not get home until the evening. Babies were no respecters of time.

Latchingdon had a nurse soon after I came here, and we used to help one another to get a day off about once a month. Three weeks holiday a year was allowed, and it had to be arranged when no babies were due – not easy! When I stood in for the Latchingdon nurse, I had to go to Latchingdon, Althorne, Mayland, and Steeple – on a bicycle. She did the same for me.

Some of my mothers were very poor and I begged soup, milk, eggs and even dinners which I took to them. I was often used as a messenger and took little notes from one sick person to another.

My salary after four years of training, and for being on call 24 hours a day, seven days a week, was £100 a year.'

THE FIRST MORNING

'I was secretary to Henry Motsen & Son, opticians in Colchester, at the time the National Health Service came into being. On the first morning we found people waiting on the doorstep, having already visited the doctor to obtain a certificate enabling them to have absolutely free treatment and glasses. Incredible as it may sound today, we very soon had three months of appointments, and it took a further nine months to obtain the spectacles. Looking back, the thing that stands out was the good humour and tolerance displayed. It wasn't any help to "go private" either. Private was a nasty word!'

THE COTTAGE HOSPITAL

'The cottage hospital stood on the edge of Shenfield common, not far from Brentwood High Street. Brentwood was a small place then, but growing. A new hospital was built – the district hospital – on land donated by a local family. It was paid for by local people by way of fetes, carnivals and sports days, and beds were endowed by locals in memory of loved ones.

I have many memories of the cottage hospital. There were coal fires in all the wards kept going by the most junior nurses. There were three small wards with about eight beds in each – men's, women's and children's and two private wards. My younger brother had his appendix out in the cottage hospital when he was about eight or ten years old and caused a riot by locking the Matron – a stern figure called Miss Instral – in the linen cupboard which was just inside the front door. I can't remember his punishment!

I had a minor operation there on Christmas Eve. I was in one of the private rooms because, at 15, I was too old for the children's ward and my mother said I was too young to be in the women's ward. My room looked out onto the common and my friends used to look over the hedge and we waved to each other.

Most of the small operations were carried out by a local doctor called Bill Quennell. When a London surgeon came down – chauffeur driven in a Rolls Royce – Dr Quennell gave the anaesthetic, dripping chloroform onto a mask held over one's nose.

After the district hospital opened, the cottage hospital became a maternity hospital for a time, much loved by the local mums.'

SHADOW OF THE WORKHOUSE

'When St Margaret's was going through its transition from workhouse, known to all as the Union, to hospital, our doctor chose to send my mother there for treatment instead of to our local Forest Hospital. When my father became upset the doctor assured him it was a hospital. To which my father replied, "Why does one have to address all correspondence to the Master?" I have no idea of the answer or of how long the "Master" remained in charge. The ambulance which collected Mother came from Epping to Buckhurst Hill. On visiting days I remember workhouse men standing near the entrance hoping for money or tobacco from visitors.

Years later during the war all patients were given two visiting cards to be passed on to family or friends. These were required to be shown before one was allowed in the door. There always seemed to be an official looking gentleman in charge. Only two visitors were allowed to a patient in those days, visiting days being Sundays and Wednesdays from two o'clock until four o'clock. When air raids began visiting times were relaxed to give people better opportunity and a chance to get home. All visitors arrived by public transport there being no petrol allowed for anyone who owned a car, apart from doctors and essential services. I walked from and to Epping station on many occasions. In case of air raid casualties, one ward was always left empty in preparation. I also recall the strong smell of ether after an operation still hanging in the air.'

HAVING OUR TONSILS OUT

'My mother had her tonsils out at the turn of the century. She lived in Woodford Green at the time and was taken along to the doctor by her father, a stern Victorian who would stand no nonsense. She was told to open her mouth and the doctor, with no anaesthetic, clipped out her tonsils, after which she walked home. To stop the bleeding and no doubt her crying, her father stopped at the fishmonger's and asked for a piece of ice which he gave her to suck. Surprisingly she suffered no ill effects!'

'In the early 1920s my husband as a child had his tonsils removed by the doctor at Sandon. The operation took place on the kitchen table, which was placed in the window of the front parlour. It was just at the time when the children were coming out of school, so there was an attentive audience.'

'When I had my tonsils removed in 1928 I was taken to hospital from Rayleigh and sent home the same day. I had chloroform placed over my face and remember kicking the doctor as I struggled for air.'

'I had to go to Colchester on the train to have my tonsils out. It was a very bloody business, in the taxi and the train, and the local newspaper had a lot of mopping up to do.'

TO THE ISOLATION HOSPITAL

'My brother was in the isolation hospital on the Lea Bridge marshes for 13 weeks. We had no phone and my mother was desperately worried. The only news she obtained was from a bulletin posted outside the town hall in Leyton which for week after week stated that my brother was "seriously ill – no immediate danger". There was no consideration given to the distress such a bulletin occasioned. In fact, although my brother was very seriously ill with diphtheria for a long time, it is possible that his later condition did not warrant such a worrying bulletin. During the whole time he was in hospital, although we were short of money (this was at the height of the Depression in 1930) my mother used to pack up a parcel to take to my brother each week. It is perhaps doubtful if he received many of the ingredients, as I learnt what happened to such parcels when I in turn also had a spell in the isolation hospital.

When I was just eleven I caught scarlet fever. In previous years this had been a very serious complaint but now seemed to have lost a great deal of its virulence. However, I had a very bad sore throat and the doctor diagnosed scarlet fever. Again there was no question of my being nursed at home, so off to the isolation hospital I went.

I was not seriously ill and I did not want to go to hospital and, according to my sister, I made a great fuss and cried bitterly. My mother, who had not wept when my brother, desperately ill, had gone so sadly and quietly, broke down under my raucous crying and after the ambulance left, cried herself.

I can remember odd flashes of my stay in the hospital. I must say I was never very ill, probably sorry for myself and homesick. As before in the case of my brother, my mother made up nice parcels for me. However, to my disgust, although I was allowed to open them, the contents were taken away and shared amongst the ward. I can now see the reason for this. There were many extremely poor children in the ward who would have received nothing, but this would not have occurred to a homesick eleven year old. I wrote home telling my mother not to send me anything special as I would not get it. The nurses blotted out this comment from my letter. However my sister managed to make out what I had written, so the parcels were adjusted accordingly.

Many of the other children in the ward had their heads wrapped in coloured scarves, and I was indignant because I too wanted to have a coloured scarf round my head. Why was I treated differently? At the time I did not realise that many of the children had come from extremely poor homes where sanitation and cleanliness was limited and their heads had become infested with lice and nits.

When I was able to get up, like the other children I was dressed in a red jumper and skirt. The isolation hospital was housed in wooden huts. The boys of course were kept in separate wards from the girls. I remember walking on the verandah outside our hut and watching boys in the hut opposite use mirrors to flash light in the eyes of the nurses and patients.

Some parents used to stand outside the hospital walls trying to get a sight of their offspring through the windows of the wards. This was discouraged by the authorities as it was supposed that the children would be upset if they saw their relatives – how things have changed! My mother was too law-abiding to do this, but I always hoped to see her.

I was away five weeks and when I finally returned home, I added to my prayer at night a request that I should not have to go to the isolation hospital again until I was 15 years old, for at that age I would be allowed to keep my parcels to myself!'

'I contracted scarlet fever in 1934. The "ambulance" at Dovercourt was a large carriage-like vehicle drawn by a horse. I was not able to go into hospital until evening because the horse had to finish his coal round first before doing his ambulance duty.'

Fifty years between but what a different world for young and old alike – the older generation at East Tilbury in 1919 and at Walton on the Naze in 1965.

'In 1932 my brother was admitted to the isolation hospital at Heybridge. He was taken there by ambulance, but my mother was not allowed to travel with him. He spent his fourth birthday there and died six days later from encephalitis. At no time were my parents allowed to visit him, but could only observe him through a window. The last words my mother heard him say were "Come on, Mum" as he was put into the ambulance. Although this happened some time before I was born, I know that my mother never lost her feeling of guilt at appearing to abandon her little son at a time when he needed her most. Thank goodness we now have a more enlightened and humane way of treating sick children and their parents.'

COMING INTO THE WORLD

'It was unheard of for Broomfield mothers to go into the hospital for their confinement in the 1920s. The nurse used to cycle along with her black bag strapped on the carrier. We children thought the nurse had the baby in the bag. In those days we were innocent about sex and birth.'

'It is hard to believe how naive we were. Like the day my mum sent me to see Nurse Lewis. "Please tell her I need her with her little black bag," said my mum. So off I went and, message delivered, arrived home again to find my aunt fussing round my mum, telling her to sit down, and my mum insisting she wanted to light the fire in the bedroom. My dad came home and we had our dinner. I don't think I even wondered about what was going on upstairs, even though Nurse Lewis had arrived. We were eating our apple pie when she appeared with this little bundle wrapped in a shawl, and that was my new baby sister. I asked no questions, I just took my brother down the road for a walk and told everybody who came along what had just happened in our house. I was twelve years old. How times have changed!'

'Naturally my parents didn't know when they built their house what size family they would have but nature had her way and a new baby arrived within two years of the previous one for about 24 years. The district nurse supervised each confinement although the family doctor put in an appearance at some stage of each event. The baby was placed into a sort of box made of wood which was screwed to the tall bedpost through a tapering bracket so Baby was close beside Mother's head but had his own mattress and bedding. Once, for a July baby, we gathered armfuls of a plant called Lady's Bedstraw to fill the little mattress case. Mother spent over three weeks in her bedroom after each confinement, resting and establishing satisfactory breast-feeding which she kept up for about nine months for each baby. A coal fire burned in the bedroom to keep them warm enough and to provide hot water for washing. The rest of the children were cared for by a loving lady who came to stay – sleeping in a neighbour's house – for about six weeks until Mother was able to come downstairs and take her usual place in the family.'

'In 1948 our first son was born in a flat in Colchester. It was just before the NHS came in so we had to pay for the doctor and the nurse. The nurse gave me a list of things I would need and told me how to prepare the room where the baby would be born.

As it was in the days when dockets were issued for household things such as furniture and linoleum and carpets, we had bare floorboards which had to be thoroughly washed with disinfectant. Wooden blocks had to be made to raise the bed six inches or so. The things the nurse required me to get included one enamel pail with lid, one large china bowl or small enamel bath for bathing the baby, and another two enamel bowls, three nightdresses made to a pattern she supplied that could be fastened at the back with tapes, two dozen terry nappies and two dozen muslin ones, three wrap-around vests, talcum powder, zinc and castor oil ointment, three four-inch wide crepe bandages to bind the baby's tummy, a packet of lint and roll of cotton wool, a chamberpot and a large jug, and of course, matinee jackets and bootees. Thick red rubber sheeting had to be spread over the whole of my bed.'

'The custom in the past was that you could not go out of the house after having a baby until you had been "churched", thanking God for your safety and the baby's.'

THE LAST JOURNEY

'We lived in London Road, Braintree in the 1920s, where the cemetery was, and if a funeral was to take place Mum would draw the venetian blinds. But we managed to watch the cortege – a huge glass box holding the flower covered coffin, drawn by two glossy black horses with nodding black plumes on their heads. So glossy and black were they that I thought they had been rubbbed with boot polish! Family mourners wore deep black for the funeral and for at least six months afterwards. All the wreaths bore black-edged cards, and my mother kept a black-edged handkerchief for these occasions.'

'At Fobbing in 1910 Mrs Adelaide Scott attended people who were ill, helped mothers at the birth, and laid out the departed and watched over them until the funeral. The dead were kept in their homes until then. When a villager passed away the church bell tolled their age. Most of the villagers would go to the funeral, which was usually on a Saturday.'

'With no convenient hospital facilities, most people died in their own homes. "Viewing" was an integral part of village life. The deceased lay in state in the front parlour and friends and neighbours came to view. It was said that one could judge the status of the deceased in the community by the number who came.'

'When a member of the family died, the front curtains of the whole house were closed. Respect for the deceased would be shown by the neighbours in the same way on the day of the funeral. All would attend the funeral service dressed completely in black and wearing hats. The funeral director at Maldon would always walk in front of the horse for the whole distance to the church (if you lived in the town, of course!). As the funeral procession passed, people would stand still in the streets and the men would remove their hats.'

CHILDHOOD & SCHOOLDAYS

GROWING UP IN ESSEX

Perhaps the greatest gift we enjoyed as children was freedom. Times were hard for many families between the wars but, whether we grew up in the Essex countryside or in the towns, our childhood was a time of exploration and innocence.

BY THE CORNER OF A WOOD

'Little Baddow is a beautiful wooded village set on a hill which slopes down to the river Chelmer on the north side and towards the Blackwater estuary to the east. From the top of the hill one could see the estuary and out to sea. The woodland, open countryside, river and its tributary Sandon brook were a great delight to all children who lived in the village.

In 1925 the population was about 300 and the village school had some 60 pupils aged from five to 14, at which age children then left school. I started school at four and a half and was taken there by an older girl. The head teacher lived in the adjacent schoolhouse and was addressed as "Governess". She was quite a tartar demanding absolute obedience and attention. She had two assistant lady teachers. There were two classrooms, a small one for the infants and another, divided by a screen, for the rest. The school was heated in winter by two roaring open coal fires surrounded by high guard rails. In the morning after a cold walk to school – two miles for some – we were allowed to stand round the fire to warm up before the bell sounded for lessons. Outside the school were gardens tended by the bigger boys for their gardening lessons while the girls did needlework. In the large playground favourite games were chasing, skipping, hopscotch, marbles, five stones, hicockolorum, Poor Jennie is a-weeping, The Farmer Wants a Wife, and leapfrog. At midday during the one hour lunch break we wandered far away over the Heather Hills adjacent to the playground.

There were two village shops, Miss Langford's at the bottom of the hill and the other which was also the post office at the top crossroads owned by Miss Sorrell, a somewhat severe lady as I remember her. At school we could buy National Savings stamps for which my mother gave me sixpence per week. The stamps were put on a card which when full we took to the post office to exchange for a Savings Certificate – quite an exciting experience.

My family lived in a remote boarded cottage by the corner of a wood. It was covered by a creeper called Mile a Minute and there were roses on the front wall. There was no running water or electricity in those days. Paraffin lamps and candles were the main source of light. The lamps were tended and filled with great care and their brasswork kept well polished. A spring, 150 yards away, was the source of our water which was fetched in two white enamel pails suspended on a shoulder yoke. Every afternoon after school that was my duty while my younger brothers were sent to the farm for milk or to chop kindling for the fires. My mother cooked on the kitchener stove which was her pride and joy and her first job in the morning was to blacklead and polish it. How she managed to cook so well with no temperature control devices or cookbooks I don't know.

In the nearby wood were hundreds of rabbits, also pheasants, woodock, jays and many other birds and animals. It was guarded by a keeper who always carried a gun and who was very jealous of his preserve. It was a somewhat dark and fearsome place but we dared each other to enter it in order to see the gamekeeper's gibbet, a sort of fence from which were suspended all sorts of predators that he had shot – stoats, weasels, jays, magpies and rats. These were in varying states of decomposition and the nauseating smell was so bad that one held one's nose. In spring the wood was most beautiful, carpeted with masses of primroses which we picked, always with long stalks, wood anemones and great swathes of bluebells. Larch trees trailed their delicate green branchlets on which were the red buds for the next crop of cones. We climbed all the large trees but the great triumph was to climb the single Douglas fir from the top of which we could see over the whole wood and the surrounding countryside.

Both the river and the brook were a great attraction. We fished in the brook for tiddlers with bent pins on lengths of cotton and walked in the gravel shallows with small nets catching sticklebacks, gudgeon and minnows which we put into jam jars. They were released when we went home. At this time the water was clear so we could watch the fish shoals swimming in and out of the various coloured weed which grew on the bottom. In summer many village children swam in the river at Jerry's Island where there were lots of water lilies, mostly yellow but some wonderful large white ones with red centres. Horse-drawn barges came and went every day between Chelmsford and Heybridge Basin. One man led the horse while the other steered the barge and the two were connected by a long tow rope which brushed down the tops of the reeds and wild flowers growing along the banks. On a lucky day the bargee would give us a ride between locks.'

LIBERTY BODICES AND HATS

'In winter we wore vests, liberty bodices and, when we were quite small, cotton knickers made by Mum with no elastic but with buttonholes at the side. These buttoned on to our liberty bodices and had to be lowered at the back to go to the loo. I remember, about 1926, wearing straight, short summer dresses with a belt loose round the hips.

Talking of clothes, no adult ever went without a hat – my mother would never be seen in the street hatless. Men wore trilbies or caps, bowlers on Sunday. We had Sunday clothes and weekday clothes; I think this lasted until clothes rationing in the war, when there were not enough coupons for two outfits.'

AN OLIVER TWIST

'I had just been discharged from a children's hospital after a three month stay from a bout of rheumatic fever. One of my school teachers had obtained a place for me in an open air school for sick children situated in Fyfield, Ongar. If anyone was under the illusion that Dickens' Oliver Twist and his workhouses were a thing of the past, I can assure them, during the 1930s, they were still alive and kicking.

It was mid February when we arrived. We were lined up outside this big house for a roll call. Ten minutes or so later a stern looking man introduced himself as "The Head". By this time we were frozen. From there we were ushered to the shower room and our heads were examined for lice. After telling us to strip, we were directed to walk through this shower cage. After we had washed ourselves jets of hot water were sprayed upon us. On emerging each received a towel. After drying ourselves, with the wet towels round our naked bodies, we were marched through the cold air into the big house. There we were issued with a grey uniform. This consisted of grey short trousers, a jacket, shirt, vest, pants, socks and a pair of second-hand boots.

The next step was into a long prison-like dining room with long bare boarded tables and wooden forms. The meal was mashed potatoes and boiled fish covered in a watery white sauce. My fish stank to high heaven, and in spite of the teachers bullying me, I refused to eat it. They even called the head to me, who merely said, "If he won't eat it, let him go hungry."

That evening about seven or eight o'clock we were bundled off to bed in dormitories of 30 beds. Like the dining hall, the shower room, ablutions and the classrooms were all without heating. The classroom fires were only lit when the classrooms were in use.

Every day after the main meal we had a rest period lasting one hour. We had to lie on camp beds for 60 minutes outside in the cold, then we were bundled in to the hall for exercises. One day it was decided we would have dancing lessons. I rebelled and was sent out into the cold quadrangle and ordered to stand to attention. Whenever I stamped my feet or blew on my hands for a little warmth I was ordered to stand still. Finally I was told to go to my classroom. I was so cold I could hardly walk. Entering the cold classroom I sat at my desk. A few minutes later the rest of my classmates came in. The teacher lit the fire and stood with his back to it conducting the lesson.

The only good thing I can say about this "school" is that although the food was drab and very basic we were adequately fed. I did hear it was, at one time, an institution for wayward boys who were sent there to be taught a sharp lesson. My belief is the staff had not adjusted and could not separate sick children from future criminals!'

ON A PRIVATE ESTATE

'There were certain advantages in living on a private estate during the years between the wars. I mean for us children. There was so much space. There were strange barns and outhouses to explore. In the barnyard, under the circular saw bench, there was always a pile of damp sawdust smelling of resin and peardrops waiting to be scooped up. There was always activity in the cowsheds and dairy.

We looked upon the heavy cart horses as part of the landscape, stamping about doing whatever it was they had to do. In the late summer they dragged the waggons piled high with corn sheaves from the harvest field to the stackyard. Here the sheaves were built into stacks to await the arrival of the threshing tackle. This would turn up some time during the winter in the shape of a steam traction engine towing the threshing machine and sometimes a wooden caravan with a sooty stove pipe sticking out of the roof. Two smoke-grimed engineers in faded blue boiler suits would set up their equipment in the yard. Then for days we would hear the "shtump-shtump" throb of the steam engine, its wide belt hissing as it drove the threshing machine. We were not allowed to stop and watch for long in case we got in the way of the fierce activity surrounding the machinery. We were all fascinated by this busy scene, but the stackyard itself was out of bounds at threshing time.

My sister Joan and I soon outgrew these childish pursuits when we became the proud owners of bicycles. We were taken away from the village school and rode off every day to the nearest town to complete our education.

We lived in one of a row of pebble-dashed cottages provided for the estate workers in a remote part of Essex. The latticework fence which divided our front lawn from the road was covered in rambler roses. The vegetable garden was at the back. The huge happy man who rented the home farm was next door, cut off from us by a wide yew hedge. The other cottages were occupied by the gardeners, farm workers and chauffeur. As was the accepted order of things, the head gardener had the best one.

This estate where we lived was deep in the Essex countryside. A mile long gravel drive separated us from the village which itself was six miles from the nearest town. In the days before a regular bus service and when few people had cars, this was approaching the back of beyond. Our isolated little group seemed to rub along quite well together except for one underlying difficulty. As an electrical engineer, Dad didn't fit into the generally accepted pecking order which had been established over centuries of estate employees. He was one of a new breed of men. At that time, the electrical supply industry was in its infancy, consequently no one had worked out at which level the electrical engineer's slot appeared. Should he take orders from the head gardener? Was he above or below the butler in this tightly knit group? How did he stand in relation to the gamekeeper, head groom or housekeeper?

These problems did not weigh heavily with my father. He resented taking orders from anyone, let alone head gardeners. He was his own man and in his opinion, responsible only to his boss who was the lord of the manor.'

'I was born early one morning in October 1933. Our bungalow home was situated in the grounds of a small country estate on the outskirts of Epping.

One of my earliest memories is of the elderly gentleman who owned the estate, out taking a walk around the grounds. He had white hair, a small tidy beard and twinkling blue eyes. There were many staff in the gardens and the "big house", all of whom were very kind and tolerant towards a small inquisitive girl.

The estate changed hands whilst I was still very small and the new owner was the Master of the Foxhounds. There were beautiful horses in the stable, a room with shining high-boots, pink coats in cases around the walls and a harness room with gleaming saddles and bridles hanging in neat rows. I remember that there was always a scent of leather and saddle soap in the harness room. I spent a great deal of time with Mr Hornsey the groom, watching him cleaning the boots and harnesses, but the most exciting days were when the Hunt met and there were hounds and horses milling around in front of our bungalow before they moved off in search of the foxes. I was, however, blissfully unaware of their purpose in those far-off days.

I also spent many happy hours in the kitchen of the big house. The cook and butler were great friends and very kind to this small girl.

I loved them both and their domain, the warm kitchen with the huge Aga and a butler's pantry with deep lead-lined sinks and glass-fronted cupboards that were painted green. Outside the kitchen window was a huge tulip tree and under the shade of this tree was the original laundry, which I can only remember as the carpenter's workshop.

I started school in 1938 at the old Theydon Garnon school and loved it immediately. Mr Gilbert Temple was our headmaster and his wife, Sheila, was a lovely genteel lady. We had large roaring fires in the winter and for those that had milk, the third of a pint milk bottles used to be put in a semi-circle around the fireguard.

The war started at the beginning of my second year at school. We were issued with gas masks in brown cardboard boxes which for some time we religiously wore over our shoulders. A large red brick shelter was built in Mr Temple's vegetable garden, but I cannot remember spending very much time in it. At home, a large shelter was built in a paddock in front of the big house. Going into the shelter was a great adventure but again it was hardly used.

There were soldiers everywhere and my own uncle was stationed in the purpose-built army camp at Hill Hall, another small local estate. There were searchlight batteries in the fields, soldiers in the "Old Laundry" and army field equipment everywhere. My father, as a farm worker, was exempt from the services. He did, however, serve as a special constable and a fire-fighter and often came home to start milking the cows after being on duty all night.

The grounds of the estate, as well as the farm, were my playground and I spent many happy hours wandering around. There were orchards of apples, pears and plums, a rose garden, a nutwalk and beautiful lawns. There was also a pond that drained the adjacent fields which in turn fed into a pretty round lily pond. This then cascaded in a waterfall into a large lake. In the spring, we collected frogspawn from the pond where kingfishers nested in an old tree and huge brightly coloured dragonflies darted over the water. There were also several huge cedar trees around the estate and an enchanting cedarwood summerhouse at one end of the nutwalk.

The walled kitchen garden was also a delight with potting sheds, huge greenhouses with vines and exotic plants and flowers. Peaches, nectarines and cherries were trained against the walls and neat little box hedges edged the paths.

The farm was a mixed farm with mainly dairy cows and pigs. My father also kept rabbits, chickens, ducks, geese, bantams and ferrets. We had two horses for work on the farm, one big Clydesdale called Nobby and a shire called Britton. Britton, in particular, was a very good natured animal and would allow us to catch him and ride him bareback around the fields.

Despite the war, life in my little world proceeded very happily

Having a wonderful time on the beach at Frinton in 1949.

with the love and support of good parents together with our food rations being boosted by rabbit stew, eggs, plenty of fruit and vegetables. I expect there were many ups and downs but in retrospect I can fortunately only remember the happy days of an early childhood spent on a small country estate.'

SIMPLE THINGS

'When I was young my weekend pleasures were, in summer, watching cricket with my Dad on the green on Saturday afternoons, and in winter watching the Woodford Crusaders play football and then in the evening listening to the band on the Bank corner. Sundays meant church, four services, walking a mile each way. We had no wireless, television or cinema but enjoyed the simple things of life such as swimming in the river Roding, conkering in the autumn, skipping and hoops. The local policeman knew everyone and if we had been naughty "scrumping" he just clipped our legs with his leather gloves, which hurt, and then when we arrived home we had another hiding for thievery.'

A DAY ON A BARGE

'I was born and brought up in a public house called The Old English Garden which stands to this day on the side of the river Lea at

Waltham Abbey. In those days most of the coal, grain and timber was transported in barges pulled by horses. Attached to the pub was a row of stables where the horses were rested overnight before continuing their journey the next day.

One lovely hot summer's day in the late 1940s during the school holidays, my friend and I were asked by the lightermen, as they were called, if we would like to spend the day on the barge as it made its way to Broxbourne in Hertfordshire. So armed with our sandwiches and drink, we began a truly memorable trip. Just gliding through the water, listening to the clip-clop of the horses' hooves on the gravel towpath and the water lapping against the barge. We watched with awe as the lock-keeper opened the heavy lock gates and got us to pass into the lock. He would open the sluice gates and the barge would magically rise up to the next level of the river, then he closed the lock gates behind us and ran to the other end of the lock and opened the second set of gates and we were on our way again.

Although it was only a short distance the journey took all day and we stopped at one or two pubs situated on the side of the river; there was never any thought that we would come to harm in the company of those men. Of course, none of this is possible now, thanks to "progress", but I still remember it as if it was yesterday.'

HELPING IN THE FIELDS

'My grandfather was an old-fashioned farmer at Stisted with about 170 acres. We lived in a house on the farm and at harvest time, everyone helped. My most vivid memories are working from 10 am to 6 pm, earning two shillings and sixpence a week. I was ten years old.

Grandfather didn't believe in tractors and had four cart horses which I loved – two Suffolk, one Percheron and a Shire. Summer-time they were at work from dawn to dusk. Having cut the corn in the field with a binder, leaving the sheaves in lines, we all lent a hand and stood sheaves up in eights to form traves or stooks as some people call them. These were left to dry and then, and this is what I remember best, three men in the field loaded the carts which were then taken to the barn to be unloaded. It was my job to take the empty waggons from the barn down to the fields and then return with the full ones. It was great with the empty ones because I could ride on the cart, driving the horse with long reins. I must have walked miles each day. One day, one old horse called Gilbert ran away with me and my father said it was the funniest thing he'd ever seen – this old horse lumbering down the cart track, me hanging onto the cart and reins for dear life, using language he didn't know I knew! The horse came to the ditch which he jumped, leaving me and the cart behind in the mud. I was fine but the cart was unrepairable!'

DURING THE DEPRESSION

'Life was very different when I was a child. It was during the depression of the 1930s; my father's business had failed and, after all liabilities and debts were discharged, we had no choice but to move to the cheapest rented accommodation we could find. This was a small wooden four-roomed bungalow at the end of an unmade and unlit road in a derelict area of southeast Essex. The lavatory was a pail in a tiny shed 20 yards from the bungalow and water was from a well in the garden. There was no bathroom, there was no gas supply, there was no kitchen but we had an old black kitchen range and one central electric light in each room. The place was quite isolated.

I was an only child and had just started attending Westcliff High School, to which I had won a scholarship otherwise it would not have been possible for me to go there. How well I recall getting up at half past six in a freezing bedroom to wash in a bowl of lukewarm water, to hurry into my clothes, still shaking with cold, swallow a hasty breakfast and leave home just after seven o'clock. I had three-quarters of a mile to walk to the bus stop and after getting off the bus there was another three-quarters of a mile to walk, in all weathers, to reach school by a quarter to nine – all this for a solitary little girl of ten! In those days, though, I don't think this was considered to be exceptional hardship.

We grew our own vegetables and kept chickens and ducks or our diet would have been very meagre as my father was unable to find employment for several years. We exchanged eggs with our nearest neighbour for goat's milk and bought cheap windfall apples. I scavenged the fields and woods for everything eatable – chestnuts and hazelnuts, mushrooms, sloes and blackberries, bullaces and wild strawberries, elderberries and crab apples. We also gleaned in the fields after the corn was harvested and, of course, collected dead wood and twigs for the fire.

There were gypsies in the area who tethered their semi-wild piebald horses with long chains which would stretch across the rough, muddy road and were a constant terror to me walking home alone from school in the winter darkness.

Life as I grew up in those days was very harsh and frugal, but there were such compensations! The freedom to roam alone safely through fields and woods, winter and summer; the gossamer shimmering on the grasses in the autumn sun; the rattle of a woodpecker in the silent wood; a carpet of white anemones in the spring and then the bluebells, knee deep, and the scent of them. All the wild flowers I collected and pressed and all the varied butterflies and moths – I used to keep caterpillars and watch the wonderful process from chrysalis to winged beauty. I would stand outside on winter evenings and wonder at the myriad of stars; how they twinkled! I was sure there must be life up there! Once I watched the Aurora Borealis.

I have watched chicks and ducklings struggling to hatch from their shells and shuddered in shock as an adder crossed my path! I was born in a London suburb, not on a farm, but those years of poverty and hardship in the depression years of the 1930s gave me, in spite of all, the most wonderful childhood to remember all my life.'

CLACTON CLIFFS AND LAMPS

'I moved to Clacton on Sea at the age of six in the 1930s. Together with two cousins I played and made dens in the cliffs, and was disappointed when steps and slopes to these were repaired, and the cliff bushes pruned and landscaped. I can remember being taken on a rowing boat through the gap in the pier, severed along its length to delay any enemy landing force once war was declared. There were warnings of what to do if mines were washed up on the shore or uncovered in the sand on the beach.

The family home was in Rosemary Road and each evening the lamplighter came cycling up Ellis Road with what seemed a magic wand to light the gas street lamp outside our house.'

WHAT A HOUSE

'I was brought up in the Medway Towns in Kent but my happiest memories revolve around my grandmother's house, No 1 Bishops Green Villas, on the road between Barnston and High Easter. Today the journey would only take a couple of hours but then it involved four buses, a ferry and a two and a half mile walk.

What a house and so many memories. The front door was always spotless with beautiful red steps but I don't ever remember going in or out of it – we always used the back door. As soon as we entered there would be a wonderful smell of cooking. There was a large butler sink in one corner with just the one cold tap, any hot water had to be from the huge kettle on the range. I remember having a bath on a Sunday evening in the tin bath in front of the range. After being rubbed down with a lovely warm towel I would sit on my Grandad's lap and watch my uncles play cards or listen to the radio. We would sit by the warm glow of the oil lamps as there was no electricity. When it was time for bed I would be allowed to carry my candle up to the bedroom I shared with my aunt who was only two years older than me and we would cuddle down into the huge soft mattress. The bedstead was iron and always creaked whenever you moved. I used to lie awake at night and look at the stars and listen for any wildlife that might be around. I remember seeing badgers and foxes around the dustbins and hearing owls in the trees. There was no toilet or bathroom so if we needed to "spend a penny" we had to go down the garden, but at night it was the china pot under the bed.

Every morning I would wake up to the lovely smell of bacon cooking. It was always a fried breakfast and porridge as well if we were hungry. If it was Monday I would watch my gran light the fire under the copper in the outhouse and then boil up the sheets and the whites and put them through the old mangle. I used to stand on an old wooden stump under the greengage trees and watch the washing blowing in the wind. When the sheets were dry I would help to stretch them back into shape and put them in the huge wicker basket. After lunch the flat irons would come out and the huge oak table would become the ironing table.

Tuesdays we would go by Lodge's coach to Dunmow for shopping. I remember the smell of the butcher's shop with the sawdust on the floor, the ground coffee in the grocer's and the steam trains at the railway station if we had to go and pay for the coal. If the weather was good we would go for a walk to Bacon End to see my gran's sister and get some eggs from her farm, or it would be High Roding to see her brother or another sister whose husband ran a bakery. There was always a cup of tea and a cake at someone's house.

On a fine summer's evening all the children would get together and play cricket in the road; not much traffic in those days. Sometimes I was allowed to walk down the road to the Spotted Dog pub to get my grandad some tobacco and I was allowed to have a bottle of Vimto for myself. Little did I realise that while I was in the public bar getting my Vimto my future husband was in the public bar drinking with his friends. It was a good few years before we met but that public house has extra special memories for me.'

OUR NEW HOME

'When we first moved into our new home in Colchester in the 1950s it was in the first road of a new estate built on farm land – Home Farm. Nearly all the houses had young families and I suddenly had freedom to play out with many friends of all ages. A popular game was to build forts and dens out of the huge piles of bricks until we were chased off by the site foreman. A favourite time was sharing a mug of hot sweet tea with the builders in their hut or having a ride on the dumper truck.

At the end of the day we went home for tea, which was bread, butter, jam and cake. Our house had a through lounge but it was divided by a heavy curtain to keep the lounge warm during the evening. Heating was by an open fire and tea round the fire was a weekend treat. Doors to other rooms were always kept shut to keep the warmth in and draughts out, so when you needed to go to the toilet you felt very isolated from the bosom of your family and night demons hiding behind the doors and under the beds sent you scurrying down the stairs two at a time before they caught you.

Winter mornings I would jump out of bed onto the rug – avoiding the lino – pick up my clothes and rush downstairs to get dressed in front of the fire. Chilblains on my toes were part of my childhood, standing on the coconut mat and scratching my feet till they throbbed. Black ointment like tar from a cardboard pot was applied to bring relief, which was preferable to my grandfather's remedy which was to immerse the foot in a po containing your own wee!'

THE UNMADE ROADS

'After the war my parents and a number of relatives and friends moved to London to buy four of the five alternate semi-detached bungalows being newly built in an unmade road "in the countryside" – Thundersley.

My strongest memories are of the unmade roads – clay soil that turned to slimy, boggy, treacherous stretches in the winter and then set like concrete in the summer and developed cracks big enough to break your ankle in.

I can still remember the terror of finding myself stuck in the mud in the road outside my home. My wellingtons were deep in the gloop and I couldn't free my feet or take a step. I struggled for ages to move just one foot without falling over. Eventually out came a sockless foot and there was no option but to put it down into the glutinous mess of a road surface, and work at freeing the other foot and then excavating the wellingtons themselves. Yuk – I still shudder.

The summer gave quite different problems and I recall being sent on an errand to the butcher's to buy "four lean lamb chops" and setting off clutching a florin (two shillings). Halfway there I dropped the coin and watched in horror as it disappeared down one of a maze of large bottomless cracks in the earth. I tried to excavate the crack to retrieve the coin but with no tools or stick to hand the earth was far too hard to make any impression on. Eventually I had to go home and report the problem, and my father accompanied me back to the point of loss, but although I had been totally confident of identifying the crack that swallowed the coin, they suddenly all looked alike! Dad was not pleased and made the simple observation that if I had stuck a stalk of grass in the crack then we'd be able to find it now!

Our road was often used as a short-cut by a rag and bone man, who had a wooden cart and a chestnut horse that rejoiced in the name "Never-Too-Late-For-Breakfast" – he'd happily accept a handful of fresh-picked grass from a child or a crust or a tit-bit from anyone at any time of the day. Never-Too-Late-For-Breakfast plodded on, behind a set of ancient leather blinkers, and I don't remember him needing telling when to stop and start – years of routine had become ingrained and he was at one with his owner.'

THE ROAD FROM CHELMSFORD

'The road leading from Chelmsford towards Waltham where you could branch left to Dunmow or right to Braintree played an important part in my childhood. My grandparents lived at the Chelmsford end, Broomfield Road, in a small two-bedroomed semi-detached house in which they raised six children. I loved to go to the house with its wild extremes, for although in the 1950s my nanna still cooked on a range, blackened to a shine once a week, and had no hot water or inside loo, in the front room, into which we were rarely allowed to wander, was a telephone!

The house had no electricity supply, they refused to have it installed when it was offered, and oil lamps, burned to give light, were only replaced by calor gas when my grandad died in the mid-1960s.

Living further along the road at Broomfield, we were never without entertainment supplied by the day to day world of a major route. At Essex Show time it was impossible to cross over the road as the sheer volume of traffic going to and fro from Great Leighs trundled by. What sights we saw! Traction engines rumbling along with angry drivers following, unable to overtake, caravans, lorries, fairground equipment . . . we watched it all with such excitement. Of course the life of the road was not always happy, and there were times when living so close brought sadness, although to us young children the sheer excitement of the crashes and the rescues that followed, sometimes overshadowed the consequences.'

HOW INNOCENT WE WERE

'My teenage years were in the 1950s and how innocent we were! When a boy first kissed me I thought I might get pregnant. We loved to jive at the Ilford Palais and it was quite a lively place with Ted Heath and his band regularly playing there. I often walked a mile home late at night in bare feet because my stiletto heeled shoes were hurting me, without any fear of being out alone. There were occasional scuffles at the Palais even in those days and I remember one night boys fighting with broken bottles and someone being thrown over the balcony. But of course there wasn't much publicity about that sort of thing (which was just as well or my mother would not have allowed me to go there!). There were more discreet "proper" dance places to go like East Ham town hall or Ilford town hall, but our gang thought these places rather "square".

The clothes I wore went from very full skirts and nipped-in waists to very tight tapered-in skirts with a slit in the back in which you could hardly walk, let alone get on a bus. When courting we went everywhere by bus.'

GAMES, TREATS AND CHORES

With little equipment and few bought toys, our games were mostly created from imagination and custom, but we had the roads as our playgrounds and the occasional treats were great occasions. We had our chores to do as well, and pocket money usually had to be earned.

MILK AND WEDDINGS

'When I was old enough, just after the First World War, I had to go to the farm at Broomfield each morning before eight o'clock to fetch the milk. After the farm was sold a milkman called at the door with a big pail of milk.

Summer evenings and holidays would find us out in the meadows, or, mostly the boys, bathing in the river. Many a cricket match was played between us in the light evenings and sometimes a "wedding" would take place. An old net curtain would make a veil for the bride and wild flowers such as buttercups, cow parsley or daisies would make up the bouquets. When bride and groom were pronounced husband and wife, we would all proceed behind them up the meadow path to the main road, then walk along to another entrance of the meadow and back to where we started. It was surprising how many mums and neighbours would just happen to be out in the garden or talking at the gate when we went along. All too soon the big clock on the estate stables would strike eight o'clock, time to go in for bed, and if we didn't go straight away first one mother and then another would start to call us in.'

'We had no running water in the cottage at Black Notley and water had to be fetched from the pump at the farm, a journey of ten minutes each way. My sister and I had to cycle along a farm track to the Green Dragon to catch the school bus, while we waited we would watch the blacksmith at work. We were also paid to carry the milk in cans, one on each handlebar, from the farm to the cottages where we lived, fivepence a week.'

DELIVERING FAGGOTS

'My grandfather was a woodman and much of my time was spent in Bendyshe Woods with him while he cut faggots and stakes, and we often brought home pigeons or rabbits for our dinner. Other days were taken up with delivering the faggots to various villages – Hempstead, Ashdon, Wimbish and Radwinter. We would have to walk to the destination, accompanied by Bob the old mongrel dog. The ride back was the thing, with a stop for home-made ginger beer at the Red Lion or Plough.'

GOATS AND SPARROWS

'My mother grew up in the early years of the century in north-west Essex. As the children got older they each had specific tasks such as feeding chickens, pigs, ducks, turkeys and goats, or household tasks such as scrubbing or polishing. The particular task for the boys was to tether the goats on the village green before they went to school. The boys also had to catch sparrows in the thatched roof of the cottage and their mother made sparrow pie. Some of the children never had new clothes as they always had to wear hand-me-downs. Each year at harvest their father earned extra money, although his main job was as horse-keeper. After harvest the whole family went in a waggonette to the local town to buy new shoes and boots and anything else which could be afforded at the time. The children were taken to the local public gardens to have a picnic lunch and they each had a few pence to spend which they had earned gleaning in the fields after harvest.'

ON THE MARSHES

'When my father went shooting over the Fobbing marshes on hot Saturday afternoons in the 1920s, my mother prepared sandwiches for tea and we all went to the seawall. My sister and I gathered brushwood, Dad put up a tripod to hang the kettle on, and we lit the fire and boiled the kettle for a cup of tea before Dad went shooting for wild duck, partridge or rabbit.'

'Writtle children, before the First World War, visited the local piggery and obtained a pig's bladder which they inflated and used as a football.'

'As we were four children and we had a mother who loved children we always had a party during the Christmas holidays. Mother was full of ideas. One was "Frog in the middle and you can't get out". We held hands in a circle, moving slowly round, and a frog (one of us) on hands and knees, had to break through the circle. When they did so a new frog was found. Another was – make the noise of a particular animal or bird. This time we all sat on chairs in a circle. A blindfolded player in the middle would hold a cushion and place it on a lap, and that person was asked to make the noise of, say, a cow. The blindfolded person would try to guess who it was by the voice.

In another game we were each given the name of a town. Mother would then call that a letter was being sent from one town to another. A blindfolded player in the middle of the circle would then try to catch the owners of those names as they changed places in the circle. Sometimes Mother would call "General Post" and everyone had to change places. Someone was always caught then.

Another game was "spin the trencher". This was a breadboard, or sometimes a circular copper tray was used. We would remain in a circle, and one child would spin the tray and call the name of a player. The player had to catch the spinning tray before it fell. If they did so they could spin it the next time. If they failed the first player would try again.'

'Games at Leyton were played in the school playground and in the road, the latter being possible because what little traffic there was, was slow moving. Hopscotch was marked out on the pavement and you had to alternately hop and jump up to the square into which you had thrown a piece of slate, or a small stone. There was a similar game where a snail-like course was marked out.

Cricket was played with a piece of roughly shaped wood as a bat, and a lamp post as a wicket. Neighbours' windows were liable to suffer. Football in the road or playground was usually with a small rubber ball which was easily punctured. Occasionally someone had a leather football, and again this could wreak havoc with the local glazing. Later in the 1920s sorbo balls arrived, and these were a great advance, having a centre of sponge rubber and a smooth outer coating of rubber, not liable to puncture.

"He" and "Release" were more playground games, He being a touch game. Whoever was he had to chase the other players, and when he touched them that child became he. Release was a team game, and usually the two sides were of equal numbers. One team had to catch the others and pen each one in a corner as he or she was caught, and continued until the whole opposition had been captured.

Cherry Hogs came when cherries were in season and you collected the kernels. It involved someone who had a wood screw sitting on the pavement with his legs apart, and the screw stood upright between them. The cherry hogs were then thrown individually at the screw, and whoever knocked the screw over had it as his prize. It wasn't always easy to get either the cherry hogs or screws.

Cigarette cards was played against a wall. The cigarette cards were flipped from between the fingers and fell on the ground. If your card covered or touched another one you picked them both up.

Peg tops and whip tops also kept us amused. The former had an iron peg at the bottom and a conical wooden top. String was wound round the upper wooden portion, and holding the end of the string, the top was tossed or flicked down to the ground. The skill took a while to acquire. Whip tops were shaped with bands of colour on the lower part. In this case the string was attached to a stick making a whip. Once again holding the whip, the top with string wound round it was cast to the ground. The top usually spun in a wobbly fashion to start, but with skilful use of the whip it could be made to spin fast, and the control of the top could be quite surprising. The younger child's humming top is still sold today.

Bus Horses was played usually with three children. The "horses" crossed and held hands behind them, and the other drove them holding the reins. The reins would range from any rough old string to the specially knitted reins made by winding wool over nails driven into a cotton reel (which in those days was made of wood). The next stage from Bus Horses was Chariot Races. Again the horses linked arms behind them, and there could be three or more horses in each team. The object was to win a race over a pre-arranged course.

Jimmie Knacker was a development of leapfrog. There would be two teams, of possibly up to six boys. The first side had one boy standing against the railings, and the others bent over with their backs level, holding on to the boy in front. The head of this boy at the front rested against the lad on the railings. The other team then ran from a reasonable distance and leapt as far as possible on to the "horses" who were bending down. Usually hands were used to gain impetus in vaulting off the last horse. If the whole team landed safely on the horses, they would rock up and down singing "Jimmie, Jimmie Knacker, one, two, three, all off and away". Alternatively, if the horses collapsed under the impact of the jumpers or their combined weight, which was often borne by the last two horses, then the cry was "weak horses" and the game restarted without the teams changing places.'

'We played the usual games of that time – hopscotch, bouncing a ball in "squares" and bouncing it against a wall, touch, hide and seek, skipping as we chanted songs, fox and goose, and statues. Other amusements of Epping children were pea-shooters made from a piece of elder wood hollowed out and using green elderberries for ammunition, catapults or "caddycrotch" made from a Y-shaped twig chosen and cut from a hedge and using a strip cut from an old cycle inner tube to shoot a small pebble at a target, and, of course, conkers using an old bootlace threaded through a horse chestnut.

We climbed trees, slid down slopes of old gravel pits, fished for tiddlers in the river, paddled in puddles and ponds, slid on the ice and sledged at "the Loop" when the snow was deep enough. We kicked a ball around, played cricket with stumps each side of the road and making our runs across it, and we played at acting, singing and dancing on a platform which was in front of a new small shop where, at first, dresses and haberdashery were sold.'

'In the summer we made cats' tails from grasses, little baskets from rushes, whistles from sheep's parsley and gleaned corn for hens and picked up acorns for pigs.'

'The highlight of summer was when the hay was cut in Mr Talworthy's fields at Chingford. This was before the 1920s. Nearly all the children in the district made for Tally's fields. Our favourite game was to make one child kneel down while the rest of us piled the hay over and around as high as we could get it. Then we would chant "Green Man, Green Man, rise up!" and this figure would erupt out of the hay!

During the summer holidays we thought it really exciting to take a picnic over to Tally's fields. All we took were a few sandwiches and some lemonade, but there was a stream along one side so we took a fishing net and caught tiddlers. We took them home in jam jars. One year I kept some from the summer holiday until well after Christmas.'

'We lived in a row of terraced houses at Leyton, with small back gardens and tiny front gardens, but the streets were our playground. There was no traffic when we moved there in 1915. We played rounders, bowled hoops and went for "outings" in small gangs. I remember one street game which was a kind of charades:

A: Please, we come to learn the trade.
B: What to do?
A: Anything better than you can do.
B: Set to work to do it.

Then we acted out a job or trade.
Our mothers left a string hanging from the front door latch, so we could put our hand through the letterbox and let ourselves in.'

'Cigarette cards were joyfully accumulated in the 1930s and stuck into albums, and we collected various coupons. "Sunny Jim", a rag doll, came courtesy of Force cornflakes. Oxo coupons provided a football and cricket bat for my brother, and a lovely plush doll clad in mauve velvet for me. Gibbs Dentifrice gave us Ivory Castle jigsaws and games, and tins of cocoa concealed woodland figures made of lead to be used for special board games.
Empire Day was celebrated with parades in the playground, each child waving red, white and blue strips of tissue paper stuck into cardboard tubes. Dark blue (Oxford) or light blue (Cambridge) favours and small kewpie dolls were bought and worn on Boat Race Day. At Christmas, Woolworths at Chadwell Heath was an Aladdin's cave of delightful stocking fillers. Cardboard "fruits" (a box of six for half a crown) were set on a small ring in the centre of our sitting room. Each one had a small wick which was ignited, and accompanied by a small "pop" the "fruit" broke in half, showering out tiny charms – absolute magic!'

THE FREEDOM WE HAD

'The freedom we had to enjoy ourselves is almost unbelievable by today's standards. My childhood was spent at Wrabness in the 1940s. Stow Woods was our playground and we would rush home from school to take our "tea" into the woods and spend hours making dens. Chestnut time brought fingers full of prickles, and how we enjoyed filling an old pram with the wood chips from where the trees had been coppiced, and collecting bundles of sere wood for the winter fires. We knew every path and track and enjoyed every season.
On hot summer days we had picnics on the shore – a small bonfire to boil an egg for baby's dinner and water for tea, and Mother teaching us all to swim in the cold river Stour, and when the tide was right collecting winkles to take home and cook for tea.
We had few toys, no pocket money, no cinema, records or homework, only the radio with "Uncle Mac" and *Family Favourites*, but what a happy childhood.'

GOING SWIMMING

'My aunt Lena was brought up at Beckingham Mill in the 1890s, where her father was the miller. She remembered going swimming at Goldhanger: "Whenever there was a good tide and a good day,

Father would drop everything. We would take a big brown basket about 20 inches long, and wide. In it were all the bathing trunks for the boys and chemises or nightdresses for the girls. In it also was a tin with tea biscuits and bottles of home-made lemonade. Father would meet us out of school. He taught the boys to swim but never attempted to teach the girls – I was so cross! We girls tied the nightdresses round ourselves and we all went in. We went down there in the miller's cart."'

'Throughout my early childhood days in Corbets Tey, our play was relatively carefree and, unlike today, without adult supervision. The main worry for our parents was the local neglected and very accessible sandpits full of stagnant water and dead animals. We children were all constantly being admonished not to swim in them but the temptation was great as the only swimming pool was the tiny indoor pool at Mawney Road, Rochford, which was beyond our sights in more ways than one – distance and cost.'

WOODING AND WORDS

'We spent hours on imaginary journeys to exotic places, with many "adventures" on the way. Always on our walks, we "wooded", picking up any pieces we saw for burning on the fire. Everyone went wooding. Most homes had a box cart, a wooden box on wheels with two handles, and children were sent out to fill it with wood, to fetch and carry generally, and small, tired-legged brothers and sisters were glad of a ride at the end of the day. Whenever a horse passed by and "obliged", someone was soon outside with bucket and spade to pick up the spoils, the garden was so important. The box cart would be used to scour the roads between villages and bring home the valuable by-product.

Snail races, raindrops down the window pane races, spinning tops, bowling our hoops all amused us, and my brother and I spent hours playing "it reminds me of", eg sugar reminds me of tea, tea reminds me of . . . and you must not say the same thing twice; word chains, when the last letter of one word was the first of the next and so on, and once more, no repetition or you were out. Such simple things, and no cost.'

SO MUCH TIME

'We had a stream at the bottom of our lane which in those days ran over the road. We used to block it up with stones and mud to make the water deep enough to swim in. We wore swimming costumes knitted by Auntie Doris out of hundreds of scraps of odd wool – all colours. They stretched nearly to our ankles when they got wet. We always came home with a jar of sticklebacks or tadpoles, or some other thing we'd found in the stream. Each evening the farmer, Gordon Schwier, would have to unblock the stream to stop a flood; then we would repeat it again the next day. We also used to spend hours in the woods a few hundred yards from our home. The seasons for bluebells, primroses and chestnuts were always our favourite times. I used to pick a huge bunch of each flower in season, wrap them in moss in a shoe box, and post them to Granny in London. Two days later a letter would arrive saying how lovely they were, and that they were as fresh as when I had picked them.

Saturday mornings our mother wrote a shopping list and we walked the mile or so to the Little Maplestead shop. We would stop at Auntie Doris's house and collect her list and be given threepence between us. Our mother had already given us threepence. We would go to the shop and Marjorie Felton would serve us. She had no voice and used to whisper to us. We always spent ages choosing our sweets; they were the only ones we had all week. Either Auntie or Mummy would provide the sweet coupon. I usually had bright yellow lemon crystals in a cone of paper; you licked your finger and dipped it in . . . lovely! I also managed a couple of bullseyes, because they took a long while to eat. It usually took us all Saturday morning to do the shopping because we never hurried, and there was always something to look at. Sometimes if we were really lucky we would have a short ride with Mr Ward who lived down Wards Lane. He had a pony and trap and used to do his shopping in Halstead; on his way home he would sometimes give us a lift as far as his lane. These were the best days.'

THERE WAS NO TRAFFIC

'In our early days there was no traffic, except for the occasional bicycle, or horse-drawn vehicle, so most of our outdoor games were played in the road.

As well as individual skipping ropes, we used a long stout rope which had come from a wooden crate of oranges, or an abandoned washing-line. This was stretched right across the road in Bridge Street (Great Bardfield) and one end tied to a garden gatepost. One girl or boy turned the loose end and a group at a time skipped and sang "All in together, all sorts of weather" etc until somebody tripped the rope. We also skipped individually, and sang: "My mother said, I never should, play with gypsies in the wood. If I did, she would say, naughty little girl to disobey, your hair won't curl, your boots won't shine, naughty little girl, you shan't be mine".

Hoops were wooden, and graded in size. We bowled our hoops with a piece of wood, all the way down to the bridge and along other streets. Boys whose fathers worked at the foundry had iron hoops and a skimmer with a hook to guide the hoop.

Marbles were kept in a draw-string bag, made by our mother, and we could buy coloured marbles. "A penn'orth o' marbles please", would be the request at the general shop. Ginger beer bottles had a glass marble under the stopper, but you had to smash the neck to get it out. You had status if you owned large coloured "glassies".

On summer evenings, before it was the custom to alter the clocks, it would get dark earlier and then the bats came out in Bridge Street. We threw our hats and caps into the air and shouted the words my mother taught me (it must have been an old pastime!): "Bat, Bat, come under my hat, and I'll give you a slice of bacon. If that won't do, I'll give two, so Bat, Bat, come under my hat." Needless to say, the bats evaded our hats. We also played hide and seek, in the twilight, creeping round people's backyards, and alleyways, until our mothers called us in.'

SCHOOLDAYS – THE BEST YEARS OF OUR LIVES?

Long walks to school, clothes drying in front of the fire, slates and chalk, large classes and small schools – familiar subjects for generations of Essex children.

A HAPPY PLACE

'School for my mother, in the early 1900s in Colchester, was a happy place. The infants classroom had hammocks for the tired and sleepy. At age seven the class had 72 children. If the teacher was away the class was divided between two others, which meant three to a desk instead of two. The headmistress wore a long skirt, which she usually draped over her arm.'

CANN HALL ROAD SCHOOL

'School started at the age of five, and during the First World War I went to Cann Hall Road school in Leyton which was about half a mile from home. Recollections of what we did in the infants school are very vague. One of the lady teachers was elderly, and always dressed in a long black dress. After a lesson about animals and cats she asked who had a cat, and whether we had any questions. I must have been very young, but I remember her horror when I asked her why our cat had two "spots" under its tail! She certainly did not answer the question. Our earliest writing was done on slates with slate pencils, and consisted of what we called pothooks and hangers.

Most of the learning in junior school was by rote, tables and spelling recited, but occasionally we had a "spelling bee" and surprisingly I sometimes did well at that. With some of the teachers there was very little imagination, but being war time they were mostly elderly and possibly not too well qualified.

We were always sent off to school in time, but picking up friends on the way led to delays. There was really plenty of warning that time was running out, as the school bell started ringing as much as ten minutes before time for arrival, and then shortly before the end the pace of the tolling bell quickened so that provided you were near enough you could make the final dash to get into your class line in the playground before the gate was closed. Those who arrived in time marched in step – or officially in step – to their classes, and then the late arrivals were admitted and conducted to the headmaster's corridor. The headmaster came out, cane in hand, hands were held out and we duly took our punishment, which as far as I recall was only one swish of the cane and not too bad at that!'

THE WAR WAS STILL ON

'My earliest memory of Bardfield school was the white painted slogan, in large capital letters, on the frontage: "Remember Our Boys". The war was not over when I started school at the age of four and learned the significance of those large white words. We "babies" (as we were called) stood for evening prayer, before going home at 4 pm, "hands together, eyes closed", and we prayed for "our soldiers and sailors, father and mother, brothers and sisters and all whom we love. Amen."

We sat in dual desks, in orderly rows. The only time we moved in a session was when we stood around the blackboard and easel, over which hung a heavy reading chart. What pleasure when we had mastered "Kate is at the gate. She is late." We waited in anticipation for the page to be turned. There was Kate again in her white pinafore, black boots and stockings, and her hair tied with a ribbon bow on top; a contemporary picture! Most of us girls wore starched pinafores with broderie anglaise. Our winter socks were kept up with garters. The boys' boots were studded with hobnails, heel irons and blakeys. Some of us girls coveted such footwear when we watched the boys kicking sparks against every hearthstoned doorstep down Bridge Street. Knee-length corduroy or serge trousers, with Norfolk jackets or woollen "ganseys" with high necks were boys' wear. If a jacket was worn, a deep celluloid or rubberised collar was worn attached with studs. What a fright, one Guy Fawkes night, when young Percy Hornsby's celluloid collar went up in flames, caused by a thrown coloured match. He was unhurt!

Back in my early days we walked home, but children from long distances, such as Oxen End, Walthams Cross, Great and Little Lodge, had to stay and bring their slices of bread and dripping, or slabs of cold bread pudding, and eat sitting on the causeway railings, or in the school porch if it rained. For drink, the fountain was nearby. Some poorer families stayed and bought "a penn'orth of scrips" from Mr Bone the butcher. These scrips or scraps, which were the crisp remains of fat after being rendered down for dripping, were once considered as toothsome as the potato crisps of today. "Give us a scrip, gal, and I'll swap ye a fag card," was a common plea.

The worst horror of early infancy was the sawdust-operated closet seat. Sit down, and the seat collapsed and clanged with you; stand up, and the seat rattled back. This contraption caused a hopper at the back to release sawdust into the bucket. Toilet paper was not provided and there was no water for washing or drinking. If you fell on the rough stony playground and cut your knee, you spat on your hanky and wiped off the blood and dirt.'

TIP HAT AND PETTICOAT DAY

'I was born in Rochford in 1911. We walked to school, a good mile, going home for dinner at twelve o'clock. May 1st was Tip Hat Day and the next day was Petticoat Day, when the boys would pull down the hems of our petticoats!'

ON THE WAY

'At the age of five I had a mile to walk to school, four times a day. Woe betide us if we were only just turning into the lane at Broomfield as the bell went. Cries of "Bell!" would be called back to others behind us and there would be one mad race to get there before the lines had filed in.

Friday was market day in Chelmsford and our walk to school would often find us behind someone's gate as cows and sheep were driven along the road to market, coming from outlying village farms. We also had to be on the alert going home in the afternoon, for the bought or unsold cattle were driven back. Being a sandy road many potholes would form, filling with water when it rained, icing over when cold. We would slide on our way to school. When spring came, whip tops and hoops came out and after the road was tarmacadamed there was much rivalry as to who could whip their top farthest down the road. Cars were still few and far between, but many a top ended up under a cartwheel.'

FUND RAISING

'Several old photographs of Stansted village school show that the numbers remained steady at around 40 pupils during the first 30 years or so of the century. In the early days most of them wore boots, some laced, some buttoned. I am told that, at one time, a travelling bootmaker would drive round with a pony and trap, selling cheap boots which were not right and left "handed", but straight, and could be worn on either foot. Many of the girls wore voluminous pinafores, and some curled their hair in long ringlets tied with ribbons.

There were two teachers, the "governess" and her assistant, who were in charge of the "big" and "little" rooms respectively. (The adjectives referred to the size of the pupils as well as to the space within the rooms.) In the big room was a large tortoise stove which gave out a comforting heat in winter to those who were near it. It also gave out an all-pervading appetising smell as the forerunner of school dinners, as we know them, were cooked thereon. Vegetable, often lentil, soup and roly-poly jam pudding or similar nourishing food simmered there in the morning and it cost a penny halfpenny to partake at dinner time.

Pupils and teachers in the classroom at Broomfield school in 1926.

The school had been built by public subscription on land given to the village by the Countess of Warwick. Each year there was a fund raising effort, organised by the school managers and teachers for maintenance and equipment. This took the form of a whist drive, an "invitation only" affair. Guests came from far and near, bearing their invitation cards, which had been carefully written by the senior pupils and which inevitably began with "The pleasure of the company of .... is requested". On the afternoon of the event the senior boys went round the village borrowing tables and chairs, returning with the oddest assortment. The big room was filled beyond capacity and moving between the tables was quite a struggle. Halfway through the evening there was an interval for refreshments with the senior girls acting as waitresses. There were sandwiches, mince pies and cakes and tea. Toilet facilities were meagre and to be avoided if possible. The men used the outside lavatories, and the ladies were provided with a large commode in the annexe to the back kitchen where the coal was usually stored. At the end of the card playing there were speeches of thanks and of appreciation and everyone went home. Next morning the boys returned the tables and chairs and then came back to demolish the "left-overs".'

CHRISTIANS AND HEATHENS

'The church school I attended at Hutton boasted 16 pupils in all, with ages ranging from five to 14 years. When I reached the age of eleven however, scholarships had come into being and those pupils who did not pass the test were sent to Shenfield school.

There was another very large residential school in the area known as the Poplar school. I believe George Lansbury was its main founder and it housed orphan and poor children from the London area. It covered many acres and the children lived in "houses" with a housemother and housefather, and was very self sufficient. There were a swimming pool, laundry, workshops and a large sewing room where all the children's clothing was made. A Mr Dean was the headmaster at one time, a much respected man and on Sunday mornings the children would march to church accompanied by their own school brass band. The school building and dining hall are all that remain of this complex, the school being used as the Adult Education Centre. A few local children were permitted to attend the school and rivalry between the church school and these children was strong. We considered them heathen!

Our classroom was one large room heated in winter by two large coal fires, lit by our teacher each morning before we arrived. She was a large benign lady who lived with her sister in the school house next door. It was a treat to be sent to the house on an errand as a piece of fruit cake was nearly always the reward. On saints' days we would walk along a stony footpath, flanked by huge elm trees, to church. The rector visited the school daily, often with his sister with whom he lived. Every summer he gave us a school treat with swings from the old oak trees, organised races and we were given a lavish tea at the end of the afternoon.'

WE MADE OUR OWN WAY

'I arrived in Harold Wood in 1925 from North London, aged six years. It could have been a daunting prospect, what with unmade roads and lots of mud (it was February), but my memories are of finding another small girl who had arrived three months before. We became friends and remain so to this day.

Our mothers enrolled us at the local school which was in Harold Wood, one and a half miles walking distance from where we lived. The journey was mainly made along an unmade country lane with a few houses here and there and a cinder path.

The school was very much the village school and, apart from a hot drink in the winter, no provision was made for meals. Our respective mothers used to bring us sandwiches and hand them through the railings (rather like feeding animals at the zoo). Later, arrangements were made for us to have a dinner nearby. Lessons were the basic three Rs. I cannot remember a great deal of the learning process but do remember seasonal games in the playground: skipping, ball games, spinning tops and five stones, all played at specific times of the year.

The other pleasures were our walks to and from school through the season. I remember picking wild flowers and wild fruits and running past the field where the cows were in case they were let out to cross the lane (we were not very brave when faced by a cow!). Our special treat was when my friend's father walked with us en route to the railway station. At the foot of the station steps there was a cabin which sold cigarettes and sweets. He would tell us to wait while he purchased a milk chocolate flake for a penny which we would consume on the remainder of the journey to school. Sometimes our mothers would meet us from school but mostly we made our own way in complete safety.'

A TINY SCHOOL

'The catchment area of Bush End school was approximately three miles; all was done on foot. My journey was two miles in hobnailed boots and short trousers up to my leaving age of 14. I started at three and a half years and I was first taught to tie shoelaces and write on a slate. The school was just one room measuring 32 feet by 18 feet by 14 feet high. At times some 50 to 60 children attended and planks were placed between desks to accommodate the pupils. The infants classes were screened from the seniors by a curtain which could be raised. Heating was a large tortoise stove along one wall. This was surrounded by an iron guard. On the stove stood a large iron kettle from which a senior filled our mugs at mealtimes. We all brought sandwiches. The water supply to the school had always been a problem and it was obtained from the village tap, half a mile away. From the age of eleven it became my lot to fetch a pail of water for the school during the first morning break and one for the school house during the afternoon period.

Bush End school was opened in 1877. At first each child was charged one penny per week for education but elementary education became free in 1891. Up to 1918 children could leave at 13 provided they reached a certain standard. With every penny needed in the poorer households, it is not surprising that parents gave education a low priority. The school diary is studded with entries such as acorning (for the garden pig), gleaning (for bread making), five mile journeys to get yeast, and truancy (following the hunt). Couple this with bad weather conditions, snow and floods, and absenteeism was rife. On more than one occasion our hamlet has been completely snowbound for up to a fortnight for digging out had to be done by hand.

Two teachers at the school, Miss Jarvis and Miss Harwin, remained for 30 years and both my father and myself benefited from their "three Rs" teaching.'

SPECIAL DAYS

'I was born in 1921 and went to St Mary's church school in Woodham Ferrers when I was five. There were three classrooms, one of which was divided by a curtain which made teaching rather difficult. The children of several families had to walk from Bicknacre and back each day. I was able to go home to dinner, but often the teachers would heat soup and bake potatoes on the tortoise stove in the "big" room. It was also useful for drying wet clothes.

We always celebrated Empire Day and on one occasion I remember we were dressed in outfits typical of the countries of the Empire and we stood in front of a large map of the world clutching a cord which was fastened with a pin to our appropriate country. We all paraded to church on Ash Wednesday and Ascension Day, then the rest of the day was a holiday. We were also taken to the war memorial on Armistice Day. We were all aware that almost every family had had a relative in the war, and that some had lost loved ones.'

SCHOOLDAYS DURING THE 1930s AND 1940s

Little had changed for the next generation of schoolchildren, though war brought its own experiences and dangers to everyday life.

SAND, SLATES AND INKWELLS

'The school I went to in Coggeshall in the 1930s was built in 1914, quite modern compared to the previous school which was early Victorian. First and second year children were in the same room and we had sand trays given to us and a meat skewer, so that we could learn to write by copying from the board. Later we were allowed to use slates and pencils and eventually graduated to copybooks. The classroom was quite plain, no pictures on the walls and very high windows so you couldn't see out.

Some children walked three or four miles to school. Shoes were expensive and some owned only plimsolls, which could be bought for one shilling and elevenpence a pair.'

'Our school was the Bell, Upminster. We had slates to write on. My earliest academic stumbling block was that I could not write "W" but my character soon asserted itself as I realised that by turning my slate round and writing "M" all would be well. As I progressed up the school my clearest recollection is of inkwells and all the pitfalls these brought in their wake – nibs crossing, nibs falling into the inkwells, too much ink and the consequent blots and hands that looked as if I was about to start finger painting. But the inkwells had their plus side. "You've done well this week so you may fill the inkwells" – little Miss Somebody at last!'

OPEN FIRES

'I was born in a cottage down Weald Road, Brentwood and I went to the local school. It had big open fires and if anyone wet their knickers or the boys their trousers, the teachers would hang the clothes on the fire guard to dry. I can remember the smell now. Hot drinks were also kept round the fire for fourpence a week, if Mums could afford it. There was a tuck shop outside school: if you had a halfpenny or penny you could get a lovely selection of sweets including pink and white coconut chips, sherbet dabs and brown tobacco.'

UNIFORMS AND HATS

'During my schooldays at Colchester in the 1930s hats were worn travelling to and from school – panama in the summer, velour in the winter. The school uniform was almost sacred! If walking, *only* two abreast, and certainly no eating sweets, or anything else, when in uniform.'

PRIVATE AND COUNCIL

'There was a school at Ramsden Heath, but my sisters went daily to a private school run by an elderly lady who shall be nameless. It was about a hundred yards past the White Horse on the right-hand side of the road to Billericay. They walked there and back every day, but Miss B was probably well past retiring age, and they received a pretty poor education. My sisters remember that in the afternoon, Miss B set them work to do, and then retired to have forty winks. Needless to say very little work got done – more time being spent on giggling and peering in at her bedroom door. Sanitary arrangements at this school consisted of a chamber pot in the good lady's bedroom!

In 1926 Ramsden Crays council school was built (now Crays Hill county primary), to take children from five to 14 years. My eldest sister, Margaret was sent to Brentwood County High School, where the headmistress told my mother that she was well below standard, and suggested that the rest of the family should be educated away from Miss B – so off they went to Ramsden Crays and I duly followed in 1931.

I loved my schooldays here, starting with dear old Mrs Clark in one of the little upstairs rooms. My only horror (and 25 years later my daughter's horror) was the toilets, which had no locks and smelled because they were buckets under wooden seats. It was very difficult for a little girl to answer the call of nature with a hand or a foot on the door to secure it against intruders! In the bitterly cold cloakrooms, about four bowls of icy water were put out each day, with "school soap". My memory is that the water was not changed all day, and no one with any sensitivity washed in the afternoon when the scum and smell of those bowls of water was repulsive.

In 1936 Billericay senior school was built (now Billericay School), and took all the pupils from the age of eleven except those who passed the eleven-plus, who usually went to Brentwood Grammar School for Boys, Brentwood High School for Girls or Brentwood Ursuline.

I remember with great nostalgia the journeys to and from school. There were no school dinners though we could take sandwiches – but mostly we made the journey of one and half miles four times a day. I never remembered my mother taking me, but I suppose she did the first day. The bus fare was one penny to Jackson's corner, but if you started out ten minutes early and ran all the way to school, you then still had your penny to spend at Smith's sweet shop which was opposite the school in Gardiners Lane.

If you came home to dinner you were allowed out five minutes early to catch the bus at Jackson's corner. The bus back to school went about 1.15 and again you could run and save a penny to buy your farthing blackjacks from Mrs Smith. But walks home were best – no running to save pennies – we wandered along paddling in the ditches (probably filled with sewage), trekking through leaves, fishing for tiddlers in the river (I once fell in and arrived home covered in foul smelling slime!), gathering wild flowers, passing love letters to the boys, searching for conkers, popping tar bubbles, talking to Mr Graves who was our roadman, walking round the churchyard and watching the steam-rollers making up the road (I can still smell them). I often feel sorry for today's children who, owing to traffic and "undesirable characters" are whisked in a few minutes from school to home – what a wealth of childhood experiences they miss.'

SENT TO SCHOOL AT DOWNHAM

'Although my family lived in the north of Scotland we – my sister and I – were sent to school in England. My father always thought that a Scots education was the best, but all the same he eventually decided to send us south so in the late 1930s I found myself in the Essex countryside – a far cry from the hills and lochs of Inverness-shire. The land was flat and to my eyes uninteresting, but school I loved.

The school was called Downham – its original name was Down Hall but because there was another well known school of this name it was changed to Downham – and it was situated near the little village of Matching near Bishop's Stortford.

When my parents visited the school they were swayed by the fact that on the dining room tables there were quart jugs of fresh milk and great plates holding about two pounds of butter so they thought we would probably survive!

The headmistress, Mrs Houison Crauford, affectionately known to all as Mrs C, was a wonderful woman. She had been Chief Guide for Scotland and before she became headmistress of the girls' school Westonbirt in Gloucestershire she ran a prize herd of Ayrshire cows in Scotland – a splendid qualification for running a girls' school!

When she left Westonbirt the parents of some 70 girls would not leave them there without her and encouraged her to start her own school, which she did at Downham. I thought she was marvellous because she could put two fingers in her mouth and give a piercing whistle. It took me years before I was able to emulate her! She also had terrific eyebrows like Mr Healey which curled up over her forehead. Her son had been in the same Highland Regiment as my father and in later years we thought that this must have been the reason we were accepted as every other girl had either a grand title or was very rich and we qualified on neither count!

My sister followed me to Downham about a year after I got there and we really enjoyed our school days which were pretty unorthodox. In the winter if we heard the hounds of the local hunt – the Puckeridge – giving tongue anywhere near the school, without question every class downed tools and we all put on our boots and joined the hunt on foot. Those who "took" riding hunted anyway and were allowed the whole day off lessons. The hunt were all very friendly and would allow us to grab a stirrup leather and rush alongside – a bit scary and looking back I suppose a bit dangerous but great fun and we came home red cheeked and ravenous. We were also allowed to join the beagles and I remember a "sporting parson" who wore a crew cut, very unusual in those days, a checked waistcoat with his dog collar and bright yellow stockings with his knickerbockers! I can see him now standing on the top of a hill watching the hare and beagles go round him. Among the hunt was the previous owner of Downham, Mrs Calvery, a most elegant 80 year old who rode side saddle and wore a top hat with veil and always with a lovely bunch of violets in her buttonhole.

On Sundays we all walked to Matching where there was a charming little church for which we provided the choir and the greater part of the congregation. On Saturday evenings a lady came down from Madame Vacani's school in London to teach us dancing. She would be fetched from the station in the school Daimler which was large and high and dark maroon like the Royal Daimlers. We all wore blue silk frocks with white collars and we had to dance with each other or our form mistress. It was all taken very seriously and we learnt formal ballroom dances. I remember that my form mistress wore very hard stays and I disliked dancing with her, she was so stiff!

The chauffeur's son was the school butler called Rodney and when we had stewed apples from which the cores had not been properly taken out the little bits were known as "Rodney's toenails"!

We played lacrosse and netball in the winter and cricket and tennis in the summer and we also had athletics. I was in the lacrosse team and we played matches against various schools in Essex including Poles Convent and another convent I think called New Hall near

Chelmsford. We always loved the away matches as we got a good tea. I hated cricket as I always got my hands hurt and I was only a very average tennis player though I enjoyed it. There was no swimming pool while I was at Downham so we used to swim in the summer at Harlow Mill once a week.

In the old stable block there was a zoo and the girls owned all sorts of pets. There were guinea pigs, rabbits, gerbils, hamsters, mice, rats, different birds and a lovely monkey with black curly hair. If you had a pet you were not required to walk to the main gate and back after breakfast – about a mile – so my sister had a half share in a gerbil to avoid this.

There was a very good domestic science block and the non-academic stream did sewing, laundry, housewifery and cookery. There was an excellent kitchen fitted out with every sort of stove, and on Wednesday afternoons, our half day, we would have voluntary cookery classes which I really enjoyed. We learnt to make walnut cakes with "Fullers" icing and beautiful Christmas cakes with lacy decorations. It was a very good grounding. I was a so-called academic and it was a refreshing break from studying. There was also a very good science lab and the science mistress Miss J-B always made the lessons fun.

In the summer Mrs C and her deputy and perhaps a lucky member of the "Parlour", that is the prefects, went off to Wisbech and brought back vast baskets of strawberries for our supper, a great treat.

Of course going to school laid one open to childish diseases, none of which I had had. One Christmas term a member of my

Wickham St Paul schoolchildren in front of the school in 1948.

dormitory went down with chickenpox and the whole dormitory was incarcerated in the bedroom for three weeks, quarantine being very strict in those days. Our meals and lessons were sent up to us. I suppose we were allowed out of doors at some time though I do not remember it. I occupied my free time knitting a cable stitch pullover for my father. It came down to his knees when it was finished but I was very proud of it. At the end of the three weeks another member of the room was laid low and to our horror it meant we had to undergo another three weeks' imprisonment. Luckily I got the pox before the three weeks were up, in time to get over it before I went home for Christmas. Actually I think I cheated and picked my last remaining spots and filled them with talcum powder so that I would be allowed home.

I left school rather sadly after being head girl for a year. After doing a "mini" season when I was presented at Court in feathers and long white dress, I went to university which I did not like and then it was the war and the whole world changed.

The school closed during the late 1960s after the death of Mrs C and her deputy. Downham has now reverted to its old name of Down Hall and is a very smart hotel. I visited it with my god-daughter, also an old girl, and we had fun reminiscing about our respective childhoods. They really were happy days.'

STRICT DISCIPLINE

'At Sheering school we sat in desks in pairs. The desk had a hinged seat which had to be raised silently when we stood. We were in trouble if the seats or the desk lids were moved noisily. We were not allowed to speak in class, and had to sit up straight when not working, hands behind backs. Playtimes could be forfeited or worse punishment meted out for failure. Severe misdemeanour warranted the cane for boys, lesser ones a strapping on the hands regardless of the sex of the offender.

Spelling tests were given every week on Friday afternoons. If we got all the words correct we were allowed to go home early. We had shoe and hair tidiness inspections to keep us up to scratch.

If visitors came we all had to stand. The rector used to come for assembly once a week (more if we were unlucky) and he would keep us standing for perhaps an hour sometimes. One girl used to pass out before he had finished. This was a welcome diversion to us all and I suspect even the headmaster felt some relief.'

OPPOSITE THE FOREST

'I was fortunate, not only in living opposite Epping Forest, but in having my school in the same road. Its three departments served all the Loughton children from five years to 14 years.

The infants department had a distinctive aroma of chalk dust, pastels and plasticine. We used child-size blackboards and knobbly scraps of chalk for our first efforts at writing. There were small squares of fuzzy felt-like material to rub out mistakes. Cowrie shells, kept in match boxes, served as counters.

At seven years old I moved into the girls department designated "The Big Girls" by the pupils. The headmistress was strict and feared by most girls. She was ahead of her time in many ways, however. On sunny summer afternoons there would be a school walk for everyone, through the forest. We learned the names of the trees, flowers and birds in this way. Once she held a mock-election, with the older girls as candidates making speeches, and proper voting procedures. Each May there was maypole dancing in the playground.

We received a good formal education, with much emphasis on rote learning of tables and spellings. In 1938 I passed the scholarship examination and went to grammar school. By now Loughton was beginning to change. The open spaces in the main road were filled with a variety of shops. Many of the surrounding fields had become estates of newly built homes. Woolworths opened its doors. Loughton retained its village-like character, however, until 1939 and beyond. Then the changes became more rapid and a small suburban town took shape.'

THE WORST DAY

'Starting school is recorded in my memory as being the worst day of my life. Preparation started weeks beforehand with my mother making over dresses and gym slips of my sister's to fit me as rationing of everything meant that new ones were out of the question. Shoes had the soles and heels covered in studs to ensure longer wear. It was over two miles to the village school, and the walk ruined shoe leather. There were no pavements and no street lights from Mill Green to Fryerning school; we used to walk the distance between two telegraph poles, then run between four to make the journey go quicker.

Fryerning had two schools, one for girls and mixed infants, and one a short distance away for boys. On reaching eleven years old, we had to catch a bus into Chelmsford to go to Moulsham schools, but we still had one and a half miles to walk or cycle to reach the bus stop. School meals in the early 1940s consisted of sandwiches of home-made jam, or pickles and chutney, wrapped in newspaper, as paper bags were almost non-existent. Milk was delivered to the schools in third of a pint dumpy bottles with cardboard tops, and these tops were used later to make all manner of craft-type things.

Cod liver oil and malt was dished out daily by the teachers, each child taking their own spoon. When cooked school meals were first introduced to Fryerning, we had to walk into Ingatestone village to a special hall where the dinners were delivered in metal containers.'

JUST AFTER THE WAR

'I have vivid memories of my schooldays just after the Second World War. My family had returned to Chelmsford after several years' absence. I was nine years old at the time, and so attended the local primary school. The Moulsham schools had been built just before the war, and were regarded as very modern. Each school (infants, junior and secondary) was built, single storey, round a grassy quadrangle. At that time, juniors and seniors were segregated according to sex, so I found myself in Moulsham Junior Girls' School.

Classes were large, and the 48 of us only just fitted into the classroom. The desks were in pairs in straight rows, all facing the front. Our desks contained all our books and pencils, and each had an inkwell, which was ceremonially filled by a "monitor" before handwriting lessons. The ink was rather watery, and tended to come out brown, rather than the intended black. However, handwriting lessons were a treat: for these we had coloured inks in addition to the brown/black standard issue. The added delights came in the form of yellow, green, purple and red inks. When you had completed your patterns and writing, copied from the board, you could suitably "fill-in" with the various colours (discreetly, of course – no big splashes of colour, materials were still in short supply). Pen nibs were a trial. A new nib had to be wetted, between finger and thumb, to remove the thin layer of wax which protected the nib. After that, you had to press the nib with just the right amount of firmness to produce a legible stroke, but not so hard that the two parts splayed out, producing a double line. And if you somehow managed to "cross" the precious nib, and so spoil it, you were in real trouble.

A lot of work was copied from the board, and text books were not much in evidence. Sums for the day were on the board; English exercises were on the board; history notes were on the board – and so on. Being a "modern" school, the board was of the very latest design. It was green, for a start, and went from floor to ceiling on a roller system. The great advantage of this, for the teacher, was that work could be prepared earlier, and then brought into view when required. One section of the board had lines on, for handwriting, and another had lines for music.

The one text book I do remember, was a geography one. It encompassed the world, from hot steamy jungles to frozen wastes. To this day I recall the sepia pictures that told how rubber was tapped from trees, cotton was picked from bushes, and Eskimos built igloos. In the pre-television era in which we lived this book was an eye-opener to the world outside. We did little art work. The urge to express oneself was not yet in vogue in education. You could illustrate your writing with pencil drawings, but that was about as far as it went. I do remember colouring printed papers produced by the National Savings. The pictures were usually on a nursery rhyme theme, aimed at appealing to young children. For example: "Humpty Dumpty sat on a wall, he saved all he could, and did not have a fall." To us, those pictures were a real treat. We coloured them with care, even the lettering. Unfortunately, the propaganda was lost on us – most of our families couldn't afford to send any money to be entered on the weekly cards.

Country dancing was very popular at the time, and we did it with a will. Dancing to records on a wind-up gramophone, we learnt the intricacies of "Strip the Willow" and "Gathering Peascods". Our mothers were persuaded to turn the old blackout curtains into full gathered skirts, made pretty by the addition of two or three rows of coloured braid. And so we swirled and twirled, happy in our flouncing garments. In the top class, the most fleet of foot were taught Scottish dancing, and the less athletic among us stood and admired as they pranced this way and that, using the special wooden swords. A lump came into the throat as the leader finally held aloft the mesh of swords, proving that the detailed movements had been accurate. In spring, the most reliable dancers were let loose on the maypole. In and out we went, clutching our ribbons, until they wove a pattern close to the pole. Then we turned about, and retraced our steps, until we were once again in a wide circle. A steady nerve was of paramount importance: woe betide anyone who caused a confusion so that the ribbons didn't plait evenly.

At my other, more old-fashioned schools, PT (physical training) had meant no more than "drill", on the hard asphalt of the playground. At this school PT included apparatus work, and I was not very happy leapfrogging over stools, or balancing on benches. Just as we had blackout curtain skirts for dancing, so we had blackout curtain knickers for PT! On the top half of ourselves we had string vests, knitted by ourselves. Well, we called them "string", but I guess they were really a kind of thick cotton. Mine was a deep pink, I remember, and we had to embroider our initials in chain stitch with a contrasting colour.

In those days, little girls were expected to sew and knit, while the boys did woodwork and handicraft. I should have thought that a class of 48 little girls wielding knitting needles would have been a recipe for disaster, but I don't remember it being so. After the vests, we knitted mittens, ready for the winter. To our delight, we were shown how to make lovely stripes, with odds and ends brought from home. But if you wanted matching mittens, you had to leave yourself enough wool to make similar stripes on the second mitten! If you were really adept, you were let loose on gloves, with all the fiddly finger bits. I never was very good: one thumb on each mitten was about my limit. I was better at needlework. My piece de resistance was a pink flannelette nightgown, which I wore for years. It had magyar sleeves (that word "magyar" fascinated me) and interminable seams from top to toe, all done in the smallest running and hemming stitches. We had to do French seams, so there were no frayed edges on show. There was blue bias binding round the neck, and the whole creation was finished with some matching blue flowers, executed in lazy daisy stitch.

The three Rs – reading, 'riting and 'rithmetic, were considered to be of the greatest importance. Our progress was constantly monitored. There were weekly and monthly tests. Your seat in the classroom varied according to your performance in the tests: the brightest children sat in the row next to the corridor, and the two cleverest children always sat right by the door. Presumably, this was so that visitors and Inspectors should be favourably impressed. Because of the war I had travelled about and been in several schools. It was my bitter experience that records of your achievements never preceded you, so that every time I went to a new school I was put in the back corner of the room, and had to work my way through the "rank and file" until I ended up nearer the top of the class. In those days reports were simple. At the end of the year you had special tests, to be marked out of 20. You were given your marks, which you had laboriously written out in your "best" writing. The teacher wrote the comments on the board, and you just put the appropriate word in the correct space. So, 20 out of 20 was "excellent", 19 and 18 were "very good", and so on. You were under no delusions as to how you had fared, and how your work was regarded!

But life was not all work. We enjoyed our playtimes, and simple pleasures. First, there was a bottle of milk (frozen, in winter!) to be drunk with a straw. Then, out we went to play jacks and five stones, squatting on the asphalt surface of the playground. For a more active game we tucked our full dresses into our knickers and jumped over balls as they were bounced against a wall. We made little dolls by winding wool round card, then slipping it off and tying it to make head, body, arms and legs. Some of us had whole families of woolly dolls! Dolls' house furniture, made out of match boxes, was another abiding passion. For entertainment, we pored over our monthly copies of *Sunny Stories* by Enid Blyton, and exchanged copies of *The Secret Seven* and *The Famous Five*.

For me, life has come full circle, as I now teach in a primary school. Children today have so much more than we ever had: computers, calculators and televisions are part of their lives. They are surrounded by beautiful books, and amazing toys. Colourful writing and artistic materials are readily available. Air travel to exotic resorts is the norm for many. But life is not necessarily sweeter. Fifty years ago, life was good as far as we children were concerned. We revelled in our simple pleasures. We certainly didn't feel deprived because of lack of toys or entertainment. "I'm bored" was not a phrase that sprang to our lips. Traditional family life and values gave us security. I, for one, look back at that time in my life with affection and happiness.'

A LIFE IN TEACHING

And, lastly, a look at the other side of the teacher's desk from one man who spent his life in teaching in Essex schools.

'My experiences as a teacher began when I left Braintree high school and went as a student teacher at Kelvedon boys' school. Here I not only had the chance of watching other teachers, but was also given the responsibility of taking a class in all subjects, and this proved very helpful to me later on. I started a course at St John's teacher training college in Battersea, but this was interrupted by the First World War.

On my return I had to give up any idea of studying for a degree as I had intended, and was appointed as assistant master at Epping boys' school at a salary of under £2 a week. There were about 210 boys in Epping school aged from eight to 14 plus. The staff consisted of a headmaster, two lady teachers, both uncertificated, and myself. The ladies each had about 45 pupils, and I had 50. I couldn't grumble as the headmaster had over 60. It was an old church school with few teaching facilities, there was no piano, and the old harmonium was not working. It certainly was hard work, and after a few weeks I told the head I thought I should go back to college for more training. He said, "You will never learn how to *teach* in a training college – you must get in front of a class for that!" I took his advice, and after a short time I settled down, got married, and would have been happy to have stayed at Epping, which was a very pleasant part of Essex, where I had made many friends. However, the old head retired and the new man who came was very different. I asked to be put in the promotion list for a headship, and after two unsuccessful interviews at Great Stambridge and Bradwell on Sea, I was appointed on 1st April 1930 to the headship of Purleigh council school.

As far as money was concerned I was actually worse off, as the rent and rates of the house at Purleigh were £65 a year, whereas I had had a pleasant house at Epping for £25 inclusive. The increase in salary was only £20, so I was £20 worse off. Still it was worth it! Purleigh was in delightful rural surroundings, and the Purleigh school building was then one of the best in the county. The classrooms were modern, there was a staff room, staff toilet and cloakroom, spare classrooms for dinners and cookery lessons, good store cupboard, garden plots for older boys, playground and extensive grass plots for games etc, and good washing facilities for children. There was a fence between the boys' and girls' playgrounds, and when I suggested it might be removed, one or two managers were very much against it. They thought it might lead to trouble.

There were 105 children on the books, of all ages from five to 14, with three teachers, Miss V. Cottee, Miss Burton and myself. We each had about 35 pupils. Children were admitted at any time and could leave immediately after their fourteenth birthday. Those who passed the examination for grammar school could leave at eleven plus.

Nearly all the children brought their dinners to school. Some came from North Fambridge by bus, and many had to walk the long distance from Round Bush and Cock Clarks. Few children lived near the school and the lunch problem worried my wife and me. My wife initiated a cooked meal for a charge of twopence. The older girls (twelve to 13 years) got to school early and helped to prepare vegetables and washed up afterwards. We got the bread, flour and milk locally at cost price, and some of the vegetables were grown by the older boys in the school gardens. This enabled us to charge the very low cost and the dinners became very popular. The Education Committee sent a letter of thanks for voluntarily doing this work at such a low cost for the children. Sadly, my wife died in 1936, and kind Mrs Nevard continued doing the dinners for a time until a cook could be appointed and paid.

In 1937 the school was reorganised as a junior school, and only 67 scholars were left. I still had two teachers and my class now numbered only 22 – the lowest number I have ever had. Their ages were from nine to eleven. Although the school had always had over 100 scholars the Committee had never upgraded the school because of the financial difficulties in the country. Now I had a small school and smaller class and received the same salary, so who was I to grumble!

Soon after this came the Second World War, and strangely enough the school numbers began to rise. Several evacuees came from London and stayed in Purleigh. War brought many difficulties, especially the air raids. Shelters were provided, and when the warning on the siren went, children packed themselves into two shelters with a teacher in charge of each shelter. The third teacher listened for the all clear and sometimes failed to hear it and consequently those in the shelters stayed down there for a long time. Sometimes the first warning we had was a loud bang and then the children would immediately sit under the desks and the teacher under a table! One day a German aeroplane which had been hit came very low just over the school but managed to hedge-hop as far as Purleigh Wash and came down in a field.

In spite of many interruptions, following nights of wakefulness, life went on in much the same way, but there were handicaps. Books were difficult to get, paper was rationed and so was food. It was certainly a wonderful day in May 1945 when we heard that the war in Europe was over and there would be no more raids.

There were still many difficulties, numbers had risen and there was a shortage of teachers, and there were many changes of staff. I still had a large class of about 40, and my sister came over to help. It had been necessary to have a class in the small hall, and this was my "classroom". We had had the telephone installed during the war, and in 1948 electricity was laid on. We had toiled on with oil lamps which didn't work and hurricane lanterns, and it was almost impossible to do anything in the school after dark. Also about this time a number of "Emergency Trained" men became available, and these proved quite an acquisition. Though they had not had much college training they proved good teachers and at least three who came to Purleigh school are now headmasters and doing well.

Towards the end of the 1950s I found myself without actually taking a class all the time, and there was a definite promise that the school would be enlarged. However, I felt I had had a long innings and must declare it closed. Having obtained a suitable house in Maldon, I handed over to Mr Dewison in 1959. The farewell presentations and parties are happy memories, and I think if I had my time again, I should still choose to be a teacher and come to Purleigh.'

THE WORLD OF WORK

ON THE LAND

Generations of Essex families have worked the land, a way of life which changed little until the introduction of new machinery became common after the Second World War. Before that horses or steam engines still provided the power on the land and the year followed the seasons as it always had. It was often a hard life and poorly paid, but satisfying for all that and highlights such as threshing day are still fondly remembered.

A WAY OF LIFE

"Then, farm work was a way of life, more leisurely but with lots of hard work. Water for the house was carried from the garden pump by the pailful, extra ones for the dairy on churning days. Cows and horses grazed in the meadows, hens scratched happily round the stockyard, where sometimes lovely nests of eggs were discovered in the straw. Collecting them in a pail with a little straw at the bottom was a pleasant daily chore.

Cows were milked twice a day by hand, a skilled job, but for an amateur almost literally like getting blood out of a stone! Youngsters enjoyed watching from the doorway, as those jets of milk were directed rhythmically into the pail, the cowman sitting on his three-legged stool, with head pressed to the cow's warm body – sometimes old Buttercup would object and kick the pail, then there was a rumpus. But usually the job was completed successfully and the milk brought into the dairy where it was put through the separating machine, cream through one pipe and skimmed milk the other.

During the dark days of winter, a hurricane lamp lit up the cowshed casting strange shadows around as it swung from a hook on the wall or beam, no easy "switching on" then – Great Sampford wasn't "electrified" until 1950. Oil lamps were used in the house; also oil stoves for cooking, these being considered quite an improvement when first introduced about 1930. Previously the old kitchen range burnt wood or coal, although earlier than this delicious bread, cakes and pies were baked on the embers of a burnt faggot (a bundle of wood cut from the hedgerow and tied with a strip of green hazel) on the spacious floor of a bread oven; quite a few are still to be seen in old houses. Embedded in the wall was a large flintstone which became white with the heat signalling it was time to put in the bread.

A service of thanksgiving in the harvest field at Bushes Farm, Magdalen Laver during the Second World War.

Each day's cream was saved in an earthenware pot and once a week, by which time it was sour, was poured into the wooden barrel-shaped churn and turned over and over. Washed with cold pump water, the resulting lump of butter was placed on a butter worker (a wooden tray on a stand with a ridged wooden roller), to be turned to and fro to work in the salt and press out the moisture – one can be seen today in Thaxted Windmill Museum. Weighed up, and patted into shape, the butter was ready for use – nothing was quite so delicious as farmhouse butter, especially in the spring time when the cows were turned out into the lush green meadows.

Churning day was a busy one, with the clatter of pails, pots and pans and the scrubbing of the wooden utensils with the final washing down of the brick floor, leaving it fresh and bright – hard work but very satisfying in every sense of the word.

Surplus butter and eggs were taken to Saffron Walden market in the pony cart before cars came into general use (only the doctor, the parson or the local squire possessed such a luxury).

Heavy carthorses were used for most jobs on the farm until tractors gradually replaced them in the 1920s and 1930s. Horse-keepers had been the key workers, arriving on foot by 6.30 am to feed and prepare the horses for the day's work – oats and chaff with sliced mangolds were brought from the barn and mixed in the manger where the horses munched and crunched until satisfied. The children often had great fun turning the old mangold-slicer – what nostalgic scents it conjures up.

According to the season, the horses went to "plough, reap or sow"; then, the day's work finished, they eagerly made their way with loosened, clanking harness across the road to quench their thirst at the old horse pond (no traffic to worry about). Then they went ambling back to the stable for a grooming down and a meal, or in summer, out to the meadows to graze or laze in the shade of the horse chestnut tree.'

THRESHING DAY AT BOXTED

'Great excitement gripped the farm household – the "throshen 'chine was a-coming." Small boys (I was among them) were rushing hither and thither peering into the distance for the tell-tale puff of smoke which would tell them the threshing machine was on its way.

A threshing set consisted of a steam traction engine which pulled a threshing drum and elevator. The steam engine was the power source, the drum or stationary thresher separated the corn from the straw, and the elevator or pitcher carried the straw away from the scene of the threshing so that it could be built into a stack.

During the summer that had passed the fields of corn had been bindered or cut by a reaping machine which tied the corn into sheaves ready for stooking, built into heaps of six to eight sheaves to finish drying ready for carting. Then the teams of horses, waggons and men would move in to cart the corn to the stackyard to be built into ricks. When this operation was complete the thatchers arrived to thatch the ricks so that the corn would keep dry and in good condition.

Now the great day had arrived and soon, not only the puff of smoke could be seen, but the chuff, chuff, chuff of the steam engine could be heard coupled with the rattling of iron wheels on hard roads. Then the smoking monster hove into sight! Two oily, blackfaced men stood on the footplate, one steering the engine while the other shovelled coal into its blazing furnace. Following on behind the drum and pitcher was a motley collection of men hoping to get a job "throsh-en".

The threshing set was cleverly manoeuvred between the lines of cornstacks, until the drum was opposite the first stack to be threshed. Then the drum had to be set. This meant it had to be absolutely level. A number of spirit levels were placed on the framework of the machine, and the wheels either raised or lowered until the machine was level.

In the meantime the steam engine had been unhitched from the drum and was pulling the elevator into position so that the straw could be built into a stack a safe distance from the threshing operation. Soon all preliminaries were completed and the machine was ready for a start the next morning.

The engine driver and his mate now retired to the farmhouse kitchen for the customary harvest cakes (large oblong scones, heavily fruited and coated with sugar) and home-brewed beer.

The farmer was busy with interviewing the "machine followers" to set on sufficient workers for tomorrow's threshing. He would need two men to work on the cornstack to pitch the sheaves onto the threshing drum, one man to assist the engine driver's mate by cutting the strings on the sheaves so that he could feed the drum, two men to work with his own head horseman to build the stack of straw, one man to work with himself bagging the threshed grain and assisting in carting it to the barn, and finally someone to rake the "caven" (small pieces of straw) and bag the chaff if wheat was being threshed. After some time bickering as to hourly payment, and the quantity of beer to be consumed plus harvest cakes, the farmer engaged seven men to work. All in all, eleven men would be needed to operate the threshing set.

Next morning dawned bright and sunny, typical of early March. The engine men had been there since dawn, seeing that their shiny black monster had sufficient water and that the furnace had been well stoked so that steam was up ready for starting. Soon the workers began to arrive and the large belt was put on the engine flywheel.

By 7.30 am all the men were in position and with a mighty chuff, chuff, chuff, the steam engine was "let go", the drum whirred, the elevator clanked, and threshing had begun.

At 11 am a "skivvy" (kitchen maid) would bring out harvest cakes and home-brewed beer. The men would stop their work for 15 minutes. At one o'clock all threshing would stop for one hour for the men to consume a packed lunch that they had brought with them. This would be accompanied by more beer. A further stop was at 4 pm for "fourses" of harvest cakes and extra strong tea.

Threshing would normally end for the day at 5 pm, or when the cornstack being threshed was finished. It was sometimes not considered wise to remove the thatch from a stack late in the day. And so it would continue until all the cornstacks were threshed.

A far different procedure rules today, when the combine harvester harvests and threshes all in one operation.

FARMS AND SMALLHOLDINGS

'There were four principal farms in Boxted and a dozen or more smallholdings laid out on both sides of the long, straight main road to Colchester. Traditional mixed farming was the order of the day, a pattern broken by my father when he started the fashion of fruit farming in Essex. Between the wars a mixed farm of, say, 600 to 800 acres would employ 30 to 35 men and more at harvest time. Fruit farming being more labour intensive, my father employed about 40 people all the year round up till 1970.

In the 1920s and 1930s the horse was king, finally giving way to the tractor only after the war. In Boxted, Lt Col Guy Blewitt bred a famous line of Suffolk Punches as well as a notable herd of dairy shorthorns. At harvest time the horse-drawn binder would clank round and round the fields of wheat, barley or oats followed by a motley crew of women and boys who picked up the sheaves and propped them in stooks to dry in the sun, before being carted away (horse-power again) to the stackyard.'

PEA PICKING

'In the summer holidays most families in Purleigh went pea picking earlier this century. It was wise to get into the fields early for we had really hot summers and by nine o'clock it would be quite hot. One particular occasion stays in my memory. My mother had taken us to a pea field in Barons Lane, it was misty which meant heat, and as we worked I heard Purleigh church clock strike three. I had never been up so early in the morning before.

The advent of the threshing machine on the farm was always an exciting time. The men would bring two little terrier dogs which would run after the rats and mice that came out in all directions from the disturbed stacks. This was a time for every home to get out its rat and mouse traps.'

IN THE FAMILY

'Both my grandfathers were labourers at the beginning of the century and my father began his life the same way. It was very hard work for very little pay and he began keeping pigs in the garden at the age of 14, saving all the profit from them. In 1926 he was able to rent a 90 acre farm near Barnston and grew wheat, oats, barley, potatoes and sugar beet. He also had two horses, a cow, pigs and chickens. During the recession he had a very difficult time, and many farmers went bankrupt. He always said he was saved by the higgler who bought and sold pigs and chickens. He would bring a litter of about 20 pigs to the farm and expect no payment until they were old enough to see and this helped my father remain afloat.

During the summer holidays as we got older we helped in the harvest field, riding on the binder, setting up the traves of corn and helping load the trailers which were taken to the farm to be stacked. When a field was almost cut all the local children came to catch rabbits hiding in the corn – everyone was pleased to have one to eat

A few more rabbits for the pot at Barnston.

in those days. In the autumn we picked potatoes which were carted to a clamp in the field and covered with straw and earth to protect them from frost during the winter months. In the spring we singled out the weakest and smallest sugar beet which had been chopped out by the men. I also enjoyed rabbiting with my father, usually crouched in a ditch with the dog, watching the holes, waiting for the ferret to send the rabbit scurrying out.'

DOCKER AND LABOURER

'Uncle was a casual docker and presented himself for work at Tilbury about six o'clock in the morning. On the days when work was not available he was home again on Orsett Heath at breakfast time, and would then go to the fields for a day's work. I can remember him donning gaiters which were lined with many sheets of newspaper; I think this was extra leg protection when using a scythe for hedge laying or similar work. Potato digging was also available, and harvest time was a manual affair with stooks in line across the fields. When the fields were cleared, Auntie and other nearby ladies went gleaning in the fields.'

VERY DIFFERENT

'We moved to Essex from the East End in 1936, to a cottage owned by Lord Petre of Ingatestone Hall. Having worked with military horses and later as a drayman on the four-horse flour drays, my father found farm work very different. He had to learn to plough, harrow, rake, and sow seeds by horse-drawn tools, walking miles each day behind the horses over clinging clay soil.

The horses were mostly Suffolk Punch breeds, occasionally

Percherons or Shires were used. Apart from the obvious field work, the horseman had to keep all the tack clean and in good repair, stables cleaned daily and feed the horses. It was also an asset to be able to cold shoe if and when a shoe was lost, or required new nails. To take a horse to the smith for just one shoe was not done as it meant about two miles walk each way, which resulted in valuable working time being lost.

Pay in those early days was approximately £2 a week with a rent free cottage. For an extra two shillings and sixpence and a pint of free milk, it was better to be a second cowman, which my father soon became.

He learned to milk the cows by hand, cleaning the udders before milking started, donning a white cap and overalls (somewhat like today's surgeon's dress in operating theatres) and sitting on a three-legged stool with a stainless steel bucket between his legs. This soon brought the farm cats to the cowsheds as they heard the zing and plop as the milk squirted into the bucket. The cats would sit and wait for the milker to turn the teat their way and direct a stream of milk straight into their mouths.

In the winter months, fields were walked to check gates and fences for repairs, ditches were dug by hand to ensure free drainage, and hedges cut and layered by hand, each taller growth being carefully cut just enough so it could be bent and woven into the hedge, thus enabling it to continue its growth and keeping the hedge thick enough to keep livestock in the fields with safety. These thick hedges made good wind and snow breaks to shield young crops just starting to grow. As a bonus the hedge also made homes for wildlife, which in its turn ate many of the pests the farmers now have to spray to control.

We moved house 14 times from 1936 to 1948, sometimes returning to the same cottage more than once. Farm jobs were easy to obtain if you were willing to work hard.'

BINDERS AND PLOUGHS

'Horses, magnificent gentle giants, provided the power for all the tasks on the farms in Stansted in the early years of the century. Of all the machinery they pulled, the one I remember best was the binder used at harvest time. It was a rather Heath Robinson, but effective, contraption which cut the corn at ground level with an oscillating toothed blade while its flails clacked round beating down the cut corn on to a moving belt which bore it back to the ball of binder string for tying into sheaves. These were thrown out at the side by a rotating fork. Men, women and children stood the sheaves up in groups, called stooks, for drying.

Steam took over from horses the hardest part of the work. The village grew accustomed to the arrival of the ploughing tackle which consisted of two engines with their crew and living quarters. Each engine carried an enormous drum under its boiler between the wheels. These drums rotated to release or take in a strong cable long enough to reach across the widest field. The engines were stationed opposite each other on opposite sides of the field, and the implement (eg the plough) was fixed to the cable. The ploughs varied in size, being able to cut up to eight furrows at a time. Signals to stop winding, or to reverse the implement, were given by whistles from the engines and the work was done much more quickly and with less effort than ploughman and horses would take.'

BY HAND

'Most men in Sheering village worked on the farms, at the maltings or in the joinery works.

Tractors were beginning to appear on the farms by the late 1920s. Yet even in the 1930s I remember seeing Will Cook, who had the most beautiful blue eyes shining out of his weathered face, walking up and down the field behind our cottage all day either behind a team of horses ploughing, or broadcasting by hand crop seeds with a lovely steady rhythm of pace and arm.

Wives used to harvest the pea crop, rising very early to pick their quota of peas at sixpence a bag before going home to get the children off to school. Potato picking was also a job for the women, and backbreaking it was. The tractor would turn out the potatoes, the women with sack aprons would snatch up the potatoes on their stretch before the tractor came round again. There could be no hold-ups preventing the pickers making their quota for the day. Women also worked when the potatoes came out of the clamp for riddling. This was sorting them out for marketable size, the small and damaged ones being kept for the pigs when the rest were sacked up for sale.'

FIVE GENERATIONS

'My own grandparents died before I was born and my grandmother's sister, Emily, and her husband James Redgewell at Great Warley became my precious "replacements", my great aunt and uncle.

James, one of seven children, left school at seven years of age and at eight was minding cows for threepence a day. Later he worked on Lord Rayleigh's estate for sixpence a day as ploughman. At twelve he was able to drive a team of horses. He had all manner of farming capabilities and became farm bailiff. In 1914 his failing eyesight forced him to give up work. He worked for 40 years six months and

Menu

GOLDEN WEDDING

OF

Mr. and Mrs. J. Redgewell,

SEPTEMBER 27TH, 1910.

HARVEST DINNER

AT

Dickenson's Farm, Great Warley,

TO

COMMEMORATE THE EVENT.

A special Harvest Dinner was held to celebrate the Golden Wedding of Emily and James Redgewell.

only had one week's holiday! If he wanted to go to a fair he was up at dawn to do a day's ploughing, then walk seven miles to get there.

He brought up six children on ten shillings a week as farm bailiff. The girls were all in service, getting up at 4 am to stand at the washtub, make bread and brew beer for sixpence a week.

At one time there were five generations living in the village. James lived to be 101 years of age, his wife Emily 93. His coffin was borne on a farm waggon with labourers as bearers; horses were the only form of transport available.'

A SMALL FARM IN PAGLESHAM

'I was born before the Second World War on a small farm in Paglesham. The village is almost surrounded by rivers and marshes, the river Roach having given it its previous prosperity with the oyster industry.

When war started my father was a market gardener. However, Southend was evacuated soon after Dunkirk. With so many people gone, vegetables could not be sold and were left rotting in the ground. My father had a twelve acre field of lettuces which were ready to be cut – they had to be ploughed in. Those people that were left were encouraged to grow their own vegetables, so he grew corn, potatoes and roots and my mother looked after up to 1,000 head of chickens and ducks. We first had goats for milk, then a cow, making our own butter. I often turned the handle of the churn; if the cream was not at the right temperature, it would not "make" into butter. Even though farmers were allowed extra petrol coupons, it was not much, so we drove around in a pony and trap.

I recorded in a school nature book I filled up in 1944 for the third week of May: "Daddy was out shooting rooks. The chestnuts are coming out. I saw three rooks chasing a heron, it just looked like three fighters chasing a bomber" – a sign of the times. We had a large rookery on the farm and a heronry. There was always rook shooting after 12th May, the day the young are meant to fly, as many rooks did such a lot of damage eating newly sown corn. Rook pie was popular then. In the end the rooks drove away the herons.

As I got older I helped my mother with the chickens – the cleaning of the eggs was a big chore as they got very muddy in bad weather. The chickens were running free in large runs. Eggs could only be sold to the packing station. The lorry came every week to collect the wooden boxes, divided into halves, each with six trays, each tray holding 30 eggs so there were 360 eggs in the box.

My father was very interested in mechanisation and had one of the early combines just after the war, pulled by a tractor. He had a cabbage planter which, if one wasn't careful, would plant the roots uppermost instead of the leaves! Potatoes were planted by machine – two of us sitting either side with the box of potatoes in the middle – but harvesting was by hand. The women had opened-out hessian sacks tied around their waists which, when full of potatoes, were emptied into hundredweight sacks. I only managed buckets. At the end of the day these were usually weighed in the field and then two men with a strong stick between them would toss them on the trailer or lorry. I was often the driver from a very early age and if I jerked when starting my father would say, "The flies are biting badly today", a reminder that it wasn't long since the days of the horse – on many farms it still was.

Sugar beet was singled by hand – a monotonous job. At the end of the day the hoes were hung over a large water butt so the wooden handles would swell and the metal clip would stay on. We soon had a harvester, a much smaller version of the ones seen today. There were still several men working on the farm, but beet singling and other jobs were done by casual women workers. By 1947, a man earned £4 10s for a 48 hour week and a casual woman 1s 5d an hour. My father again grew some market garden crops and we had an early start cutting lettuces. While he cut, I packed the boxes – six in the bottom upwards and the top six head downwards, so they didn't get damaged.

There were also the pigs, chickens and our house cow, and some beef cattle, which were run along the road to another part of the farm a mile away. There was little traffic to worry about and gardens had fences and gates.

From an early age I was always keen to earn some money. In the autumn I would go over the marshes on my own to pick mushrooms, which were sold with my father's vegetables in Southend. I also hatched chickens and ducks and fattened them for eating.'

FARM BOY

'In the 1930s the cows would be walked to pasture by the 14 year old farm boy through our bungalow estate at Corringham, leaving their trademarks on the roads and grass verges to the dismay of proud homeowners as the horned cattle butted their hedges and grazed on their shrubs. The blacksmith was two miles away and at least one of the local farmers would, with the help of his farm boy, shoe his own heavy horses. This boy was also expected, at 14, to be able to harness these horses and put them in the cart and drive it.

At the other end of the age range, Old Tom kept the verges down and was to be seen walking round with his scythe over his shoulder, trousers tied round with string just below his knees. He also caught snakes by using a piece of red rag on the end of a long stick – when fastened on the rag the snakes would release their venom and he would then put them in his sack. I never knew what he did with them after that.'

SHACKING

'Often, fields at Great Yeldham weren't ploughed until nearly Christmas. A horse team did an acre a day, hopefully, and after harvest chicken huts would be seen on most fields. The birds were "shacking", keeping themselves on what they could find after the fields had been cleared and raked, and then towards Christmas they would be brought in and fattened. Turkeys were not usually housed on the field but were driven from the farm every morning to shack, and back at night. Keeping the turkeys was a boring job.'

BEANS AND BARLEY

'Agriculture was the main source of employment at Great Canfield, and horses were used on the farms here until the 1950s. Beans and oats were grown for the horses, and barley was grown for beer. The nearest brewery was at Dunmow, Hartford End, as Ridley's owned the one and only public house in the village (which closed in the 1920s as the farm workers, so we are told, spent too much time there!).'

GROWING UP ON A SMALLHOLDING

'During the 1940s my sister and I were growing up on a smallholding in Wickham Bishops. Being too old to go to war, Dad did shift work at the Crittall factory in Witham, making supplies for the army, and also ran the smallholding, producing fruit, vegetables, poultry and eggs. A lot of the work fell to Mum because of the factory shifts. Dad also became an air raid warden.

We also had some goats and from their milk Mum made curd cheese and, using rennet, junkets too. Dinah and Peggy were very good tempered nanny goats, but Betsy could be very temperamental.

Tractors eventually took over from horses on the land – cutting corn at the Hall, Wickham St Paul.

If you forgot she was there you were liable to land flat on your face from a butt in the rear. I still have a very vivid memory of Dad showing me the birth of twin kids to Dinah by the light of a lantern, and my amazement at how soon they were able to get up and search for milk.

Work on the smallholding had to go on day in, day out; goats milked and fed, chickens fed and watered, eggs collected and graded, and all the sheds cleaned out – all done with a bucket or shovel and wheelbarrow. No automation in those days. The one piece of equipment we could not have done without, the bucket! As soon as we were able, we children had our chores as well.

Water for the chickens came from a well in the garden and was carried to the chicken runs. Dad had a wooden shoulder yoke like the old fashioned milkmaids, so that he could carry two buckets at once. Later he devised a water tank on wheels which saved time and steps. During the frosty weather the ice on the drinking troughs had to be broken several times a day, so that the chickens could drink.

Corn and the meagre poultry rations were carried in the same way with hot mash being given in the winter to encourage the hens to keep laying. Dad had to supplement these rations with whatever he could find: household scraps, old vegetables, cooked potatoes, and the sweepings from under the machines in a biscuit factory. There was also the disgusting, malodorous "Tottenham Pudding", a cooked mixture of scraps and leftovers from hospital and factory canteens. When it was delivered it had the look, and often the smell, of a heap of farmyard manure. It could contain much more than food, and had to be checked for cutlery, scissors, china, glass and even the odd used dressing!

Eggs were collected carefully in straw-lined pails, going from hen house to hen house. All our poultry was free range then. In wet weather dirty eggs were gently sponged with cold water (oh! the frozen fingers), then hand graded and packed.

We had an incubator shed where fertile eggs were incubated and hatched to provide replacement laying hens. The eggs were laid out on trays and kept at a constant temperature and turned twice a day. If things went wrong, as they did occasionally, and the heat failed, the whole batch could be lost. If successfully hatched the chicks were transferred to the brooder. This consisted of a large box-like structure with a heater in the centre with an area round it large enough to contain all the chicks. Surrounding this area were loose curtains made of flannel – usually Dad's old cut up trousers. Outside this was a cooler area where the chicks could go for water and food. Gradually over a few weeks the warmth would be reduced, and the growing chicks introduced to the outside conditions.

In later years Dad bought sexed day-old chicks and put them straight into the brooder. These were mostly female replacements for egg production. Any cocks were fattened for market, as were old laying hens past their best.

On top of the routine daily chores would be the seasonal work, growing extra vegetables and fruit. After the war had finished, Dad acquired a few extra acres and started producing soft fruits; blackcurrants, gooseberries and strawberries, most of which went to Wilkinsons jam factory at Tiptree. He also grew a few acres of corn. Dad also bought an Anzani Iron Horse. This was a motorised single plough, but guided by a man and very heavy and difficult. He never admitted how many times it had him in the ditch! I remember the reaper coming to cut the corn, and going along behind with my parents learning how to tie the sheaves and stook them to dry. Then came gleaning the fallen ears of corn to feed to the chickens.

After the sheaves were dry and stacked the hens were let out into the corn field to clear up the remains of fallen grain, and what happy hens they were! Nothing was left to waste. A few months later the threshing machine would arrive from Tom Marven's farm. That day the village boys would have great sport chasing and killing all the harvest mice escaping from the stack. Everyone ended up covered wIth sticky, dirty dust from the noisy steam driven machine. Of course, being only young I did not fully realise the amount of work my parents had to do. Basically it was a very happy childhood, but I have to say that my over-riding memories are of the cold winters and freezing, numbed hands and feet.'

FARMING FOR FUN

'After the terrible experiences of the Second World War when we lived in Chigwell, mercifully escaping the blitz, we moved to our present home at Upminster Common. We had 20 acres of land, which had to be farmed. Not knowing what to do, we had the help of the War Agricultural Committee who found us a land girl.

We bought a ewe and lamb which we brought home in the back seat of our car! Then about a dozen pigs to fatten for bacon. After a while we increased our activities. We built an agricultural cottage, employed a farm worker, purchased pig huts and a number of in-pig sows. It was interesting to rear the piglets either for pork or bacon. We weighed them each week then took them for sale to Romford or Chelmsford markets in our car trailer. On one occasion we took pigs from different litters to Romford and when they were unloaded into the pens one escaped and went over to the stalls that sold china, fish etc. It caused amusement but we did not think it funny! Fortunately the market men managed to catch it without damage.

As we had common rights we tethered sows on the common verge down Bird (now Tomkyns) Lane. They were no trouble and when unhooked made their way back to the yard for food. Once a courting couple who had not noticed them got an unexpected surprise to find one of the animals snorting around them!

We started sheep farming with pedigree Suffolk ewes. Lambing started in January and some of the early ones were taken to Romford market for sale to local butchers. We sold the last two lambs when the market closed its livestock section. The sheep were turned out on Tylers Common to graze.'

IN SERVICE

For many young girls, going into service was the only option for employment available to them when they left school. From farmhouses to the 'big house', servants were in demand and the work took some girls away from their country roots to the big city.

FROM FARM TO COUNTRY HOUSE

'At the age of 13 my aunt left school and went to live with a relative to learn how to do household tasks correctly, one particular task being to scrub the kitchen floor; if it was not done to the relative's liking it had to be done again, and on one occasion the floor was scrubbed three times. In this area if children left school before the age of 14 the local school overseer checked whether the children who had left early were gainfully employed.

The first job Aunt had at the age of 14 was at a remote farmhouse about five miles from home in north-west Essex, her position being nursery housemaid. Her tasks were to get three children up and ready for school and ensure that they had breakfast. Morning duties included household cleaning, including windows, and in the afternoon, on returning from school, the children were taken for a walk before having their tea. After tea the children's shoes had to be cleaned and then Cook was helped with the washing up. Annual pay was £12 plus keep with one day off a month. Lights had to be out every evening by 9.30 pm. Aunt worked so hard she suffered very bad chilblains in the winter and her hands often had to be bound up. On one monthly visit home the chilblains were so bad that Father wouldn't let his daughter return to work and her employer fined him one month's wages.

At the age of 17 Aunt worked as a between-maid at a large house about three miles from home. First thing in the morning Aunt had to work in the dairy and make sure the pans were clean and then skim cream off the milk and go down to the cellar and make butter. The butter and milk not used in the house was sold at the door and Aunt was responsible for dealing with the sales. On Sunday mornings she had to report to the master the weekly sales and hand over the money. After the dairy work housework also had to be done, with other help. In this particular house, when salt beef was cooked the water was retained for the following day and the vegetables cooked in the salt water.

At the age of 20 Aunt took the position of under-housemaid in a country house about twelve miles from home. Every morning Aunt was ready for work at 6.30 and her first task was to awaken the members of the household and take tea in bed to the adults and hot water for washing in the room, although there were in fact three bathrooms in the house. The dining room had to be cleaned and tidied before the household rose in the morning, and whilst breakfast was being taken the nursery and study were cleaned and tidied, together with the drawing room and hall. After breakfast the beds were made and the rooms cleaned and tidied. Each evening the beds were turned down, and shortly before the adults retired to bed hot water was again left in the bedrooms. In this position time off was one afternoon and one evening per week, but all staff had to be in bed by ten o'clock. Staff were allowed to go home for two weeks a year and at Christmas they were given a party by the master and mistress which the children of the house joined in. Morning service was attended by the staff alternately once a fortnight.'

WE HAD FUN

'I went into service at 14 in a big house at the Maplesteads as a housemaid. Our starting wage was £13 a year, but with several in the staff we had fun. I was allowed out one half day each week and every other Sunday. I went everywhere on my bicycle.'

AT THE SQUIRE'S HOUSE

'I was born in Woodham Mortimer 87 years ago; my father was head gardener at Woodham Mortimer Place, an enviable position in those days, and it was the rule that he should report to work wearing a bowler hat and starched white collar. We lived in a cottage with no water laid on, it had to be fetched from a spring in a field at the back. The water ran down a slope and there was a pipe where it came out of the ground and it could be collected in a bucket.

There were advantages in being employed at the Squire's house if the master was a kind one, and although we were poor and often in dire need of new shoes we never went short of food. We were allowed all the surplus vegetables, rabbits off the estate for the catching, and a good meal "up at the house" for all employees at Christmas time. My aunt was in service at a large and wealthy house elsewhere, and one of my most exciting memories is of being given two almost new, and good quality, suits outgrown by the son of the house, one was grey and one was brown.'

AWAY TO LONDON

'Perhaps I was one of the luckier ones, for at 14 years old, in 1922, I had to leave school for service. There was not very much else for young girls, who often found themselves working in an ordinary house and home each day after work. But I was going to a palace and no doubt expected to see all I had read about in books. My father worked for HM Office of Works and carried a pass card for entry into places such as St James's Palace (he was only a labourer), and that was how I got the job. He took me to London, complete with my belongings in a small brown tin trunk, and we reached St James's.

The house I was to be installed in was "Stable Yard" almost opposite to the London Museum, just a little way from Edward Prince of Wales Mansion. Around me was not what I anticipated, just drab grey buildings. Ah! But I hadn't been inside. I was so young I must have felt awed by the great rooms and winding staircase. Sir Douglas and Lady Dawson were really my employers, but a very strict looking head maid named Ada took charge of me, her black hair pulled tightly back and her glasses on the end of her nose. She scared me a bit, but the other maids were kind and helped me. I soon discovered the other staff: cook, kitchenmaid, scullery maid, butler, footman, hall boy, lady's maid and mademoiselle, the nursery governess for one small girl named Rosemary.

My job was in the servants' quarters, up at six o'clock in winter. It was so cold. No heated bedrooms for us, and more work to do by the breakfast gong at eight o'clock than would be done in a week now.

The butler presided at meals in the servants' hall and we had very good food, my favourite breakfast being fish kedgeree. Then work again – no vacuum cleaners or sweepers, but brush and dustpan, knee and elbow grease. We made our own polish with beeswax and turps. I saw Sir and Milady about twice, not being allowed through the green beige doors until I went up the step. Then with the head maid I could enter the vast drawing room. In here were two huge fireplaces and so many tables filled with miniatures which I dare not touch. I well remember Ada throwing a dustpan at me for some misdeed. It missed!

One half day off weekly and in by ten o'clock was the rule. All other evenings were spent with Ada and her favourite of the four pekes (Celeste), mending towels and tablecloths which I hated. My wages were £10 and all found. Eventually Sir Douglas retired and we were all moved to Henley on Thames, a lovely house called Remerham Place. There the family of one of the gardeners took me under their wing and I spent my off time in their home. I well remember my first Christmas when I received a present from home, a pair of slippers and tucked in the toe wrapped in tissue my first, very own wrist watch. A highlight at Christmas was the lovely dining room with a ceiling that looked like blue sky and clouds, used for the staff dance.

Peat was chopped and used for the fires, which were right on the hearth. In fact, the television series *Upstairs Downstairs* depicted service as I knew it very well indeed, and I certainly saw how the other half lived their lives. I left at 18 and went into shop work but had a good grounding for later years.'

HARD WORK

'Service in those days was hard work. In the house where I worked at Navestock we were up at 5.30 am to clean and set tables ready for breakfast, and did quite a few jobs before we got any break. The food was all right but we only got five shillings a week. We wore caps, a white apron and blue dress; in the afternoon we changed into a black dress, a little apron and little lace cap to wait on table. We were lucky if we got to bed by 10.30 pm.'

UNDER-HOUSEMAID

'When I left school I went into service as an under-housemaid at a large house in Sheering. It was hard work. Up at 5.30 am to take tea to the cook and head housemaid, then clean the stone flags in the entrance hall and the front steps. After this to the dining room and study to clean and lay fires ready for lighting, then to light the fire in Her Ladyship's bedroom and take up her hot water for washing in a polished copper can, after which was breakfast in the servants' hall which was very good and plentiful. This was followed by various household jobs until lunchtime, then change into afternoon dress – black dress, cap and apron – and help with the sewing or light jobs. My last job was to take up Her Ladyship's hot water last thing. I had Wednesdays off and cycled home, and also every other Sunday. I received nine shillings and eightpence a week.'

KITCHENMAID AT DEDHAM

'After I left school I was a kitchenmaid at Dedham. They'd consider it hard work now. I just took it as a matter of course. We lived in and started at 6.30, unless the sweep was coming (every three months) when I'd be up at five. The first job was to polish the ovens; two ovens – all steel. Then, halfway up the wall was painted brown. We polished it with beeswax and turps.

There was a cook and kitchenmaid (me), parlourmaid, underhouse parlourmaid, Nanny and the little boy – four in front of the house, and five at weekends. We were supposed to have a day off a month. The others were all right, but I had to do the vegetables, all of them, for lunch and dinner, and the boy had to have his food sieved. I was lucky if I got away by 11.30. I bicycled to Boxted or in to Colchester. We got paid that day – £2 a month. The stamp was taken off it, and we had to find our own uniform, a blue dress and white apron, and a hessian apron. Bessie made them for me. The insurance stamp was for the "Panel" (ie the doctor). Because we were in domestic service there was no unemployment benefit.'

OTHER WAYS WE MADE A LIVING

There were, of course, many other ways we made our living in the past and the following memories can only be a sample – from a Forest Keeper in Epping Forest to a stoker at Chelmsford gas works, or from the village barber to oysterman.

VILLAGE INDUSTRY

'Horndon on the Hill was mainly a farming community, the nearest industry being in Stanford, where there was Boorman's mill which provided flour and feeding stuffs and ran its own bakery shop where we got corn for the hens and big biscuits for the dogs. I think these contained meat of some sort as they provided an adequate diet with a few table scraps. As our dogs usually lived to 15 or 16 the biscuits must have been nutritious. There was also a cattle market and some small industries, and down on the river the oil installations. The

bigger industries were further upriver around Grays.
Apart from the shops in the village there were craftsmen such as the carpenter, plumber, tailor, blacksmith, and undertaker. In the area where we lived there were several poultry farmers all of whom seemed to make a living. There were one or two people like my father who worked in London, which necessitated a cycle ride of three miles to Laindon station. There was a yard near the station where they could leave bicycles for sixpence a week.'

'In the yard in front of the blacksmith's workshop at Stansted, still embedded in the ground, is a circular metal plate six feet in diameter, with a central hole 18 inches across. The sight of this plate brings to mind activities which took place around the turn of the century, and buildings which no longer exist.

One of these buildings was made of brick, with walls nine inches thick and a central square chimney. The inside space was six feet long, six feet high and one foot wide and it was purpose built for holding fires of faggots in which metal tyres were heated to be fitted to wooden wheels lying on the metal plate. We children always gathered around when the furnace was alight. For me it was, and always will be, the one through which Shadrach, Meshach and Abednego walked unscathed in defiance of Nebuchadnezzar, and I imagined that they emerged with the red hot waggon tyre. The wheel lay on the metal plate with its hub in the central hole and the tyre was fitted rapidly with dog-irons. It was a great privilege to be allowed to run around the perimeter with a watering can, pouring cold water making clouds of steam, to encourage shrinkage and a tight fit. The furnace was demolished around 1950 when the demand for its services ceased owing to the wider use of the pneumatic tyre.

The wooden wheels came from the wheelwright's workshop which was conveniently next door. Wheelwrights and blacksmiths combined their skills with wood and iron to produce and repair agricultural vehicles and implements.

In front of the wheelwright's workshop was a large sawpit in which, at top and bottom, sawyers could cut up great tree trunks, one at each end of the enormous saw. There was also a shed with ladders slung horizontally side by side in the roof. We used to swing like monkeys from rung to rung along these ladders, racing one another until we dropped off, exhausted.'

A STOKER AT THE GAS WORKS

'My father earned his living as a stoker. He was a Scotsman who had been a coal miner until the outbreak of the 1914-18 war, when he joined the Royal Engineers to serve his country. During his years of service he met and married an Essex girl from Boreham, so that upon his demobilisation he did not go back to Scotland but got work at the Chelmsford gas works as a stoker.

On one occasion Dad had forgotten to take his "piece" (his sandwiches) to work, so Mum sent me to take them to him. I was twelve years of age at the time. I have never forgotten the terrific heat from the huge building where I found my dad and his mate.

Once there, I stayed and got an insight into the work of a stoker. First of all Dad drove a large truck outside which he had to fill, shovel by shovel, with coal. He often said, "I may have left the mines but I'm still coal heaving." Next he drove the truck into the building where he fed the retorts. There were many of them, like very long ovens with heavy doors at either end. The coal was fed in from one end and "blown" through to the other end where Dad was waiting with another truck to catch the flaming coals. He then drove the truck outside to where, behind a high wall, were water taps, and these he turned on to douse the hot coals. I have never forgotten the clouds of smoke, the steam and the awful smell from that procedure. Lastly Dad emptied the contents of the truck outside where it became coke.

That whole process was repeated a number of times during his eight hour shift. These shifts were of one week each at 2 pm to 10 pm, 6 am to 2 pm and 10 pm to 6 am respectively.

My dad did this heavy, hot, dirty work seven days a week for 25 years and never lost one day. In those days he got no extra money for weekend work but he was allowed to take one week of *unpaid* holiday each year. It was only once in every three or four years that he was with us on Christmas Day or for New Year.

My mother plays her part in my story, as every day she carried buckets of water up the hill from our "spout" to fill the copper to heat for Dad's bath and to wash his working clothes.

Sadly, Dad sustained a very serious accident at the gas works and was never able to work again. Life then became ever harder for him.'

FAMILY JOBS

'Farm work was the main work in Wickham St Paul and Dad worked at the Hall. He would go off in the early morning with his "ninesies" which consisted of doorsteps of bread and a hunk of cheese, a flask of tea made with condensed milk and this would last him until dinner. In the summer when we came home from secondary school we took him a fresh flask and cake or more bread. Sometimes we'd stay and lay out the sugar beet for him, all to face the same way to make it easier to chop the tops off. My brothers used to help a neighbour.

We liked to watch the men harvesting, cutting the corn to build haystacks. After a field was finished we'd glean the edges for ears of corn for the chickens. The boys would collect straw for the rabbits' beds and chicken nests. Other field work was potato picking. We would go along at the end gleaning up the small ones which had been left behind. For this we earned so much a bucket. In the winter the farm workers would use spades to help clear the snowdrifts from the roads, piling it up high to the sides.

Three times a week my brothers and I would collect a pail of water for elderly ladies who lived on their own. We got paid sixpence a pail.

Some village girls worked at Courtaulds mill in Halstead and some men worked at Rippers Woodworks in Hedingham, both transported by bus. On leaving school I worked at the Co-op. I loved that job, working in the warehouse office and, when not busy, helping weigh sugar, biscuits and dried fruit into bags. Broken biscuits were cheaper! I loved the smell of the bacon room where they cut up the cheese and sliced the bacon. At the end of the day the wooden benches all had to be scrubbed down.

In 1958 I got a job nearer home at an egg packing factory, testing and packing eggs for the shops. If a bad one was dropped, the smell hung around for ages! Friday was "full scrub down day" – and I mean scrub down! Mother helped out at the small market garden in the village planting, hoeing, chopping and packing vegetables ready for market, apple picking and pruning.'

'Bluffy's Bus' which took the factory girls to work in the Halstead area.

BONDS OF CHELMSFORD

'Bonds of Chelmsford stressed in 1937 that their office staff must either have passed their scholarship and be"highly recommended" by their headmistress or come in straight from high school. The former got seven shillings and fourpence, the latter ten shillings. We worked from 8.45 am to 6.15 pm Mondays, Tuesdays and Thursdays; 8.45 am to 1.15 Wednesdays; 8.45 am to 7.15 pm Fridays and 8.45 am to 8.15 pm Saturdays. They were the shop hours.

From the minute we got into the office we were not allowed to talk to one another unless on business, with a ten minute coffee break in the morning and ten minute tea break in the afternoon. On Fridays and Saturdays we got a half hour tea break when we were given one slice of bread and butter, one small slice of cake and a cup of tea. Some of the shop staff lived in at the front of the shop, upstairs on the first floor. A very strict housekeeper made sure these girls obeyed the rules. The owner and his two sons ran the shops with the help of a very strict manager and several floor walkers.

Mistakes were not tolerated. We wore black dresses with a small white collar, black shoes and stockings both in the office and shop. Despite all this we had fun and Wednesday afternoons we went as a party to Oaklands Park to play tennis in the summer or for walks along the river. When I was sent over to the furnishing shop at Moulsham Street to work as cashier the hours were sometimes even longer. If there was a customer in the shop on Friday or Saturday night we were expected to stay in case they paid and every Saturday night I took the leather bag with any money taken after the first cash-up at 5.30 pm to the bank night safe, sometimes as much as £350. I was 15 years old then.'

THE DAIRY AND THE BANK

'We moved to Dagenham in 1932, my father being a dairy manager. In those days milk and groceries were delivered by horse and cart. The depot had over 30 horses and I used to watch them being shod, full time work for the farrier. We were always up early each morning, as my father started work at 5 am. Every Christmas and Boxing Day he worked so our Christmas dinner was always eaten late, as he had to wait for the last roundsman to come back to the depot and in very many cases it was the horse that brought the milkman home! The horses knew just where to deliver and the way home. When my father first started work as a milkman, he told me, the milk was in churns and he had brass ladles to take the milk out, which had to be kept well polished.

I started work at a local bank in 1944 earning 32 shillings and sixpence weekly. We worked long hours including Saturday mornings, and at balance time on 30th June and 31st December we were very late indeed, once or twice seeing the New Year in at work. When I was a junior clerk at the Dagenham branch, many times I had to go to Rainham with a senior member of staff with a lot of cash and books, carried in a black case – we went by bus! How times have changed.'

THE BAKERY

'My grandparents lived in Brightlingsea in the 1940s, where they ran a bakery. They had an end of terrace house and the back door of the living room led into the bakehouse. This was a long room with a stone floor. In it there was a sink with a tap over it and along each side were large wooden bins in which the flour was kept. The tops of the bins were used as work surfaces. At the far end of the bakehouse were two ovens. The top one was for baking the bread and the bottom was cooler for proving dough. The heat for the ovens came from a coal fire at the side.

Needless to say, the day began very early and they worked long hours. When all the baking was done, some of the freshly baked loaves would be put into a large wooden bin for sale in the shop and the rest were loaded onto a brown handcart. Grandad would push the cart around the streets and deliver to the door. Nan was left at home to serve in the shop. Most of our visits were just for the day but occasionally we stayed overnight and then the highlight of our stay was freshly baked rolls straight from the oven for breakfast.'

THE SAUSAGE FACTORY

'1927 saw the start of the Broad Oak Farm Sausage business at Hatfield Broad Oak, by the village doctor, who used some old stable buildings as a factory. Soon he was joined by a partner and the business began to expand until in the mid 1930s Broad Oak Farm Sausages were supplied for the maiden voyage of the *Queen Mary*.

Such was their fame that they now employed four men, and an 8hp Morris delivery van covered up to 200 miles each day, delivering to shops in nearby towns and villages and to London, where the product was gaining popularity. Local deliveries were made by bicycle. The factory itself was now a thatched, corrugated iron building in a field on the edge of the village, the animals used for the sausages being bred and slaughtered in one of the largest Essex barns, just across the field. Large White pigs, the offspring of a boar and several sows kept on the farm, were the basic ingredient. The pigs were humanely killed, then the carcases scalded in a copper and hung for a day or two, before an old Lister petrol engine operated the mincing process.

As pork does not keep well in warm weather, in these early days the factory closed during the summer months and workers were employed on the farm. After difficult war years the business was bought by village butcher Reg Simons – who would continue using the secret recipe for many years to come.'

THE VILLAGE BARBER

'Every village had its local barber and in the 1930s my grandfather William Salmon of Park Road, known as "Trugle", was Little Easton's. He was a well built man and worked at Brook End Farm, where he was head cowman. He wore collarless flannel shirts, thick tweed breeches supported by braces and a leather belt made from an old cut-down horse girth, with leather leggings over brown boots on Sunday and black boots during the week. A tweed jacket and flat cap completed the picture.

On Sunday morning after he had walked or cycled from early morning milking, he would be ready to start. The outhouse, which was a small enclosed division between the two cottages which housed the fitted bath, was the local hairdresser's. There was no hot or cold water piped in, water having to be heated in the washhouse copper down the yard and carried to the outhouse in buckets, but my father installed a waste pipe draining into the field ditch.

Men were charged threepence or fourpence and boys paid a penny or twopence. He didn't cut ladies' hair. One of the kitchen chairs was brought out and a rather superior cloak made by my grandma was put into use. In the summer the cutting was done in the backyard. Styles were all much the same – short back and sides or very short back and sides. Any wisps that wouldn't settle were plastered down with spittle. We boys were threatened with, "If you don't sit still boy, I'll cut your head off."

Should your toenails need cutting he would oblige. But his speciality was cutting corns for which he made a small charge, and his customers were well satisfied. Cully Moore, a farm worker, Arch Harris, a horseman, Tom Baker, another horseman employed at Easton Lodge, and Leggs Buttle, who was retired, were some of his regulars. Another was Isaac Baker, a very old man who was found dead at Tinge Ho after his haircut, and was carried home on a field gate which the men lifted off its hinges.

Grandfather continued to cut hair until he was about 70 years old.'

LIFE ON THE TOOLS

'The building trade has always been seasonal, and in the 1930s employment was obtained through the Labour Exchange, word of mouth and the old pals act. The rates of pay were set by an agreement with the Master Builders Federation, which in the 1930s were around one shilling and sixpence per hour. This was honoured by all builders in the Master Builders Federation but many didn't belong and few paid overtime rates. Rates of pay were regional, ie in Suffolk you would get twopence less per hour.

Most local builders were engaged on building "a pair" on an isolated plot and hours were from 7.30 am to 5 pm, less in the winter. There was no sick pay and the men had to rely on private arrangements such as slate clubs, no loss of earnings when wet. But the men were treated as men and both sides treated the other with respect. Many employers endeavoured to retain a good man.

The rates being hourly the men were entitled to an hour's notice when dismissed and in the case of carpenters, they were entitled to one hour extra to sharpen their tools. This custom was the norm and always honoured.

Apart from local builders, the local councils, the Gas Company, and the Electricity Boards had their own maintenance staff and paid according to the working rule agreement. They also had pension schemes and naturally the vacancies were sought after.

Public works contracts were also very popular with the workers of the day, top rates and conditions being assured. But as in life there were others, some employers left much to be desired and the well known tradesmen kept clear of them, and those who gave them a go invariably told the employer "to lick em and stick em" which meant "I want my cards, I'm off". The casual nature of the job made one become philosophical, becoming hardened to the way of life.

The Labour Exchanges were vastly different from today's Job Centres. You had to sign on twice a week with about 8,000 others at Southend and when you finally reached the counter there was a notice which read: "If no work, say no work". Vacancies were on the board, but you had to ask for a green card in order to apply. The staff decided if you were fit to apply, ie if you had been trained as a carpenter, they would not send you for a job in a joiner's shop, or if you were experienced as a soft wood joiner, they would not send you to a high class hard wood shop.

Men were not forced to take a job when the firm would not pay the trade union rate. I once left a job only to fall out again about three months later. The Labour Exchange offered me my old job back but I refused and was summoned before the manager. I was told I was not compelled to return unless the trade union rate was being paid. Also the Labour Exchange would not compel you to travel further than 15 miles to work.

Working conditions were very basic, you worked during the winter if in employment in the wet and cold, with meals in the cement shed or under a tarpaulin. But the summer made it all worth while, and you cannot beat an outdoor life. There was comradeship, for the men worked in an environment where legendary figures were prominent in the trade – the craftsmen who could erect a roof in record time or hang a door in under the hour, a joiner to make a door in three hours. I once met a pair of plasterers on a housing site who could render and set a house in three days and the work was perfect; the brothers had a well earned reputation.'

WE NEVER WENT OUT

'We never went out when we were first married, except to cycle from Broxted over to Mother in Ardleigh and have a cup of tea. The horses needed feeding Sundays as well as weekdays. Before he was married Bob lived over the stables at Cheshunts. For our one week's holiday a year we went to Bob's mother. There were two horses when he started, seven in the end. When they'd been hunting, at about ten o'clock at night, after a meal, Bob would say, "Let's go and see the horses." They always knew he was coming.'

THE FOREST KEEPER

'My married life as a Forest Keeper's wife started in the early 1950s. The house in Epping that went with the job was rather large. It stood in a quiet lane backing on to forest land. It was offered to us at a very low rent with an extremely low salary to go with it. My husband's full uniform was provided as well. Times then were very hard, but that is how things were generally.

The Keepers were on 24 hour call, and very often were out late into the night for whatever reason. They walked on patrol for many miles in the course of the day, and on occasion used a push bike. Their job was, and still is, I guess, similar to a policeman's. They had the power to apprehend and arrest anyone on forest land if necessary. The Keepers would also work in the forest with the wood gang, ditching, felling trees, cutting back and generally doing whatever needed to be done. They had to keep and make daily reports, these reports used in court on occasions.

After about four years of living in Epping, the Superintendent wanted my husband to transfer further south, so we moved to Buckhurst Hill. A lovely semi-detached house, overlooking parts of Chingford, went with the job. I never tired of the smashing view from my kitchen window and to see the seasons come and go – sometimes dramatically – was, to me, wonderful.

Living as we did on forest land, meant darkness early. No street lamps to light our country lanes; this bothered me at times in the winter months, having two daughters coming and going. I always felt a little on edge until they were home again. The road we lived in then was very lonely with ditches either side and a stretch of forest land near to a small caravan site, but we became used to it after a while, and spring never seemed far away once we got into February.

My husband's job took him, after Christmas, to Copt Hall estate in Epping, firstly to count the deer roaming there and also to help feed them if the weather was really bad.

Keepers also dealt with the public just as a policeman on his beat would. They would be in charge of the very large fairs that came to Chingford and Wanstead throughout the year. Another part of their work was to patrol the lakes and ponds to check on the fishing, and the illegal fishing that would take place, also the collecting of fishing fees. They would go out very late at night to patrol certain areas. They dealt with many injured animals too, usually deer, foxes, dogs and cats – they never refused a call out, even when off duty.

The Keepers then had a good knowledge of guns and took great care and pride in looking after them. Most of the Keepers in our day were ex-servicemen. How they took pride in their uniforms, their badges, boots and leggings; much spit and polish went on. There were times when the Super would want a "shoot" to take place. Then some of the men would be away for a day.

Very often in the summer months there would be very bad forest fires, often due to a carelessly thrown away cigarette. The fires would spread deeper and wider over large areas, especially when it was tinder box dry. The men would think they had put all the fires out only to find another one breaking out some distance away, and so it would go on.

Hard work and hard days, out in all weathers and sometimes at

Volunteers would be called for to clear the snow along local roads in winter, here at Wickham St Paul.

risk from someone up to no good, my husband came home at times having had to put up a fight or be left badly injured. All in all he enjoyed his life as a Keeper. It would have been easier for us though, if in the early days we had had a decent salary to live on. All that changed when the union took over. The wages were improved, the hours were slightly less, and, after some years, some of the Keepers had motor bikes to patrol on. The bikes were of the type that would take the rough terrain. They covered many miles that much more easily and efficiently. They also had walkie-talkie radios, as we called them then, which meant they could radio for information or help. The only drawback that I could see, was that they did get terribly wet and cold as they didn't have the excellent waterproofed clothing of today.

We always thought ourselves fortunate to live on the forest with its spectacular beauty, bringing up our children in such peaceful surroundings. Thanks, originally, to Queen Victoria who was on the throne when the forest was given to the people in 1878 – and to the Corporation of London who care for and maintain this part of Essex we take so much for granted. May it always stay – as it was intended – for the enjoyment of the people.'

SCRUBBING THE DECKS

'When ocean-going liners docked at Tilbury, local women were employed to scrub the wooden decks, for two shillings and sixpence a day. My grandmother was one of them because she was a widow with six children to support.'

TEACHING THE PHYSICALLY HANDICAPPED

'From school in the 1930s I went to college and qualified as a teacher. I taught physically handicapped children at the Benton open air school at Ilford. The building was bungalow style, the north side being brick built as were the east and west walls but the south wall was wood and glass and always open. The internal partitions were also wood and glass and folded back so that two or more areas could be made into one. In summer we worked completely out of doors and for most of the rest of the year too, in cold weather being dressed in fine layers of wool, cotton and then wool again with thigh-length hand-knitted wool stockings and mittens on our hands. We broke off work every quarter of an hour to exercise fingers and toes with singing rhymes and some other physical movement to keep our circulation going. The children arrived around 8.30 am and in winter we started the day with hot cocoa if the temperature was below 40°. We all went into the dining room together for lunch; our kitchen staff were wonderful and always gave us good nourishing meals. After lunch, bed rest was compulsory for one hour before the classes returned to work. If the weather was wet, foggy or snowing we were in the shelter of the partitioned rooms and on very few rare occasions were the south shutters ever closed. I don't remember ever having a cold or feeling ill in all the years I worked there.'

FROM SEA TO SHORE

'All the villages that I have ever come across generally had their own local tradesmen; in most cases a blacksmith, carpenter, bricklayer, plumber and in some cases, a thatcher. Most of them had left school and gone to work with Dad, inheriting his skills and his knowledge. My father was a brick moulder making bricks by hand, so in 1919 I found myself working in a brickfield. The employment though was for summer only, so early in September looking for work, I wandered around Ipswich docks and accepted a job on a sailing barge as a third hand and found myself bound for London, little knowing that when we sailed down the river Orwell I was practically severing my ties with Suffolk for those of Essex.

For the winter of 1919-1920 I remained on that barge, but after two trips the mate left and I was promoted. That may sound glamorous, but then most of the coastal barges were manned by only two men, the very large ones requiring three.

With trips to Yarmouth, Mistley and Ipswich the winter passed, but as a living it was very uncertain. If the work was plentiful and the weather not too unkind, a living could be good but time spent in hanging on the buoys opposite the Victoria Gardens at Woolwich soon exhausted any money previously earned. On the barge it was a case of no work, no pay. The bargemen always spoke of being on "starvation buoys".

By the end of March 1920 I decided that perhaps a shore job would be of more profit as I was rapidly needing new clothes, so on reaching Grays I told the skipper that while I had a pound or so I would leave and try ashore. Buying a copy of the local paper I found in "situations vacant" an advertisement for brick moulders with an address in Grays to apply to. I found that it was a firm of builders who owned the field at Low Street, a little place on the railway between Tilbury and Stanford le Hope. It was only after a great deal of thought that I decided to go and apply for the job. There was quite a lot to consider. In those days working men did not own cars, in most cases they were confined to working within walking distance of their homes – although I suppose there must be a lot of present day workers who would not consider four miles reasonable walking distance. The only other way to increase the area of employment was a cycle.

While I found getting employment in the summer months no

problem, as a small town or large village generally had a brickworks fairly near, there was also the task of finding work in the winter months. The building of new estates of houses meant road construction, the laying of sewer and drainage pipes needing in those times (that is the 1920s) quite a large number of men, most of the work being done by hand instead of the large machines much used today. The wages of the time would be regarded as a pittance today, the present hourly rate being more than we could earn in a week. The men using pick and shovel were paid one shilling and threepence an hour, while the more skilled men who put the timber in to make the trench safe and the men who laid and jointed the pipes could be paid one shilling and sixpence. A large number of men without immediate ties would make a practice of finding where large construction jobs were taking place and travelling to the vicinity to keep in work, I might add not to the pleasure of the local workforce.

In the winter of 1923 I had finished working at Galleywood in a brickworks surrounded by, of all things, a racetrack, when I struck lucky and got a job on a liner bound for Australia. When a seaman signed on he was given a cheque, known as an advance note, for a month's wages. They were always dated for three days after the ship's sailing, so if the man was not there it could be stopped.

There were men, however, near the Board of Trade office, who would gamble and change your cheque for two shillings in the pound, a facility seized on by some of the younger single men. If he did not sail, the "changer" was the loser, not the shipping company. The ships of the Orient Steam Navigation Company used to lock out of Tilbury docks on a Friday night, load passengers by tender and sail Saturday morning. It was the custom then for the ship's officer to come on the dock head pier to find a replacement for anyone who had not been aboard when locking out on Friday. That morning, being bitter cold, I was the only one there. When I assured the ship's officer I could use a shovel I was recruited to be a coal trimmer, to wheel coal from the bunker to the stoker. At £15 a month and a trip to Australia, I thought I was in clover, but I found out I earned every penny of it. The trip out and back took 13 weeks and on my return I found that the whole crew were paid off, another way of saying we had got the sack. A few were kept on to maintain steam for essential services, but what I was most interested in was I got a discharge book with a good character and was told that they would be signing on again in two weeks' time, and that if I applied I would be engaged.'

WOODEN TOYS

'My father's occupation was making wooden toys. He would cycle out into the countryside around Colchester where willow trees were being felled, buy them by the cart load and have them delivered to his wood-yard where the trunks stood in "wigwams" to season. He had a factory with machinery to cut, shape, smooth and paint the wood to make engines, horses, barrows, scooters, trucks and baby-walkers. The factory was some distance from home and, so that some of his work could be done in the evenings and at weekends, he built a large workshop on the side of the house, heated by a tortoise stove using waste wood and sawdust for fuel. When more sleeping accommodation was needed for the children, he extended the workshop at the back making a dormitory with room for five beds in it.

The work which was done at home was mostly finishing the decorations on the toys. Coloured strips were painted onto the red engines and paper stripes and cut-out saddle shapes were pasted on to the horses which also had pieces of animal hair nailed on for manes and tails. In the 1930s we made thousands of wooden yo-yos. At the factory the wood was cut to size, rounded at the edges on a lathe and a central hole bored halfway through each piece. They were laid out on large trays, painted with a mechanical sprayer and, when dry, they were stacked up partly overlapping and sprayed with a different colour. At home we cut string into lengths and, using short lengths of dowelling, put the end of the string in one hole, pushed in the dowel and pressed another painted half on to it. We tested each one to ensure that it would spin up and down the string evenly. If one of them didn't spin, it was taken apart and the halves were matched up with different ones of a more even weight. When satisfactory, they were stacked in boxes of a dozen or a gross to be taken with other toys to shops all over East Anglia and North London.

For delivering the toys to the shops, my father had a one-ton Ford open-backed lorry. In those days there were no direction indicators on vehicles so Father made a "long arm" of wood painted at the end to look like a pointing hand which he stuck out at the left side of the cab when he was intending to turn in that direction! If I went on a journey with him I was thrilled to stick out my own arm to indicate for him.'

OH YEA!

'My grandparents lived in the little cottage next to Grayton's shop at Epping at the beginning of the century. Grandfather was employed by Ben Cowlin & Son, house decorators, as head man over all the painters. Cowlin's works were on the site which is now the Epping Forest council offices. He was responsible for the efficiency of the painters and he had great diffculty with one man who was always late for work, so he thought of something which might cure Sid of this very bad habit.

Grandfather secured the interest of the town crier, who agreed to shout a message walking down the middle of the High Street. "Oh yea! Oh yea! Oh yea! Lost – a man by the name of Sid E . . ." This brought all the lazy stay-in-beds to their windows, including Sid. When he realised he was the subject of the call he couldn't get to work quick enough. He was never late again!'

TO COURTAULDS BY HORSE AND CART

'Courtaulds' workers went to Halstead from outlying villages by horse and cart on Monday morning and stayed with mill workers in the top floor of the three-storey cottages. Their wives cooked food which they took with them. Then they came home again on Friday night.'

LOCAL WORK

'My mother did not work until I passed the scholarship and a school uniform was needed. She did field work – hard work and in all weathers, but she enjoyed the companionship of the other women. It became acceptable in wartime for women to work and she then moved on to the Bata shoe factory at Corringham, which employed many women from the area. There was a local firm making chestnut fencing, Bata's or engine cleaning at the Tilbury railway yards where boys might find work. For girls there was, again, Bata's, or locally as shop assistants. For the better educated girls there were opportunities for nursing, teaching or office work.'

FARMS AND OYSTERS

'Paglesham is a small village at the edge of the Rochford Hundred situated on the river Roach, which is a waterway meandering towards Rochford from the river Crouch. The village is divided into two parts approximately one mile apart. Churchend was centred on the farming community and Eastend, being nearer the waterside, supported the fishing and oyster industry. At the turn of the century life was about one thing, survival. The men would work long hard days on either the land or the water.

Most of the farms in the area had tracts of marshes and saltings which were used to fatten cattle. In other areas they ran smaller numbers of sheep and pigs. When the cattle were mature, some would be slaughtered on the farm but the rest would have to be walked to market in Rochford, a distance of some five miles. Having sold the first herd on the stockmen would then have to walk new young stock back to graze the marshes of Paglesham.

On better land nearer the farmhouses arable crops would be grown of wheat, barley, oats, mangolds and kale. In modern times we rarely see the last three crops in Essex although I suppose sugar beet looks similar to mangolds. At that time the workforce on the farms in the area was between 40 and 50 men. Today the number does not run into double figures and is probably between five and eight.

One of the obligations the farmers had to fulfil was to maintain the seawall that happened to be on their property. About two months of every year was allocated to this task. The men just used spades and wheelbarrows which had to be loaded and pushed up the wall by means of a series of wooden planks. There were no bulldozers and mechanical diggers then.

Because Eastend was nearer to the waterside most of the men from this area worked for the oyster merchants. This industry thrived until the 1953 East Anglian floods decimated the oyster beds. Although some people continued after the disaster it never fully regained the productivity of the earlier years. In its heyday a lot of the oysters were packed and transported by horse and cart to Rochford railway station and put on the train for London.

For ten months of the year the men worked on the water, but in July and August they all worked on the farms helping to get the harvest in. Come September they returned to the water. Their first job would be to sail round to Burnham on Crouch to a particular outfitter's shop so that they could be fitted out with new knee-length leather boots. Rubber wellington boots were not available then.

The women of the village also had a very hard life. The families lived in very small cottages rented from their employers. In fact the oyster merchants owned most of Eastend. There was no mains drainage, water or electricity laid on, and there were mostly between eight and ten children in every family. It is hard to comprehend what it was like to have such a large family in so small a dwelling.

Besides running their homes the women also had jobs such as housework, cooking and needlework in the big houses or worked in the fields and in the dairies on the farms. Their wages were very small so they lived very frugally, making meals out of next to nothing. They rarely had meat but would use wild rabbit and fish when they could get it. When it was necessary to go shopping it was a round trip of ten miles to Rochford and back, which they usually did on foot.

If any of the villagers worked for a church-going employer they were expected to attend church as well, and woe betide anybody who neglected to bow or curtsey to the said employer. There would be no job for them the next day.'

WAR & PEACE

THE GREAT WAR 1914-18

Zeppelins over Essex, air raid warnings and soldiers on the move are memories for many. The war touched every town and village in the county and when it was finally over it left a legacy of sadness well expressed in the silence which once fell over the land on Remembrance Day.

OFF TO THE WAR

'As a child coming home from school it was a regular thing during the war to hear the military bands playing at North station, Colchester as the troops boarded the trains taking them to the front. The wives and families would be there in tears and the soldiers trying to cheer them up. To this day I can never hear a military band without remembering those scenes.'

AIR RAID WARNINGS

'My father was a special constable during the war and one of his duties was to patrol the promenade at Maldon with another constable, both of them on bicycles. They would listen for approaching aircraft, which used the river as a guide. They then had to cycle to a police station so a call to London could warn of an impending air raid. There weren't many phones in those days.

There were many soldiers in the town and surrounding area, and another job was to make sure the "ladies" of the town got home. Maldon was a very small town then and everyone knew everyone else. A wheelbarrow was kept in a central position, so if necessary they could be wheeled home.

There were food shortages and when word got around that margarine was for sale in the High Street, my brother and I were sent to get some, though it was grim to taste.'

GETTING AN ALLOWANCE

'My mother was a countrywoman and a clever manager. We were poor but we were well fed. To earn additional money for the household she went out scrubbing floors and took in washing. While Father was away in the army, the War Office gave Mother an allowance of £1 8s a week for rent, heat, clothes and food for us five children. I remember threepence worth of cods' heads produced enough fish left around the gills to make a fish meal for Mum and us. Meat was about a penny halfpenny a pound, and threepence of pieces made a meat pie. Lambs' breasts also cost threepence each. A bunch of pot herbs and vegetables cost a penny.'

ZEPPELIN!

'I was three years old when the war started, but I remember we were frequently alerted in the early evening by the pheasants calling in our local wood at Stansted at a time when the Zeppelins were setting off from Germany. We knew then that there would be a raid later that night. Essex was directly in their path to London. Later, towards the end of the war, I was taken from my bed one Saturday morning by my father to see one of the first daylight raids with aeroplanes having a dogfight a long way off over London.

Soldiers were billeted in the village, and Elsenham Hall was occupied by the army. My brother became friendly with many of the soldiers and invited them to supper Saturday or Sunday evenings. We usually had an enormous rabbit pie and after the meal a sing-song round the piano.'

'The war greatly changed our way of life. Soldiers were billeted in the Althorne area in farm barns, though the officers were put into the homes of people with a bedroom to spare. A Zeppelin was shot down at Wigborough. We watched it from our bedroom window and the next morning cycled to see the wreck.'

'My earliest memory is of the Zeppelin coming down at Wigborough in 1916, which my brother Eric, two years older than me, was taken to see. I was very angry because I was considered too young to go. However, he brought me back a small bunch of ripe blackberries picked from the hedge of the field where the Zeppelin came down. The German crew gave themselves up to the local police and were taken into custody as prisoners of war, and the Zeppelin caught fire and burned itself out. The skeleton framework remained in the field for some time and many photos were taken of it.'

'My husband was ten years of age at the outbreak of the war and remembers the air raids by the large silvery, cigar-like Zeppelins. He was living at Wanstead at the time and saw the first one brought down over Cuffley in Hertfordshire in 1916 by Lt Robinson. It lit up the sky for miles around. Later the Germans switched to Gotha aeroplanes which were more difficult for the anti-aircraft fire to hit. The last raid over Essex and the worst was in May 1918 when a number of planes were shot down and my husband saw one crash in flames on the Marshes. His home adjoined the City of London cemetery where the three lost in the plane were buried. The cemetery was closed to the public for the funeral but my husband climbed over the boundary fence and was the only non-combatant at the interment.'

'I was quite small but I remember the Zeppelin coming down at Billericay. We all collected bits when we were taken to see it. Four or five Germans were escorted up the station hill to be put on a train.'

'In 1915 I was carried in a blanket to the basement of the police station for shelter during an air raid. Bombs fell on Leyton during the war.'

FIRST TO LAST

'My first recollection is of 4th August 1914. My parents took me to Clacton for the day. When we boarded the train, coming home to Colchester, Mother was upset and Father comforted her. At St Botolph's station, there were a great many people about talking excitedly. I must have been distressed, because Mother said to me, "It's all right, nothing for you to worry about." It was of course the outbreak of war.

Soon we had soldiers billeted upon us. They were very good to me. I expect they were thinking of their own children. One of them,

Peace Day celebrations at East Tilbury in 1919.

Sam, was visited by his wife. That was the last time she saw him, for he was killed soon after.

In 1916 we moved to Bergholt Road, near North station, sharing a house with my aunt and uncle. My cousin Henry, the same age as myself, and I were great pals. I remember the seemingly endless columns of troops entraining at North station; for many of them it was to be a one-way journey. One day we saw a lad we knew and he waved to us. He was just 17 and three months later he was killed on the Somme.

Father did not get called up but was on munition work, night shifts, so I saw little of him. Henry and I attended North Street school. I well remember the queues for rations at the Co-op. In the field nearby the army came to practise drill. One day we found some live bullets. We used to put them in a vice, in Uncle's shed, hit them with a punch and hammer, and off they would go right through the shed wall. I often wonder why it was we did not kill someone, or ourselves. Sometimes we would watch the searchlights at night, looking for Zeppelins.

A Zeppelin came down at Peldon and Father took me out to see it. We brought home a small piece of the fuselage. The Strood was zigzagged with sandbags and there were soldiers on duty there.

About the middle of November, 1918, Mother took me into the town shopping. The streets were decorated with flags and bunting, and one notice read, "Hurrah, we won the War". I said, "I expect the Germans say, Damn, we lost." For which I received a telling off for using bad language.'

LIGHTS AND KEYS

'During the war lights on the vehicles were dimmed because of air raids, and street lights in our area in Leyton had the upper part of the exterior glass painted black. In main roads lighting was then usually by carbon arc lamps, but I do not recall if and how these were shrouded or used. The gas lighting (I am pretty sure it was gas) on London Bridge was masked on the river sides of the standards to prevent reflection in the water.

Armistice Day, timed for eleven o'clock in the morning of the eleventh day of November 1918, proved to be a damp, dull day with almost a greenish tinge in the sky. Everyone rejoiced, and I believe bells were rung at that time, and maroons were let off for a more peaceful purpose. There were no such things as fireworks, but we boys produced what we called key-bangers. These consisted of a key with a hole in the end, a piece of string with the key tied to one end, and a nail on the other. The hole in the key was filled with a mixture of sulphur and saltpetre and the nail then pressed into the mixture in the hole (the bigger the key the better). The whole thing was then swung forcibly against a wall or a lamp post producing a highly satisfactory bang. If the charge and resulting explosion was too great the end of the key disintegrated, and the problem was to get another one. To my shame I "found" one at home which was duly ruined, and it turned out to be an essential one. Punishment was swift and sure.'

COMING HOME

'I can well remember as a child at Ilford my uncle coming home from France. It was Sunday 9th November 1918. He was plastered with mud and my parents had to peel his puttees off his legs, and his khaki uniform. My mum put it in the coal oven of the kitchener to kill the fleas.

Then on Tuesday 11th November, at eleven o'clock, suddenly church bells, hooters and anything else that could make a noise told us that the Armistice had been signed and everybody started singing and cheering.'

SILENCE

'During the years between the wars Remembrance Day was always on 11th November. In the late 1930s I was working in the Bank of England and we were allowed to go up on the roof for the two minutes' silence at eleven o'clock when all the traffic stopped and there was no sound in London except the birds, and quite often they were quiet too. It was the same throughout Essex – silence for two minutes.'

THE SECOND WORLD WAR 1939-45

Just two decades later we were again at war, and Essex was once more in the front line. Bombs began to fall on our towns and villages and many a night was spent in the air raid shelters.

A LONG WAR

'My parents had been through the Great War so they knew all about bombs and soon I learnt that September 1939 was going to be the start of something horrible. "Blackout" was nailed up at windows – old blankets if you couldn't afford heavy curtaining – but Mother was adept at making it still look like home. Fortunately my boyfriend soon made me see life had plenty of happier sides to it all – and *his* family were banging in umpteen nails in their woodwork too – but the fear wasn't apparent and everyone relaxed after a bit despite the false alarm next day when all the sirens were sounded by mistake.

We had to dim all our bicycle lights, the car lights, street lights, lamp lights. Indeed all the world seemed black and we wondered at the skies – the moon and stars seemed to shine all the brighter. So many rules and regulations, hardships, shortages, basics which, even if we did not have much money, were always available. Eventually food was rationed so everyone had fair shares (black market flourished). But young people still enjoyed life. I lived in outer London (still Essex), at Chadwell Heath. We married in December 1939 and we were dreading the call-up which would separate us – surely for not *too* long? The war couldn't last long, could it?

How I hated it. Suddenly this war was personal. We lived for the "leaves" when passes had to be shown often and time was short. I worked in East London then, travelling by train, but we had about three months of snatched leaves together before Bill had to go overseas. Everyone had to do war service of some kind if you were fit and able. If we had not got a "tied" job we were made to join the services or the Land Army. My job was considered a tied occupation but we then had to do fire watching in the local area for two hours at night (with tin hat and stirrup pump!) once a week. Oh those cold nights, turning out of a warm bed at 2 am to sit with our fellow fire watcher until 4 am, hopefully then to sleep again until 6.30 for work. I was also an NFS (National Fire Service) lady waiting, watching, listening for the arrival of those fire bombs in our area. I think this was every tenth night.

Many stories filled the papers in those days, the losses on land, sea and in the air. Then *we* were getting bombed. So each of us hoped and prayed for the other and letters were our one means of saying "I love you"; news was censored anyway. Bill's letters were obviously fewer and shorter than mine but each was treasured and re-read. Some of my friends and acquaintances had sad news; some were making new contacts with the many servicemen from overseas and enjoying the fun – and the Americans all looked so *rich*! Smart uniforms of fine materials; offering chocolates, silk stockings and so many things we hadn't seen for ages.

As I travelled to London one day, a German bomber came low and strafed our train. "I wonder what it's like to be shot?" I thought as we all crouched low in the carriage – and I thought of Bill in the Middle East living through much more than a few bullets. The plane came down in flames a distance off and the train slowly continued onwards and we got to our work.

Trains were usually packed tight in those days, sometimes like sardines. One morning it ran off the rails approaching Liverpool Street. I had often wondered what it would be like to pull the communication cord. "If £5 you can afford, have a thrill and pull the cord" one wag had written, but I never thought of it when the coach grated and wobbled. Fortunately *someone* did and we stopped quickly before we tipped over. So we all got out, walked along the rails, and caught a relief train back to work.

Going home in the evenings the train was also packed but everyone accepted it, as they do now. The Battle of Britain had started then and when we reached the station we used to dash up the stairs past the ticket collector and run all the way home. By then I was sharing our house with Bill's mother and sisters. The front door was open, they were in the Anderson shelter, so I'd slam the door shut, grab the hot dinner off the cooker, out through the back door and straight into the Anderson with the others. There we would stay until morning while the ack-ack guns travelled round our roads and fired at the planes.

"Blimps" guarded the skies round London and searchlights scanned the skies but they still got through. Occasionally a bomb would drop somewhere near – it wasn't so many years ago that I heard "they found an unexploded bomb down the end of our road". Of course London had it severe, as did many other towns, and we had our share. Doodlebugs wiped out families and homes *en masse*. It's strange how one got used to all this! Many times the sirens would sound and we'd drop everything and go down to the basement shelters, but sometimes we got blasé and our bosses had to *make* us leave the offices for shelter. The doodlebugs gave no warning though; a dull thud after a moment's silence and you knew some poor folk had had it. The tube stations became second homes for hundreds and we stepped over them and through them to get to our trains.

One morning I got to A & H to find it black and ruined – the fire bombs had fallen on it – so we were eventually transferred to other premises. I went to Lombard Street in the City, sand-bagged everywhere. One evening I arrived home and the family were "different". We didn't have to dash into the shelters at that time so the dinner was ready on the dining table as I entered. "What's wrong?" I asked. They were hoping I wouldn't sense the atmosphere, that I would eat my dinner. So the telegram came out: "Missing, believed killed". I didn't eat my dinner. But, thank God, he wasn't killed. Seriously injured. They eventually found him in a distant hospital. And he got better. He was a long time coming home. He was transferred and needed in another category where his skill was used. So we had to grin and bear it for some while after the war was over. Yes, it was a long war, but he came back, and that was one of the happiest days of my life. I was "one of the lucky ones" and I thank God for it.'

A CLOSE SHAVE

'A vivid childhood memory of mine is of a time during the last war when dogfights between the enemy aircraft and ours were a regular occurrence. My sister and I were playing in Rookery View recreation ground in Grays. The sirens went off, warning us of approaching enemy aircraft. We immediately set off home. As we were running up the road an ARP warden shouted to us to keep to the side of the road. We were running as fast as we could but didn't seem to be getting anywhere. All this time the aircraft above was machine-gunning at us. We threw ourselves into the garden air raid shelter, and as we did the bullets were pinging near us. In the morning Mum found the bullets in our gutter. A very close shave!'

IN THE SHELTER

'We acquired a Morrison shelter for our house in Grange Hill, Chigwell, made of iron. A heavy metal sheet was supported by substantial angle irons at each corner, and there were less substantial end and side members also of angle iron. Across the bottom, end and side irons was wire with a six inch mesh to provide the base for a mattress. The whole thing was bolted together and was about the size of a large double bed. We did not use it all that much but it was a comfort to have it available. One of the V1 pilotless planes landed directly in the cutting adjoining Grange Hill station and did considerable damage to the station building and around. All the front tiles on our house were displaced and some of the front windows blown in, but other property nearby suffered worse.'

'Although we were surrounded by farmland and woodland at Horndon on the Hill we had our fair share of bombing, being so close to the oil refineries and on the direct route to London. One farmhouse on the edge of the village sustained a direct hit and the farm across the road from us had a bomb in the farmyard, a piece of which travelled across the field, through our asbestos wall and into the side of a dresser cupboard full of china.

My father was an air raid warden at night when he got home from work in London. I went out with him one night when I was home on leave, because someone had reported seeing something that looked like a landmine coming down in the fields near us. We did not find anything, luckily, but it was one of the few times I felt really frightened.'

POWs

'I lived in Purleigh and we had two "trusty" German POWs living in the groom's room next to the stables. They had been taken straight from university to fight in the war and they were 23 when they came to live and work on our farm. They were supposed to make their own meals and I was given 25 shillings a week for each prisoner, to do their shopping. I used to cook for them anyway as they were hard workers. They joined us one Christmas Day and I remember them singing *Lily Marlene* and *Silent Night*. There were four Germans and two Italians at Raven's Farm at Purleigh Wash and others were brought out from the camps on a daily basis, but they were under guard.'

'My father had prisoners of war working for him on the farm at Abridge; they were billeted on Hainault golf club land and they loved the onion soup my mother made in a big copper. One of them stayed on after the war and married a local girl.'

COMMANDEERED

'The house where I now live, St Helen, was commandeered by the War Office during the Second World War. Why such interest in a modest house in an Essex village? The secret is of course that Ramsden Heath lies on a direct line between Germany and London.

A gigantic searchlight was stationed just north of the village to pick up enemy planes on their way to bomb the capital. A lookout point was established on a hill south of the village and when a bomber was spotted the information was transmitted to the searchlight crew. This operation was manned by a small army detachment, officers being billeted at St Helen. Other ranks slept either in the outbuildings of a farm further down the lane or in portable barracks which had been erected close to the searchlight. My grandparents, who lived at the farm, became very attached to these boys and one in particular, who played the piano in the evenings when not on duty, became like another son and often visited them after the war.

The village was made famous by the notorious Lord Haw-Haw during many of his nightly broadcasts when he threatened that the light would be extinguished, together with the village. Although a number of landmines and rockets were dropped in the area the attacks were unsuccessful.

Today the house shows no signs of its wartime experience other than the leaded windows on the side of the house which are slightly bowed as a result of a landmine falling in a neighbouring field. The flagpole raised defiantly in the front garden survived the Nazi threat only to be felled by a stronger force on the night of 14th October 1987.'

HARD WORK

'Prior to the war I was a chiropodist at Leigh on Sea. For the first few months I carried on with my work and joined the local ARP.

In the spring of 1940 the danger of invasion became imminent, and many people left the town, so my practice gradually became less and less. In May a friend – a farmer's daughter – rang up to ask if my father and I would like to spend a week at their farm at Shalford in north Essex and help with the haymaking. At that time I suffered badly from hay fever and I was not keen, but after talking it over we decided to go.

We had been there only a few days when a friend from home rang up to say that the Invasion Notices were up in the town and many people had left. We hurried home, and consulted the police and our vicar (who had already sent his wife away). The police told us that in the event of invasion we would have to leave, taking with us just one suitcase and leaving our animals behind. This decided us, and we returned to the farm. The farmer told us he had a vacant cottage and we could have it if I would work on the farm. We paid six shillings a week for it, later reduced to three shillings, the official rate. The wife of our next door neighbour told us that her husband (a skilled agricultural labourer) had never received three shillings a week in his life!

It was hard work, but I enjoyed it. I had two horses to look after and work with and took part in all aspects of farm work, helping with the milking, washing all the utensils, mucking out the cowsheds and carting the muck up a steep hill to the muck heap. (Once I tipped myself on it with the muck.) After that it was hoeing, carting, more muck spreading and haymaking till the evening milking.

Our first air raid warning came when I was having my weekly bath in the outside shed which we shared with my neighbour (having first locked the door). The bath was a long tin one filled with hot water carried from the kitchen. The warning came from our local ARP warden cycling round and blowing his whistle.

In January the farmer was able to get one of his old farm workers back and we were given notice to leave. After a lengthy search we moved to the old school house in Blackmore End. We still had an outside toilet (a bucket) but we had a real hot bath. It was in the kitchen and had to be filled from kettles heated on the stove, but it was luxury. Then the lid came down and formed the kitchen table.

Shortly after we moved in I was asked to do a milk round for a week. I agreed and did it for the next four years. I had an old fashioned milk churn with brass top and tap, and a can and measure, and did about 30 miles a day round the neighbouring villages in a shocker of an old van. It had a hole in the floor through which one could see the road, and the tyres were worn until the

We carried identity cards at all times during the war.

inner tubes were exposed. I had five punctures in a week, and I had plenty of practice in changing wheels, including once when the local garage had not put the wheel on properly. The front wheel came off and rolled along the country lane ahead of me. I put it on again taking one nut off each of the other wheels, and all was well.

I finished about 2 pm, took up my chiropody bag and visited patients in the local hospital and various villages round about.'

FROM THE FRYING PAN

'Living in Southend, quite soon the area was evacuated due to the threat of invasion. My family, with all our belongings, went to Poplar in East London to stay with my uncle. It wasn't long before we realised we had gone from the frying pan into the fire, as the London Blitz started and we were in the line of fire while Southend seemed to remain intact. After a while we obtained a house in Romford but did not fare much better.

Life was quite hard really and yet the spirit and courage of people was amazing. I joined the Fire Service and travelled each day to Stifford (near Grays) by a bus which was able to run, not on petrol, but by using a large gas cylinder. Needless to say, it was always breaking down, especially on the hills.'

CLOSE CALLS

'The aerodrome at North Weald loomed large in our lives. The first time I entered it was an Open Day in 1938, when all I recall was a long line of Gloster Gladiators, stretched out along the runway. But after 1940 how it changed. First we had Beaufighters roaring through the dark nights, and then the Hurricanes zooming low over the house.

I remember also a bombing raid during the middle of a cricket match, with players, children and all tumbling on one another in the ditch. There was the tragedy of a bomb falling on an air raid shelter on the 'drome itself, when WAAFs and airmen lost their lives together.

Luckily, our closest call was a line of incendiaries across the lawn. When the runway was extended, it closed our road to through traffic to North Weald. However, residents were allowed to drive round the perimeter and out the other side. One foggy night we set out, but missed the road and finished up in a dispersal hangar. We hurriedly backed out and tore out of the 'drome, expecting to hear a plane coming for us, though why we thought they would be flying in the fog, I don't know.

My husband's parents kept the local pub, and the army camp was up the lane at the side. You can imagine how busy it was at times with all the family literally "all hands to the pumps". Sometimes we had the airmen, but they mostly stayed in North Weald though sometimes the Norwegians came round for apples, which they would stuff down the front of their battledress. One of the public houses in North Weald, The Woolpack, was also bombed and never opened again.

When the war was over we had a party along the lane, and finished up with fireworks. Where my husband obtained them, I have no idea, but what a finish for the children.'

BOXTED UNDER FIRE

'Some years ago I had access to the official logs of the Royal Observer Corps at Boxted and these help to set the scene for one terrible day in August 1940.

Friday 30th August dawned with skies not so blue as on many mornings of the past month; in fact large areas of cloud drifted across eastern England. The Luftwaffe blitz on airfields and radar stations had reached its crescendo on "Eagle Day" (13th August) and was now losing some of its intensity. However, attacks were still being mounted on Fighter Command airfields and on this Friday morning the Germans had launched several attacks on airfields south of the Thames, making use of the patchy cloud cover.

At about 3.30 pm radar detected a force of 70 raiders approaching the Essex coast and all units were alerted. Douglas Bader's "Big Wing" of 12 Group Hurricanes were already airborne from Duxford and were directed south to intercept. The German raiders were identified as Dornier Do 17s and as they crossed the Essex coast they were joined by a force of Me 109 fighters.

In Boxted things had been very quiet. Although the battle raged around them little had happened in the village, just numerous warnings followed by all clears. The villagers took all this in their stride. On this Friday the area had been on "red alert" most of the afternoon and aircraft had been heard but not seen owing to the cloud cover.

At 4.55 pm, when many villagers were at tea and others just leaving off work in the fields, all hell broke loose. The air was filled with the screeching of bombs and explosions. Yet within ten minutes all was quiet, the raiders had jettisoned their bombs and gone.

Fortunately there were no casualties and no damage to property, the bombs falling to the south of the village on agricultural land. Four high explosive bombs fell near Enfields Lane leaving sizeable craters and two more fell on land near Barritts Farm but failed to explode, which was lucky as they were very large bombs. Three more dropped on Ellis farm but all failed to explode. When the pigman went to tend the pigs he saw them standing looking down the hole made by the unexploded bomb! Two bombs fell on land north of the old Queen's Head and again they failed to explode. Had they done so the devastation would have been considerable to local properties.

On land south of the Queen's Head and the Horkesley road, an area of market gardens and smallholdings, many hundreds of incendiary bombs fell, few of them igniting. Some incendiaries that did ignite fell in a cornfield, where that afternoon the farmer had completed carting and stacking his wheat. Two farm workers were still in the field when the bombs started to fall and three incendiaries fell close to the newly completed cornstack. The two men bravely threw the bombs away from the stack with their forks and smothered them with earth. Some 40 incendiaries fell in this field and ignited but the two men, helped by others from neighbouring farms, walked across the field putting out the fires and smothering the bombs.

All emergencies have their amusing side and this was no exception. When the bombs began to fall a local family retreated to their newly constructed shelter. It was then discovered Grandma was not with them. Rushing out to see what had happened the dutiful son found Grandma in the pantry. Asked why she had not gone with the rest of them into the shelter she replied: "Well, I could not come in there with you and leave the butter on the table – the old cat might have got it!"

Later that evening Lord Haw-Haw (William Joyce) reported on his broadcast to Britain that German aircraft had bombed "military objectives" at Colchester causing considerable damage; one aircraft was missing! A lesson on how to turn defeat into victory. This brought to an end Friday 30th August 1940.'

FIRST DOODLEBUG

'My husband George, who was in the Fire Brigade at Romford, was on night duty. During the night I was awakened by a loud noise, which also woke my mother in law. There hadn't been an air raid warning, but looking out of the window we could see a flame going across the sky and disappearing in the distance.

Next morning I mentioned it to my husband who was alarmed that we had stood and watched it. It was the first doodlebug and it fell on a railway bridge at Cobham Road.'

STRANGERS AND BOMBS

'At the beginning of the war the evacuees arrived in Danbury village. They were grammar school boys but they didn't stay long. Then the soldiers arrived. The first were the Scottish Highland Light Infantry. A lot of big houses were taken over including the Manor, the

Spinney, the Dainties Cafe and Gaybowers chapel. My Dad stored the forms and chairs in his barn, the books and organ we had in the sitting room. Some of the tunes we played on it were a lot different than hymns.

The Palace at Danbury Park was used as a maternity hospital during the war. The Queen Mother came and visited the mothers there.

One night our village had three bombs dropped on it, one in the middle of the road in Mill Lane, one in the churchyard close to the church, and the third behind the Bell public house. A doodlebug fell behind houses in Hyde Lane and a lot of incendiaries on Danbury common which the Home Guard picked up. Luckily there were no casualties but plenty of damage, especially to the church.'

IN THE SKY

'On a cloudless warm September day in 1940, a friend and I decided to cycle to the nearby beauty spot of High Beech. Suddenly gunfire peppered the sky. As it became louder we got off our bikes and sheltered in a ditch until things quietened. Then we continued to a farmer friend. After a welcome cup of tea, we went out into the garden and watched a terrific air battle raging in the sky – a never to be forgotten sight and experience. In the distance a lone pilot was parachuting from a height, and within my heart I wished him a safe landing whether he be friend or foe. As we neared home the sky over the London docks was brilliant red with blazing fires from the bombing at the commencement of the Battle of Britain. Many people were evacuated, some to Buckhurst Hill, where they eventually settled. My friend and I were thankful to arrive home safely.'

NO TIME TO BE FRIGHTENED

'Hope Cottages at Boxted were built 70 years ago. My parents were the first to move in. It was near there the doodlebug fell. I had just had my tea and was reading in front of the windows. Mum went to shake the cloth, and called, "There's a doodlebug coming. The siren's gone, look out!" With that down it went. We didn't have time to be frightened. I scrambled to the middle wall on my knees behind the settee. My Mum cried, "Where's Phyllis?" (my sister). She was in the road. She had enough sense to fall down. The thatched cottage behind went up in flames, and poor old Mr White got a cut thumb. The Americans with fire engines arrived first. The bomb hadn't been down five minutes when there were people everywhere. They came on their bicycles from Manningtree, Mistley, and they went all over the house, and I lost my piece of shrapnel. They never stopped to say could they come in! All the ceilings and inside walls collapsed because it had lifted the roof. The County Council came that night and put tarpaulins over the roof. We all trooped round to my granny and slept on the floor'

OUR PRISONER

'We lived in the "defence area" of Essex at Althorne, and there were restrictions on those allowed in. Windows were blacked out at night, so lights could not be seen from above by enemy raiders. Moonlight nights and full tides in the rivers, we knew those conditions were helpful to enemy aircraft and tried to get to sleep before they came. We lived right on the edge of the village so it was quite a long walk or bicycle ride, but my mother joined everything in spite of the distance – WI, Guides, knitting for the forces at Women's Fellowship, collecting for the Red Cross and National Savings, also the first aid post, and the first aid lectures. My sister and I were used for them to practise on.

This training stood us in good stead as one particular cold March night we heard footsteps outside, and our neighbour called out to say that he had a wounded man and needed help. On opening the door the man, seeing the fire, stumbled past her across the room and held his hands out to it. My sister and I sat up from the mattress, and he turned round at the noise and we saw he had a terrible face wound. My mother sat him in her chair by the fireside and I helped her with the first aid, while my sister put her coat over her pyjamas and went out into the cold night and along the lane to telephone the local police from the farmhouse some distance away and tell them that we had a wounded German airman at our cottage.

When we had tended his wounds my mother suggested to the neighbour that we'd better disarm him as she had noticed a gun, so this we did via signs and he readily handed it over onto the table. A little later he stood up, and from the pocket in the leg of his flying suit, which incidentally was very poor quality, he pulled out a metal box, long and flat, and put that on the table too. We didn't know what it was, so seeing our puzzlement he took it and pressed a button and a wicked looking knife blade shot out which he immediately retracted. My sister returned from the farm, accompanied by the farmer, and we waited for the police to come. I remember Sheila getting out her knitting and sitting down to do it with great unconcern, to the amazement of our prisoner.

Eventually we heard footsteps outside again, and it was the police. He stood to attention with a blanket of ours wrapped round him, and he put his hand on my mother's shoulder as if to say "thank you" before he was taken away.

We later learned that he had been blown out of his Junkers and parachuted down into the meadow about 50 yards from our cottage.

He had crawled across the lane, almost frozen and bleeding to seek help.

Next morning we were sent to school as usual, a mile to walk up the lane, then seven miles on the bus to Maldon. Mopping up German airmen was all in a night's work it seemed.'

RATIONS AND MAKING DO

Keeping families fed and clothed was no easy task in wartime, but we managed on what we could get on and off the ration, with some very odd recipes going the rounds!

NOT VERY TASTY

'How peaceful life was at Latchingdon until that day when war was declared. My baby was just over a year old. However, we were lucky in a way that my husband was released for essential farmwork, as we got harvest rations during the summer months, which meant extra cheese, a pound of sugar and a pound of jam. We kept chickens so any surplus eggs I put in waterglass solution. We stretched the butter ration by beating it in milk and made quite good sponge cakes using liquid paraffin! One day I made a steamed pudding with potato jam in the bottom of the basin and some other ingredient. When my husband took a mouthful he spat it out into the sink and said, "What the devil was that?" I told him that Lord Woolton had given the recipe on the wireless, to which my husband replied, "Well, you tell him to eat it then, I don't want it."

Landmines were dropped at Goldhanger leaving huge craters but miraculously missing the church and houses. They were also dropped at Palepit Corner, Mundon and a farm at Latchingdon. Fortunately, I believe only a horse was killed. The noise was deafening. Then we had the flying bombs which set fire to a house in Mayland. Southminster had bad damage and people killed.

The ration books were a nightmare and caused a lot of black marketing. Some fruit was unknown. I craved for oranges when I was expecting my second child but all that was in the shops was tinned carrots. We tried bottling fruit by sealing with candlewax, and salting runner beans. Spam and processed cheese were always on sale. Manufacturers tried making mutton into bacon by calling it "macon" but it was not very popular. Whalemeat came on the market, again not very tasty.'

JAM MAKING

'My mother, Mrs Nellie May, was the founder of the Greenstead Green Women's Institute in 1919. She was a farmer's wife living at Claverings Farm. She organised and presided over the wartime jam making centre in the village hall, a converted chapel, which she helped to purchase for the village. Sugar was rationed, so fruit grown in our gardens would have been unused but for this idea.

The village hall had one cold water tap, which was a real asset, as no houses in the village except those with their own well and pump were fitted with such a luxury. Helpers brought along their own paraffin stoves and matches, and spare paraffin. Also their own preserving pans, scales and weights, small jugs for filling jars, and a good supply of jam jars. These were collected by volunteers, and had to be a recognised type that held exactly one pound in weight.

Every helper was kept busy. Some weighing in fruit, some washing and stoning plums, some washing jars and warming them, ready to receive near-boiling fruit.

Only five plumstones were allowed in a one-pound jar of jam. If stones were not removed before boiling, they had to be removed from the boiling preserving pan before "putting up" the jam. Helpers were allowed to take the stones home, to try to extract any jam stuck to them. Each jar had to be completely full, and a waxed paper circle laid on top while the jam was still warm. Next a cardboard lid with a green WI was placed on top. Then the jar was labelled of course.

The jam was sold in the local shops and was in great demand, as the Women's Institute was held in high regard locally.'

QUEUES AND LONG WALKS

'As my mother had a new baby I, being the eldest girl at seven, had to go up to the butcher's in Chelmsford at 7.30 am to queue up for our meat ration as the shop didn't open till 8 am, and then I had to go off to school. I used to get one book's worth, which was one shilling and twopence, and sometimes you were very lucky and could buy some offal. This used to be sold on an alphabet system, and as our name began with an "R" we didn't seem to be lucky very often. As we had a baby in the family we had what was known as a "Green Book" and so were able to get a few extras such as oranges and orange juice, and extra milk as well. We never went hungry as my mother knew the local poacher, so we often had pheasants, partridge and, of course, rabbits to eat.

"GROWMORE" BULLETIN No. 3
OF THE MINISTRY OF AGRICULTURE
AND FISHERIES PUBLISHED BY
HIS MAJESTY'S STATIONERY OFFICE

PRICE 4d. NET

The wartime government bombarded housewives with advice and recipes for cooking and preserving.

My grandfather also used to bring up lots of vegetables from his allotment the other side of town, and a bucket full of coal when we were down to just coal dust in our coal cellar. We made this into brickettes for the fire. Grandad's coal got the fire started, then we'd use the brickettes and logs of wood. Even though you'd order coal from the merchants, you had to wait six to eight weeks for delivery. My mother got hold of an old pram when I was about eight years old, and we'd go to the wood merchant's to buy logs, and often (if there was a kind man taking the money) we'd get a sackful on top of the full pram, and all for sixpence. Once, when my friend was helping me, we were returning through a long passage behind some houses and a wheel came off the pram, so my friend had to walk all the way back, about one and a half miles, to fetch my mother, who had to come and help push the pram back home. After these journeys, which I did about once a fortnight, I'd just love to have hot buttered toast and Shippams sardine and tomato paste for my tea. Nothing tasted quite so good on a very cold day when sitting in front of the old range fireplace, which was the only warm place in the house.

When our shoes were worn out we would cut out pieces of cardboard to cover the hole in the soles, and we'd put blakeys on the heels.'

'With colleagues from the office we used to go to London on a Saturday morning to buy our shoes. Lilley and Skinner in Oxford Street had their quota that day. Queueing was a matter of course.'

ODD RECIPES

'Like many people we kept chickens, ducks and rabbits. The chickens and ducks were fed on boiled mash and potato peelings plus odds and ends; how the smell lingers with one! The ducks came to an untimely end when my mother fed them some salted runner beans which had not "kept". We asked the advice of all around and not realising that it was possibly a surfeit of salt which had killed them, buried the bodies; my mother was very upset but the runt, Jemima, who was not strong enough to get her beak into the beans survived. Her eggs were treasured! The rabbits were exchanged by the butcher with others so that we did not eat our own pets. We were at one time the owners of a pig. Kept by friends in the village at Ramsden Heath our long thin and their short fat pig were fattened, caught with a great many squeals and bad language and taken to the slaughterhouse before being stored in the Romford cold store. The bacon proved to be delicious and well worth the effort of catching them.

When my father was at home he would enjoy shooting pigeons

and rabbits to supplement our rations but then came the nasty bit. Donning a large apron and her gas mask my mother would pluck, skin and draw. I would leave the kitchen but well remember the look of horror on a visiting gypsy's face on one occasion when my mother prepared to purchase pegs whilst still in her protective outfit.

Birthdays were celebrated with parties. We ate jellies, blancmange made from goat's milk, and always a cake made from hoarded ingredients – with disastrous results when colouring overpowered the icing once. We all ended up with purple tongues!

Christmas cakes and puddings were baked using a lot of vegetables to eke out the dried fruit and the addition of gravy browning to give the correct colour. Marzipan made from strange ingredients with almond essence always tasted right and somehow there was icing sugar in blue bags sold by Lukin Smith's the grocer's, for the snow.

Dried milk and peppermint essence made chewy mint lumps which we carefully wrapped in cellophane – just like shop sweets. These were a great treat and supplemented the weekly Mars bar which was divided into seven portions, one portion a day. Afternoon tea included eating dripping toast or sandwiches filled with reconstituted bananas before listening to Uncle Mac and *Children's Hour*. "Good night children, everywhere".'

GETTING WED

'We were married in Berners Roding church in April 1943 and held a reception in Willingale village hall. Since everything was rationed both our families collected sugar, fruit etc and I made a cake. We also collected tins of fruit and the Co-op caterers provided Spam salad for one shilling and sixpence a head and 100 small fancy cakes for a penny halfpenny each. I wore the dress I had made for my sister for her wedding, she wore a borrowed outfit and an old school friend wore the bridesmaid's dress I had for my sister's wedding. The veil and head-dress were also loaned so it wasn't just something borrowed, it was nearly everything.'

EKING OUT THE RATIONS

'I drove a canteen van at Rayleigh and helped at the British Restaurant which was in an empty house on two floors. Food was pulled up on a wooden lift by hand and a two course meal was one shilling and sixpence, very good value.

We made mince rolls with one bacon rasher and a carrot and onion all chopped together, and suet if we were lucky enough to get some. We had plenty of potatoes and vegetables and dried egg. We made blackberry and apple pies, and soup with bones from the butcher,

Weddings called for an extra effort but Hilda Smith and Frederick Palmer managed to make it a day to remember at Thundersley in 1942.

and drank lots of water. Coal was in very short supply (one hundredweight a week) so we went for walks in the woods to find logs, but we came through a very hard and often sad time and I feel we were much stronger for it.'

PARACHUTES

'When the airfield at Marks Hall was built life looked up for the village girls! We helped at the YMCA doling out beans on toast and coffee or tea. Then in 1942 the Americans came and we had dances in St Peter's hall. Our farm was close to the airfield and we saw many bad things. We had an unexploded bomb on our land and had to evacuate the livestock. The bomb exploded the next day causing a huge crater but very little damage.

We were fortunate, living on a farm, with our own poultry and eggs, plus rabbits and game. Clothing could only be bought with clothing coupons, but I was given a large amount of rayon parachute material and was able to cover all our eiderdowns in green and blue. A skirt for myself was not so successful, it was gathered at the waist but when worn it billowed out like a barrage balloon, so had to be abandoned. Later I used white nylon parachute material for underclothes, nighties and pretty embroidered blouses. We also collected the foil "window" which was thrown out of German aircraft to confuse our radar. We stripped off the paper backing and it did nicely for Christmas decorations.

We queued for our ration when sweets arrived at the village shop. Once the pressure at the counter was so great it trapped the elderly couple who owned the shop and squeezed them against the wall.'

DOING OUR BIT

We all did our bit for the war effort, whether it was by working on munitions or making jam, a variety of experiences that illustrated life on the home front.

WORKING UNDERGROUND

'I wonder how many Essex people remember working in unfinished underground Central Line tunnels during the war. The extension from Liverpool Street to Stratford was, I believe, finished by the start of war, but work was well on to completion of stations from Leytonstone to Newbury Park, and it was therefore possible to use some of this area for factory work – not from a safety point of view, but because it was there and convenient. I worked for the Aeronautical Inspection Department of the Ministry of Aircraft Production, and was attached for a time to Plessey's who made some electrical equipment down in Redbridge station, and some machines extended into tunnels either side.

The inspectors were not underground all the time as were the workers, but our "office" was Redbridge station on the street, and there were some temporary buildings attached. The noise of the machinery in this underground cavern was deafening, and I was glad not to be down there all the time. I did treat myself to a walk one lunchtime, and walked through the tunnel to Wanstead station. Quite a long walk and very damp in places where the tunnel went under the Roding. The escalator was in place at Wanstead, but of course not working, and I walked up it and back to Redbridge along the street.

Working in these conditions was not considered particularly healthy, and we were sent once a month for chest X-rays at the BMA in Tavistock Square, London. I can't say I enjoyed the experience that much, and was happy when I was moved to another Plessey factory which was a lot more conventional.'

ALL THE FAMILY

'There was talk of war for a year or two before it was actually declared; people were being urged to join the ARP as it was feared that air raids would bring gas attacks and so classes were held to instruct us in how to deal with the casualties of such a happening. At the end of the instruction course we had to pass an exam which included passing through a gas-filled chamber wearing our masks; this was not a pleasant experience!

My father was the ARP warden for the Layer de la Haye area and it was his duty to supply and fit everybody with a gas mask; for this purpose he recruited me! There were large and small ones for adults, Mickey Mouse ones for the smaller children, and the babies were put into an enclosed cradle-like mask with a pump attached which had to be kept going in order for the baby to breathe. I remember it was not at all easy as some of the children were frightened of the masks – and I don't blame them; they were quite hideous.

Soon after I married in 1939 I was called up for work since all women without family ties were expected to help in the war effort. I was sent to work at Paxmans as a progress chaser. My job was to see that the parts needed for building the engines were available in the store as needed and to order them or chase them up as the case might be. I enjoyed this work very much and the comradeship of the other women.

My husband, being an agricultural engineer, was exempt from the forces but he did serve in the Home Guard in the ack-ack on the Abbey Fields. This may sound as if he got off very lightly but, in point of fact, he worked almost a 24 hour day most days, particularly in the summer as he was in great demand by the farmers. He would leave home at 6.30 in the mornings and not get home until 9 pm most nights for a meal, a wash and then off for night duty in the ack-ack.'

FUND RAISING

'There used to be a big garage and showroom near the Crown public house at Loughton, belonging to Mr Patmore. When it was one of the fund raising weeks for the services Mr Patmore would clear the showroom and it was used for exhibitions and money-making efforts. My father made a battleship, which disintegrated if hit in the right spot with a marble, for Navy Week, and an aeroplane which bombed and shattered the target if the button was pressed at the appropriate moment. A bit bizarre, but it raised money for the appropriate forces.'

APPEALS AND CHALLENGES

'The Women's Institutes had always worked for the improvement of social and educational standards within their communities and during the war years. Buckhurst Hill WI certainly "did its bit"! There were many different areas for members to work in, so making full use of the skills and talents of all. Remember the "Dig for Victory" campaign? Gardens were turned over to vegetable growing. The County Federation provided vegetable seeds at low cost, so that as much as possible could be grown at home to make up for the shortages in the shops, thereby ensuring that families had plenty of fresh and varied produce. Many members kept chickens to provide a supply of eggs for the family, as the ration was only one egg a month for quite a long period. From time to time there were egg collections for the Forest Hospital in Roebuck Lane, and in April 1941 a total of 417 eggs were donated.

A jam and canning centre was set up in Buckhurst Hill and classes on preservation were held in Epping. Those who attended brought back their new skills and organised teams of preservers. In 1941 their first effort produced 155 lbs of jam, 124 lbs of chutney and 65 lbs of piccalilli. This was then put on sale to the community and each year it became more popular.

The West Essex Medicinal Herb Collectors organisation appealed to the WIs to collect and dry herbs. Naturally the WIs rose to the occasion and herb drying classes were set up in Epping. Rambles on summer evenings were organised for herb gathering. The herbs required included young nettles, raspberry leaves, marigold petals, foxglove seeds and yarrow. Dandelion roots were also dried in the winter months. In 1942 just over 4 cwt of herbs were collected in the area and Buckhurst Hill headed the list with a total of 1 cwt 15 ozs. This was an awful lot of herbs! How hard they must have worked.

Apart from these domestic efforts, there were also sewing and knitting groups who met weekly. A certain amount of wool was allowed to the WIs, free of ration coupons, to knit comforts for the troops. This brought forth hundreds of pairs of gloves, seamen's socks and balaclava helmets, which were all greatly appreciated. Aprons and children's clothes were made from the good parts of discarded clothing. Boxes of useful mending items were made up and distributed to local military bases and at Christmas time gift boxes were sent to men and women who were far from home.

In 1941, 1,000 refugees arrived in Chigwell. Until sufficient empty houses were found, hospitality was needed and furniture collections had to be made to make the homes habitable. General help was given when required with the evacuation of children to safe areas. Teams were ready to help with emergencies as a back-up to the ARP and first aid and tea stations were kept ready during the blitz.

Appeals for salvage were made. All paper, metal, tins, bones and rubber etc were collected and sent to the various depots. On the social side, whist drives were held monthly and the profits from these were sent to various causes. War Weapons Week received £47 8s 6d, equivalent to about £2,000 now. Wings for Victory received £74 4s 0d and Salute the Soldier Week received £97 3s 7d. Apart from these special efforts, profits were used to buy wool and other items needed in the community, and substantial contributions to the Poppy Appeal must not be overlooked.'

ST LEONARD'S LAUNDRY

'My mother in law, out walking with one of her children during the First World War, came across a young soldier doing his washing in the open at Middlewick camp, and she offered to do it for him. Next week there were two bundles, the following week, nine bundles!

The St Leonard's Laundry grew from that, and in the Second World War were official contractors to HM Government, doing most of the laundry work for the eastern England forces. Individual bundles consisted of a shirt, underwear, socks and handkerchief, wrapped in a towel, and many a time a lorry carrying clean supplies would travel miles, often through the night, to catch a regiment on the move. Devious means were used to ensure sufficient clean blankets and paliasse covers would be available, whilst maintaining secrecy regarding numbers and destinations of troops leaving or entering Colchester, (which was of course an important garrison town then) or in the other areas the laundry covered.

The work provided full employment for female members of local families, who walked and cycled to work. Daughters at an early age frequently declared their intention to follow in grandmother's and mother's footsteps. There was a good spirit. *Music while you work* broadcast twice a day by the BBC provided light relief. There was sadness and sympathy for those anxiously awaiting news of loved ones reported missing. There was humour too. It was thought a pretty face in charge of complaints would have a soothing effect. Complaints went up by leaps and bounds! Then there was a classic remark from a demonstrator with a learner, who insisted on continually smoothing a shirt before pressing it: "Don't keep patting it dear, only pat a shirt when there is a man in it!"'

'I joined the WAAF in January 1943 and, after my initial training in the north of England, I was posted to the Fighter Command 11 Group Station at Debden, near Saffron Walden. I was classified as a Clerk SD and had first to learn my trade. Clerks (Special Duties) were in fact the "plotters" that are sometimes shown in films pushing arrows about on maps of Southern England and were a vital part of the defence in the Battle of Britain. By the time I joined the Air Force, the Ops WAAFs had been issued with rods with controllable magnets on the ends which could easily pick up the little metal arrows and release them where needed. The plots were received from DF (Direction Finding) stations and other sources throughout the region. We were given a grid reference over headphones and on the grid reference we placed a little arrow pointing in the direction the aircraft were travelling. The aircraft could be either hostile or friendly. We always worked in the operations room attached to, although in some instances a considerable distance away from, an airfield.

There were other duties involved, but mainly the newcomers who had joined the WAAF after the main battle had passed over, plotted aircraft on the tables.

Shortly after that all the British personnel were moved from the Debden aerodrome which was taken over by the Americans. Several of us moved from Saffron Walden down to the North Weald aerodrome. North Weald had been at the forefront of the Battle of Britain. It was a badly-sited aerodrome, being very near a radio station with tall masts which guided the enemy raiders. Consequently the 'drome had been badly bombed and the Operations Room destroyed. The Ops Room had been moved temporarily to a hall at the back of a pub in Chipping Ongar.

All the WAAF operations staff were billeted in corrugated iron huts in the grounds of Blake Hall where eventually the new Operations Room was to be opened in the old ballroom. In the meantime we were taken by buses to Ongar each time we went on duty and if it was night duty we used to try and get some sleep in between spells of duty, lying on the floor of an adjoining room. Some airmen were also employed in the Operations Room and they were usually older men who were not suitable for a more active role.

Soon the new Operations Room in Blake Hall was ready for use and there we remained working until the end of the war.

By the time I had joined up the Battle of Britain was virtually over but there were still sporadic raids over London. Later, these were followed by the flying bomb attacks (V1s). We used to plot those horrible flying bombs (or doodlebugs, as they were nicknamed), and then suddenly the plot would disappear and we knew the bomb had exploded somewhere causing death and destruction. Whenever a doodlebug plot was received it was identified by the name "diver". When we received such a plot we would call out "Diver, diver, diver". I knew the grid reference of my home and if when I was on duty a doodlebug ended up there I would phone home immediately I was free to see if my family was all right.

After the V1s came the V2s, rockets with devastating warheads against which there was no protection. We could sometimes pick them up when they left France or Holland, but then of course they were lost until the explosion. My own home was badly damaged by one of these weapons. Luckily my mother escaped injury.

Our huts at Blake Hall were primitive. We had two toilets and cold water basins in a room at the end of a hut. The hut was heated by two black coal or coke burning round stoves which we stoked ourselves. We had narrow iron beds and three small hard mattresses called biscuits, two sheets, a small pillow and several grey blankets. Every day all bedding had to be folded up in a neat pile and put on top of the three biscuits at the top of the bed. We had metal cabinets for our clothes but we supplied our own bedside tables by converting orange boxes. These, painted or varnished and with a curtain in front, worked excellently.

The bathhouses were probably in what were originally the stables. They were not very pleasant and as we walked to them in the evening, bats used to fly round our heads. I never did like bats. On one occasion a bat got into the Ops Room and it was a good thing there were no enemy aircraft around then because it caused pandemonium!

I was sorry at the deterioration that occurred to Blake Hall during the Air Force's use of the building. It was a beautiful building and I hope is now returned to its original state. However, I know that the Ops Room has never been returned to its original purpose. It still stands as a reminder of the events of 50 years ago. I learnt to love the countryside round Blake Hall, Moreton and Ongar, and when I drive along the road from Epping to the Four Wantz I am always reminded of my days in the WAAF.'

CALLED UP

'When I was called up in March 1944 the women's services were up to full strength and women were being directed into "work of national importance". I was instructed to report to the personnel department of the Hoffmann Manufacturing Company in New Street, Chelmsford. I cannot claim to have made any direct contribution to the making of roller and ball bearings that Hoffmann's manufactured, merely doing clerical work. I remember with sadness the direct hit by a doodlebug in December 1944 and the devastation it caused. A plaque was placed in the entrance hall of the social centre in Mill Lane in memory of the people who were killed.

On the lighter side, I remember the rush down to the market in the lunch hour on Fridays to see what coupon-free bargains could be found – chiefly parachute silk for making undies, and of course nylons!'

BILLETED ON US

'I was married on 29th July 1939 and after a fortnight's honeymoon I came back to Brentwood looking forward to new furniture, new cutlery, new sheets and, of course, a new husband, all to myself. Alas, not for long!

The day after our return, down Woodman Road marched an army of soldiers – Pioneer Corps – remnants of the First World War called up to defend their country. As they marched along, so they cast off two by two, to be billeted in the houses along the road. We got landed with George and Albert and I don't know who felt the most awkward – me or them. I didn't know what to do with them or what to feed them on – I hadn't yet learned to cook. To have a husband was one thing, but three men was a disaster! However, George proved a welcome addition. He had been batman to a colonel in the First World War so off he went with sixpence and came back with herrings for breakfast. He was a great help in my early days. The sad thing was they rubbed their heels against my new settee – black marks everywhere! – and were unused to cutlery which *cut*, so my knives and forks had their silver plate chopped off their ends very quickly. Each week the captain came along to pay me – one shilling and sixpence – and, so the form said, "the manure was the property of the Government"! I *think* they meant from horses! After them I had a succession of young soldiers; they were fun, up to anything, and I have to confess that quite a few strings of sausages and bacon rashers just happened to appear in my kitchen at intervals – off the record (and the ration!) of course.

Then they were drafted and officers billeted in Weald Hall came to tea at weekends. They wrote regularly after they left and then the letters stopped – and I wondered.'

NOT JUST ENTERTAINMENT

'My sister and I, in our mid-teens in 1942, joined ENSA – Entertainment National Service Association (or as the troops referred to it: "Every night something awful"!).

Well, you can imagine, for my sister and me this was just the start of a great adventure, and that it certainly turned out to be, for in the next three years we were to travel over 75,000 miles giving I don't know how many shows to goodness knows how many people.

On the occasions I will tell you of, we were billeted in Colchester. On our first visit most of our shows seemed to be on or near the coast, and required daily trips down the main road from Colchester to Clacton. After doing this journey two or three times we started noticing the way that the roadside pill boxes (concrete machine gun emplacements) were disguised by clever camouflage. I recall that one of the shams was to build false garage doors as screens or to make the front look like a garden shed, but the one we liked best of all was the mock advertising hoarding which proclaimed "Hotel Endisnear – special rates for German visitors".

On our second visit to Colchester some ten months later, the events that overtook us were much sadder. We set off as usual all set to give our performance, but when we got to our destination, a searchlight site, we were not greeted in the usual way by an expectant group of soldiers. Apart from the solitary guard at the gate, there was no one to be seen. Needless to say we were puzzled by this unusual state of affairs, and when we talked to the guard, he said that most of the lads were in the mess hut and perhaps we had better go there. This we did, and yes, the lads were there, but only a few and they seemed dazed and not expecting us. We introduced ourselves and asked them what was amiss. At first they were hesitant to tell us, and then it all came out. A few hours before, a German plane returning from a raid had swooped low and raked the site with machine gun fire, killing some of the soldiers and wounding others. The army ambulance had taken the casualties off to the military hospital in Colchester and they were the ones left. They pointed to the row of bullet holes in the adjacent Nissen hut and then fell silent again. They were obviously in shock, and it would have been quite inappropriate to force an entertainment on them under these circumstances, so when the cook came in and asked us if we'd like a cup of tea, we accepted and sat down with the soldiers to give them a chance to tell us more of their recent experience if they wanted to. In the event, there was not much to say, they were still in shock and were chiefly concerned with their mates who had been whisked into hospital, and not knowing if they were wounded or dead.

Then it was that our mother had a bright idea. "Have you got a gramophone?" she asked. Yes, they had, it was a portable wind-up one, rather battered but serviceable. They got it out and set it up on a rickety card table and our mother asked them what music they would like (we always carried a few of our favourite records on tour with us). One shy lad plucked up courage and said, "Have you got the Warsaw Concerto?" By a stroke of good luck, we had, so we all sat round listening to it being played several times while I think we all shed tears into our mugs of tea as we shared their grief. When we left them they seemed to have regained their equilibrium somewhat, and we felt that although we had not done our show, perhaps what we had been able to offer by sharing their grief with them was of more help. With ENSA, it was not just entertainment.'

SPECIAL CONSTABLE

'When the war came in 1939 Mr H became a special constable at Ramsden Bellhouse. He took his duties very seriously, the whole village his to command. His war started quickly, for when the siren sounded within a few minutes of the broadcast telling us we were at war, it was on with the tin hat and arm bands and on to his bike. He cycled to the church and ordered everyone to go home. One cannot help feeling they were safer in the church than on the roads had there been a real threat that first Sunday morning.

Another trick of Special Constable H was to wait just inside the church gate (there was a good hedge there then) and step out right in front of you if you were riding your bike, demanding to see your identification card. He seemed to forget he had known you from babyhood, served on committees with your parents and repeatedly chased you off his grass verge!'

THE ROYAL OBSERVER CORPS

'A village organisation which played a vital function in the air defence of Great Britain was the Royal Observer Corps, whose motto "Forewarned is forearmed" led them to plot the tracks of hostile aircraft in the area, and to aid our own distressed aircraft. The village post at Hatfield Broad Oak came into existence in 1937 and by the outbreak of war had become part of Group 17 under the control of the Watford Table. Group 17 covered London north of the Thames together with large portions of Essex, Middlesex, Herts, Beds, Bucks and Berks. From high observation points information of aircraft movement was reported immediately to Watford so that vital plotting could take place. The Corps were indeed regarded as the "eyes and ears" of the RAF.

The post was built by Corps members and consisted of a concrete surround, creating a space of about six feet square, in the centre of which the plotting table was set: on this table was a grid square map and the plotting instrument. A strong-point cubby hole was attached where it was possible to boil a kettle and write up the post log.

Enemy aircraft were heard over the village for the first time in December 1939, at which time the post was cut off by snow drifts! Two members walked some eleven miles to the post, where they remained on duty for four days, being sustained by a local farmer until the snow cleared.

Ack-ack gunfire was first apparent in March 1940 over the Thames estuary, followed by the mystery Very lights and almost daily warnings of fifth columnists, and on 26th July 1940 the first bombs (whistlers) were dropped in the vicinity. This signalled the beginning of the blitz and the Battle of Britain. On 6th October (a Sunday) the post was attacked by enemy aircraft in low cloud, three bombs falling in an adjoining field. The crew on duty were impressed by the arrival of eight Hurricanes from North Weald within four minutes! During clear weather flares could be seen 50 to 60 miles away and a log entry reads: "The air battle seen in the East is reported to have been over the North Sea, 40 miles off Clacton" (80 miles from the post).

In May 1942 the unusual step was taken to resite the post to the tower of St Mary's church, 300 feet above sea level and with 360° visibility over the surrounding countryside. For a year things were comparatively quiet until the coming of the Marauders (US aircraft). One evening a squadron landed at Easton Lodge, followed by another, then more and more each day. At Willingale, at Stansted, at Matching – everywhere one looked were Marauders. From before daylight until after dusk every day, sometimes three missions a day, the tempo getting faster and faster as they shaved time off their take-offs and landings, until by D-Day they landed in at the rate of three per minute!

During June of the same year doodlebugs came into operation and on several occasions Observers had the novel experience of looking down on a "diver" as it passed by the tower on its way to London. The last sign of real enemy activity was in March 1945, and on Saturday 12th May, the crew on duty came down the 102 steps from the tower for the last time.'

THE WOMEN'S LAND ARMY

Another service into which some of us were called was the Land Army, keeping food production high at the time we needed it most. Many found it a satisfying and memorable time of their lives.

THE FIRST IN ESSEX

'At the outbreak of war I had just completed three years' training in dance and drama at the Ginner-Mawer School. Instead of taking up a teaching post I decided to go to the other extreme and applied to join the Land Army! I travelled from Loughton to my first position at Kingston's Farm at Matching Green, the home of Mr and Mrs Tom Howard. Together with three other girls I was recruited by "Mrs Tom", as she was known, and we started training on her farm. We were some of the first land girls in Essex.

We were given training in poultry and general farmwork. The poultry were all free-range, Rhode Island Reds, Black and White Leghorns; they lived in field houses which were moved from time to time. The other livestock were a house cow, the working horses and pigs. One of the other girls had constantly bruised legs from being pushed about by the pigs when she had to go in and feed them! The arable crops were wheat, barley, oats, sugar beet, peas and potatoes. November was the time for threshing and I remember all the boys standing around with sticks to try and kill the rats which ran out from the stacks as they were dismantled.

Our training was completed in January 1940 and I moved to the dairies in Little Hallingbury owned by the Roberts family. We were up at five o'clock each morning for two milk rounds in the motor van, spending the afternoons washing milk bottles and making cream. After six months I became ill and was off work for about a year.

I then joined "Will Soper" at his market garden in Harlow. We grew tomatoes in the sunny summer days but picking frozen brussels sprouts in the winter and washing leeks was not so pleasant as we had to break the ice on the water tank. Potatoes had to be planted by hand and the parsnips dug up with a fork. Later machines were introduced for planting potatoes and cabbages. Produce was transported by horse and cart although, later, tractors were used.

My days on the land ended in 1944 when my first baby arrived. We had fun and freedom and we did work hard!'

STARTING AT THE BIG HOUSE

'I joined the Land Army in 1941 and was sent to Bradfield, a small village just beyond Manningtree, and seven miles inland from Harwich. I arrived at the end of July to work at the "big house" of the village. I had an interview with the lady of the house and was told I would start work at 7 am. Breakfast was 8-8.30 am, lunch 1-2 pm, and I would finish work at 5.30 pm. It ended with: "Always use the back entrance and staircase, always be in by 10 pm and no followers."

I had worked in a large insurance office in London. Now, after deductions for board and lodging I had 19s 6d per week, out of which I sent my widowed mother 15 shillings. There were already two land girls there, and the rest of the staff consisted of a male cook (ex Merchant Navy), and Audrey, 14 years old, a general dogsbody, who worked from 6 am to 10 pm with a half-day off per week, and a whole day off every month. She did everything from washing up to mending silk underwear. Two women from the village helped out in the mornings.

We land girls had to see to the flowers, vegetables, fruit and hens, get in coal, and stoke and clean the Aga, wash the dogs and the car, and do any other jobs that came up. I can remember that in the basement were 13 buckets each holding twelve dozen eggs preserved in waterglass, which covered them in a white fur. Our "lady" decided to cook them, but every egg she used was bad, so I had the job of checking the lot and they were all bad – the smell! The cook had mixed the waterglass with hot water from the tap instead of boiling water. Not exactly war work, any of it.

I eventually left the "big house" and went to a fruit farm in the same village, lodging in a cottage.'

SENT TO FOULNESS

'It was towards the end of December 1941 and the thought of being in the country with fewer bombs sounded like heaven to me. So when my factory friend Rose asked me if I'd like to join the Land Army with her I had no doubts. "I'd love to" was my reply. It took a while to get things sorted out as I worked in a factory which exempted me from being called up for the forces. We both went to London to enrol.

I was sent to Thundersley in Essex early in March 1942 and for the next four years lived in a hostel with 39 other girls. During that time I had some strange but interesting jobs and one stands out because of a very frightening incident.

Twenty of us were sent to work on Foulness Island near Wakering. It was December and very cold. We had to dig trenches and lay

Name Miss Ruth Hirsch

No. 4[illegible]317

You are now a member of the Women's Land Army.

You are pledged to hold yourself available for service on the land for the period of the war.

You have promised to abide by the conditions of training and employment of the Women's Land Army ; its good name is in your hands.

You have made the home fields your battlefield. Your country relies on your loyalty and welcomes your help.

Signed G. Denman
Honorary Director

Signed R. E. D. Gray
Chairman Committee

Date 21.4.41.

I realise the national importance of the work which I have undertaken and I will serve well and faithfully.

Signed Ruth Hirsch.

The Women's Land Army played an essential role in the war effort – not always appreciated by their male contemporaries.

drainage pipes so that the ground could be used for growing wheat. Jock, our jovial lorry driver, would collect us from the hostel at 7.30 am and return us back to the hostel at 4.30 pm.

Our first glimpse of the island was uninviting. We first came upon a soldiers' camp and near to that an old disused house. These were the only signs of life we could see. All around was field upon field stretching for miles, it seemed. In the far distance could be seen the spire of Wakering church. The dull grey sky made everything seem bleak.

It was all great fun at first. The trenches were dug from the many pools of water to the nearest ditch. In the trenches we placed the earthenware pipes and then filled the trench. Water from the pools would seep through the soil into the pipes and hopefully run away to the ditches. We worked in pairs and were always eager to see if the pipes were doing their job. All over the field you could hear girls calling to each other, "Is your water running yet?" as they worked and waited for the first trickle of water to come through. There were about 300 acres of land waiting to be drained and it looked as if we would be there for months.

At first we spent our lunchtime out of doors but found it too cold, so the empty house was looked into. What a relief it was after that to spend the lunch time in comfort around the fire. Every day we each brought a lump of coal from the hostel to light a fire. We bought wood from a shop near the hostel and it was a real treat to warm ourselves for an hour.

Six weeks passed very quickly, then one morning as we squeezed into the lorry, we noticed the sky was much darker than normal. We finished our morning's work and returned for the afternoon session, when suddenly it began to snow. We took no notice at first and carried on working until someone pointed into the distance and we saw the spire of Wakering church had disappeared. Within minutes we were in the throes of the worst blizzard I have ever seen. The foreman called a halt and ordered us back to the empty house. It was only a 20 minute walk, but it seemed to take us hours. The wind was whipping snow into our eyes. Our cheeks were stinging and we could hardly see a step in front of us as we struggled to get under cover. Even though the wind was blowing and the snow was being thrust upon us, it was deadly quiet.

I had read of people getting lost in blizzards and my imagination ran riot. I prayed that the ones in front of us would be able to find their way. After what seemed like ages, the house was before us. By this time we were thoroughly worn out. What a bedraggled lot we looked as we went inside. Our cheeks were scarlet and our hair white and wet, but how lovely it was to be safe.'

CHELMSFORD AND DUNMOW

'I joined the Land Army in 1942. I was stationed at Chelmsford and worked for the Essex War Agricultural Department. We were sent out in gangs of eight to farmers who needed extra help for harvesting, potato picking or hoeing, or any dirty job no one else would do. We worked in a radius of about ten miles from Chelmsford and returned each night to our billet (mine was in Springfield Road). I think Essex was about the first county to try the new-fangled combine harvester. I worked on it and was delighted to be chosen. When the Americans arrived in Chelmsford the Land Army were sent to Boreham to clear fruit trees so they could make runways.'

'I came to Dunmow as a land girl. We lodged in Ackroyd Avenue in a hut that housed 40 girls. Twenty of us slept on double bunks on each side of the room, heated by a burner in the middle. Breakfast was a bowl of porridge and half a sausage and we were given a packed lunch, usually two rolls and a piece of cake.

Our first job was working for Mr Wheeler who took us hedging in the snow on 7th January – the week before we had been working in London offices! On one occasion 20 girls were taken to a particular farm and the farmer looked us over and said, "I only wanted one and that one with muck on her face can go home."'

HAPPY DAYS

'Why did I join? Because the time was drawing nigh when I would be called up for one of the military services and a friend who was already in the WLA said that she could arrange for me to work with her among the "tomatoes in the greenhouses". I thought, "What a lovely job, inside when it rains!" Alas, it wasn't to be – it took nearly three months to gain an interview for the WLA and then another three before I was posted, by which time the tomatoes had ripened and been picked! So it was that I found myself on a very large poultry farm in Essex with several other raw recruits and a boss aptly named "Mr Chicken".

After a year with all these thousands of chickens, and as some of my good workmates had left, I decided to move and was very lucky to be taken on at a nearby arable farm which also had poultry, a large horse named Captain and two dear youngsters, twin boys. At the end of that first week the farmer put me on the tractor to drive through the sugar beet field whilst he and the Italian prisoners of war with their English "ganger" loaded up the truck behind me. They all laughed at me because I kept on letting the engine stop. "I'll learn," I wrote in my diary that night, and I soon did. Not only did we have Italians working on our farm, who were very happy-go-lucky, but later German prisoners of war who, unlike the Italians, worked hard, "keeping their noses to the grindstone", even though there was only one British soldier guarding them. We were even invaded by the British Army at times! It was allowed to take over a farm without notice it seemed, dump a gun or two and carry out manoeuvres. After they had gone we would find a few chickens and some eggs missing but who could blame them?'

A CHILD'S WAR

Children soon came to accept the changes in life as normal, though the reality of war was felt by those sitting for hours in air raid shelters.

NO JOKE

'As a 13 year old, listening to Mr Chamberlain's eleven o'clock broadcast, I could not comprehend why the adults looked so gloomy and worried. After all, this was the "big adventure", the one thing that could possibly disrupt school routine! Minutes later, a siren sounded. My father, a local policeman, was on duty in Romford so my mother and I rushed outside to be greeted by our neighbour who shouted, "Oh, my God – they're here!"

He and my father were in the process of digging a shelter in the garden, to be shared between the two families. It was then just a large trench, with no cover and with six inches of water in the bottom. Clutching our masks, we obeyed orders and leapt down into this open grave, along with other adults, three children and their dog.

The neighbour, a Mancunian, had fought in the First World War, and we bowed to his superior knowledge. So that, when he raised his head above the level of the ground, sniffed and cried, "Gas – put on your masks", we did so!

We stood there, feet and ankles wet, clothes covered in mud and mask visors all steamed up – cold, terrified and waiting for the end. My "big adventure" had suddenly turned into a nightmare.

Then, the all clear sounded and we slowly emerged. We were amazed to find that things were just as we had left them. But that false alarm had taught me that war was no joke and that life would never be the same.'

HOURS IN THE SHELTER

'During the war I lived at Ilford and we had the Morrison indoor shelter, which we used as a stage on which to perform our party pieces when I had birthday parties. I only remember sleeping in this thing a few times as it was not very comfortable. We preferred to go down the garden to the Anderson shelter, although it was crowded with Mum, Dad, me, my baby sister and my grandparents all sleeping in such a tiny area. If the greengrocer, baker or milkman happened to be near when the siren went off they would come down the shelter too.'

'I was at Westleigh school when the playground was dug up for air raid shelters. These were like tunnels underground, very dark and spooky although there was electric light. We would all have to troop down there with our gas masks on (fortunately only for practice at that time). It was always very damp with pools of water on the floor under the duckboards.

Later the school was evacuated and most of my friends went up to Derbyshire, but my sister and I remained behind. When the district was considered to be a possible invasion area and evacuation of everyone became compulsory, my father took a furnished house in Middlesex, but bombing there was much worse and after six months we obtained permission to return to Leigh on Sea. By this time all the empty houses had been requisitioned by the army and there were soldiers everywhere. We were the only civilians in our road. Schools, of course, were closed but eventually about a dozen children met every morning in a private house, where a retired teacher did his best to arrange some form of education.'

GAS MASKS

'One Saturday afternoon in 1938 my father said that he was taking Neil and me to get our "gas masks". We had no idea what they were (Neil was five and I was six) and although Dad spoke of it as an exciting adventure, the more he emphasised this the more scared I became.

On arriving at the library in Paglesham we approached some gentlemen sitting at tables, surrounded by stacks of brand new cardboard boxes approximately six inches square and a little less deep. There were hundreds of them. I am not quite sure of the procedure but I imagine we had our names checked off on a list, then we were each issued with a box with a size marked on the outside. Inside was a weird contraption made of black rubber with a little window and a round base of metal with holes in it: at the back were a series of webbing straps. We were taught how to put this thing on. "Hold the straps, put the chin in and slide the straps firmly to the back of the head," the gentleman said, as he checked that the straps were correctly adjusted. When we had them on we looked like unearthly monsters with grotesque pigs' snouts.

To demonstrate the efficiency of the gas masks we were all expected to enter the test van. This was a large grey van with a double set of doors. About twelve people entered the first compartment, donned their gas masks, then the doors were opened to the second compartment and we all passed through. When we were in this section the official told us to pull the masks from the side of the face for a few seconds to allow the tear gas to get into the mask, just to prove that ordinarily the mask would hold it out. I was always a coward and this time was no exception. I cheated. Instead of pulling the mask away I only pretended to. The whole experience was very frightening to me and I was only too pleased to be out in the daylight again.'

WAR EFFORT

'When I was about eleven I heard that Winston Churchill's wife, Clementine, was raising funds to aid Russian children. I got together with some friends my own age and we arranged a programme for a concert. Two brothers had a small musical group and they provided the accompaniment for my friend and me to sing and dance. Brentwood library was the source of some short play scripts. We rehearsed in back gardens and needless to say, as it was my idea I got all the best parts! The school carpenter, Mr Baxter, was in charge of the property box and stage scenery. When we felt ready we hired a small hall in New Road and sold tickets to our parents and friends and we put the show on. We duly sent off our contribution to Mrs Churchill and were delighted to receive a letter of thanks. Handwritten from Downing Street, it said: "I am most grateful to you for the trouble you have taken to help the brave Russians in their terrible struggle and in the glorious defence of their country." That letter remains a treasured possession.

NO SWEETS

'War to me meant no sweets, and looking in shop windows decorated with dummy chocolate boxes.

In the beginning we were sent home from school at Witham each time the siren sounded but in the end we took no notice of it. Planes flew over the town at night on the way to bomb London and we slept downstairs every night at that time. Sometimes we heard the whistle of bombs being dropped, a sound one does not forget, but they mostly landed in fields surrounding the town and next day we would walk our dogs and have a look at the craters. As children we watched the Battle of Britain overhead and planes coming down. I am so thankful I was too young to think of the young men dying.'

BOMBS AND SWINGS

'We were in Woodford Green throughout the war. We lived near the recently built Broadmead Bridge and as it was almost white in colour this was a source of worry, as on clear nights we felt that the German bombers would see it clearly and bomb it. There was a big gun that travelled up and down on the railway line and fired at the Germans planes, and it was comforting to hear it boom out. After an air raid, next morning all the children would go searching for shrapnel, to see who could find the largest piece.

We had to carry our gas masks with us all the time in square cardboard boxes. They soon became battered, so waterproof cases were made to cover them. I had a very sweet tooth and the one pound a month sweet ration soon went, so I bought Horlicks and Ovaltine tablets and Zubes from the chemist and kept them in the gas mask case.

For a time the schools closed and a teacher came to our homes, with four or five children attending from neighbouring houses. After a while, when they had reinforced part of the school, we started back part time.

The girl who lived next door to me is still a friend to this day. During an all-clear we would come out of the shelter and play on her garden swing. It was exciting on moonlit nights, but we soon hurried back to the shelter when the warning went.'

SCHOOL AND PRE-SERVICE TRAINING

'I had just started at the senior school at Becontree when the war broke out and, with the exception of myself and a few other children, the pupils and teachers were evacuated. For months those of us left behind popped along to the school twice a week for homework. Gradually teachers and children returned to their homes and school was resumed part-time: mornings one week, including Saturdays, afternoons the next. By then the school looked like a fortress. Baffle walls had been built in the corridors which consisted of brick walls spaced out about a yard apart built out from alternate sides of the corridors to just over half-way across the width – the idea being that, if a bomb dropped in the vicinity, the blast would be stopped dead in its tracks.

As soon as we left school we were encouraged to join a pre-service training unit. Favouring the WRNS I joined the Girls Nautical Training Corps (GNTC), eventually becoming a standard bearer and then a side drummer in the band, cycling to the Sterling Works factory at Dagenham for band practice with my drum slung over my back like a rucksack. We had an ex-Marine bandmaster to put us through our paces and put the fear of God into us as well.

By the time I reached Third Officer it was decided that all officers would have a day's gunnery training and we were detailed to report very early on a cold winter's morning to HMS *Crysanthemum* lying alongside HMS *President,* Captain Scott's *Discovery* and the *Wellington* at London's Embankment. We had taken some provisions and, after learning how to load and fire the ship's guns and attending a lecture, we were given tea in the mess. Naturally we flirted with the sailors – as the song goes "All the nice girls love a sailor" – and I certainly hit it off with one of the crew. As we were about to leave he surreptitiously popped into my pocket a small greaseproof-wrapped parcel about four inches by two by half an inch deep, with the confusing instruction, "Keep it under your hat". I had no idea what it was and it was too dark because of the blackout to have a peek as we travelled homewards. If only he had told me. When I got indoors I discovered what it was as I pulled a very deflated piece of greaseproof paper from my pocket. It had contained two ounces of lard – a week's ration of fat! The heat of my body had melted it, as the very greasy patch on my uniform testified.'

WARTIME GUIDING

'After a lapse of a few years I resumed Guiding in 1940, prompted by the thought that the activities would provide some lighter moments for the children of the village in the dark years of the war. I took over the 1st Hatfield Peverel Company which consisted of about 20 Guides. Our meetings took place in the laundry room at the back of the old vicarage in Maldon Road. The room, about 20 feet square, contained a large cupboard and a big open fireplace.

At the time I was working as a land girl on my uncle's farm, which was my home, feeding pigs, bullocks, cows and chickens. This meant I was able to purloin any commodity I thought necessary for the needs of the Company, ranging from logs and steamcoal for the Guide room fire to milk with which to make cocoa after a cold church parade.

During the first year we practised first aid and worked for a few badges. We were also given a small piece of the vicarage kitchen garden in which we grew vegetables and flowers, taking the results to the old ladies living in the almshouses. The visits from the children gave as much pleasure as the offerings.

Then, in the spring of 1941 our thoughts turned to camp. Mr B Blunt kindly said we could use his small field adjoining the Ulting churchyard by the river. Activity then became intense. We had no camp equipment and so we set about borrowing or making our own. Screening and paliasses were made from old sacks after being washed in a large dustbin. The water was heated by standing the dustbin on bricks over a fire. The fire shelter consisted of a large stack-cover drooped over a long pole, supported by smaller poles and guyed down on either side. Cooks were apt to emerge looking rather like Red Indians.

What proved to be a most efficient cooking stove was made by placing a large sheet of iron on top of two rows of bricks. On this we boiled dixies and a huge kettle, borrowed from the grandmother of one of the Guides, without the contents being tainted by smoke, the usual product of camp fires. Tents were borrowed but as they were white, had to be camouflaged with branches of willow as the locals thought they might attract German bombers. Rations were pooled but chickens, eggs, milk and fruit arrived from the farm (a very understanding uncle!) and as one of the Guides' grandad was the village baker, there was no shortage of bread.

For entertainment we went off on our bikes to Heybridge for bathing and paddling, accompanied by two large biscuit tins of doorstep sandwiches and several bottles of lemonade.'

I STAYED

'My brother was born at two o'clock in the morning of 4th September 1939. The midwife and doctor assured my parents that he was the first baby born in Chingford during the war. I do not think this was ever officially confirmed as I suspect there were greater things to worry about at that time. His arrival was not actually scheduled for another fortnight, but when war was declared my mother decided that, "It was better to get it over with". She swallowed a two ounce bottle of castor oil and Edward was born rather rapidly, in 20 minutes, weighing in at around five pounds and rather short of finger nails but otherwise apparently sound in wind and limb. Mother was quite keen on precipitating the birth of her offspring as she had applied the same treatment five years earlier in 1934 when she got fed up with carrying me around in an August heatwave.

My fifth birthday was on 18th August 1939. Presumably I should have started school but the school was evacuated. I can remember my parents telling me that I should go away to the country to be safe from Hitler's bombs. They tried everything to persuade me, including "Mr Churchill wants you to go". Even at five I knew how important Mr Churchill was. But I said I didn't care what Mr Churchill wanted, I wanted to stay with Mummy and Daddy. I stayed.

Eventually a house school was set up on two mornings a week and seven or eight children from the road gathered around the dining room table to begin our education from Miss Thekston. Later she married a local builder and became Mrs Stevens, but she always had a wave for her former pupils long after we had grown up.

The school at Kings Road eventually reopened as children drifted back from evacuation and presumably I was not the only five year old to defy the edicts of Winston Churchill. Having been to house school I was rather proud of not having to go into the "baby class" where they lay down on mats for a rest in the afternoon.'

LIFE IN BRAINTREE

'In September 1939, soon after I started at Braintree high school, on a Sunday morning, a lone German raider dropped a string of bombs, one of which demolished a bungalow in Cressing, and one fell on the garage opposite our school. It caused damage to the face of the building, so to the delight of most of the pupils we were given a week off school.

Being at school during the war was very restrictive, especially on movement from place to place. We were not allowed to stay after school for social activities, we could not play hockey or tennis matches against other schools. We did very little practical cooking, because of rationing. Once we were taken to the local swimming baths, but because of an outbreak of polio (then known as infantile paralysis) we were never taken again. One day I got into trouble with the headmaster for going to my grandmother's house (opposite the school) instead of going home on the school bus. However, if we had misbehaved, we still were given Saturday morning detentions!

There were compensations, such as being allowed to wear fawn lisle stockings instead of thick black woollen ones, and we had a gym mistress who occasionally would allow us to play pirates on the rope ladders, or give us ballroom dancing lessons. Quite often classes were interrupted by air raid warnings, but on one occasion during the time of the doodlebugs we were in the middle of our school leaving exams, so we were told to carry on with our art exam.'

NO MORE

'Although I was only eight when the war ended I shall never forget the euphoria. No more air raid warnings (the sound of the siren still turns my stomach); no more ducking when you heard an aeroplane. No more gas masks, scrim, blackout – the long period of darkness was over and how we celebrated! Street parties, Victory concerts, and a huge feeling of neighbourliness because we'd all come to rely on each other to get through. And at last, instead of receiving letters from him, my father was coming home – though, sadly, not all our friends were so lucky.'

THE EVACUEES

Children were very quickly evacuated from areas thought to be enemy targets and some of them found a wonderful new life in the country, though experiences were not all good – on both sides!

FROM GRAYS TO FELIXSTOWE

'On 5th September 1939 the children of East Thurrock school, Grays, were evacuated. I was one of them. We had been recalled early from our summer holiday and had been given a list of things we had to pack: a change of underclothes, nightwear, washing items, one toy, a gas mask, and a packet of sandwiches for lunch. Each child had to be able to carry his or her own case.

We gathered at the school with some excitement although the sight of parents crying was disconcerting and unsettling. We were "labelled" with our names and school name securely tied on before climbing aboard charabancs. When we set off, we knew we were being evacuated but no one bothered to tell us what that meant! We arrived in Tilbury and embarked on one of the pleasure steamers. It was a beautiful sunny day and became very hot. All of us had been told to wear a coat and I was proudly wearing a hat to match my coat *and* a much-loved fur tippet, so I was sweltering in the heat! Children were crying now that they appreciated the fact that Mum was getting ever further away as we sailed down the Thames. Many were sea-sick too and the memory of that journey to Felixstowe remains vivid as sounds and smells!'

IN CHARGE OF ORGANISING

'My mother was in charge of organising the evacuees in the Boxted area. She felt we should take in a family of four. The eldest boy was nine, the youngest girl was four and had fits. They'd never slept in a bed – always underneath. They were a bit difficult I think, but they were nice children. The worst moment was when they left. They had started to enjoy being here and were given proper food. They had never sat down to a meal – just given a penny and told to go and buy whatever was at the end of the street. Of course, they were immediately put under strict control by the servants to do this and the other. They loved it. When the invasion was threatened in 1940 they were ordered back to London. Their mother came to fetch them in a car or a taxi, and there was the *most* dreadful scene. I can see it now, outside the front door. The children were screaming because they didn't want to go, the maids and ourselves were weeping because we didn't want to see them go, the mother was screaming at us that we had stolen their affection.

My father was commanding an ack-ack battery. At one time his office was in Boxted House which had been requisitioned. My father was inclined to be a *little* eccentric, and when there was a westerly wind he got on his bicycle and used his golf umbrella as a sail. The soldiers used to think this was a very peculiar thing for their Colonel to do.'

AN UNHAPPY EXPERIENCE

'I was away in the army. My wife had evacuees from Custom House, Tower Hill – full of nits they were. The mother and two children came. She was there all day and helped herself to what she wanted. The children were too young to go to school. They didn't enjoy country life. This woman's husband came down every weekend – he took stuff out of the garden and eggs to take back to London – just helped themselves. They were with us several months, then went back to London. My wife had to burn all the bedding. We didn't get paid for it – just paid for the food. "They" just came round and said "you'll have them".'

TO DEEPEST RURAL ESSEX

'When war with Germany was declared I was 13 years old and my sister eleven; our brothers were six and two. Because of the two year old's tender age, Mother was allowed to be evacuated with us.

The morning of 3rd September was fine and sunny following a wildly stormy night; many folk judged it an omen. I remember waiting with other families at the local primary school in Woodford, Essex, the chosen assembly point for intending evacuees, where a fleet of empty buses awaited us. My father looked pale and strained. Some people were tearful. Then, at 11 am the news came through from Westminster that Britain was at war with Germany. We knew then that we must leave Woodford. Suddenly, an air raid siren began to wail. We had been initiated already into its significance, but now it seemed threatening in its urgency, and we were scared. Soon we were boarding one of the buses and waving goodbye to our now tearful father. I had never seen him crying, and it made a deep impression on me. Mother was crying too.

The journey proved long and wearisome as we headed for "an unknown destination". Our first substantial stop was on Maldon Hill and by this time we were hungry and very thirsty, our small supply of food and drink long since used up. A few families were taken off, and the remaining passengers offered a welcome drink of water. At this juncture, a uniformed, bespectacled nurse boarded the bus. Without preliminary comment, she shouted from the platform, "Are there any pregnant women in here?" The effect was startling. Such an unabashed public utterance – particularly in front of children – belonged to an era yet to come. Mother was not the only one to express her outrage.

The journey then resumed, and it seemed an age before we arrived at our final destination – the village of Goldhanger, deep in rural Essex. By now, it was late afternoon. We were escorted into the village hall and told to sit in our family groups with our belongings. There had been no further refreshment since the drink of water at Maldon Hill, and we were hungry, thirsty and very tired; Mother looked exhausted. And yet I cannot recall feeling anxious at this stage; the day was turning into something of an adventure, at least for my sister and me and, after all, we had Mother with us.

Eventually, some of the local people arrived, spoke to those in charge and then moved among the assembled families and, in a curiously improvised way, began leading them away to be billeted. After a little while, only our family remained; five people were not easy to accommodate in the usually small village homes. It was the local policeman and his elder daughter who finally came to our rescue. Mother told us later that she had felt as if we were like cattle being looked over in a cattle market. Such a vehemently distasteful impression was in no sense the fault of the decent country folk who generously opened their homes and their hitherto undisturbed lives to total strangers.

Leaving the village hall with our new hosts, I recall walking to the centre of what proved to be a tiny, and to us unbelievably rural, village. I was enchanted. We then turned into the main street with its church and tiny school, and eventually stopped outside a pretty, weatherboarded, double-fronted house. This was Lavender Cottage – aptly named, since lavender bushes bordered the central pathway to the door – and there at the door was the policeman's wife to greet us.

Our hostess cooked our meals each day. She also counselled Mother from time to time on country ways: who was who in the village – namely, the landowning farmers (as opposed to the rest); where to shop in Maldon on market days; and how Tolleshunt D'Arcy – a village a few miles distant, where she had once owned a small business – was far superior to Goldhanger in every respect. She especially enjoyed Father's visits at weekends, when he would joke with her and they would have animated conversations.

From our perspective, the impact of living in a tiny village, probably little changed for generations, was striking. Amenities we had taken for granted in Woodford – mains drainage, gas supply, variety of shops, frequent buses – were simply not available. The village bus was a daily affair. A butcher, a baker, a general store met the everyday shopping needs of the community. Nevertheless, for us children the village and its surroundings held the prospect of exciting explorations during the sunny, late summer days. The sea wall and beach by the Blackwater estuary were favourite haunts but there were also the delights of wandering the lanes and meadows and discovering a rich variety of wild flowers. House martins were still busy in the cottage eaves, and I remember the magic first discovery one late evening of glow-worms. Then, there was the novel sight, for children brought up in suburbia, of a herd of cows on their twice daily journey past our cottage gate to be milked. Less pleasing were the swarms of cowflies that accompanied them, and frequently found their way into our bedroom – one of several occurrences that quickly made us realise that not all the sights, smells and experiences of country living were going to give us pleasure. Another bedroom visitor – a bat – caused us great excitement before he escaped into the night air.

Among other fragmented memories of newly found pleasures are the sight of the village blacksmith shoeing the big farm horses that worked the land, the buying of fresh walnuts from that same blacksmith (they grew on a beautiful tree outside his forge) and buying the local, luscious D'Arcy Spice apples from a little lady who grew them in her garden. Her long, untidy hair and eccentric manner somehow belied the incredible neatness of her wee cottage, bright with polished copper and brass and full of interesting and – to a child – magical objects. When she weighed out the apples, she was at pains to tell my sister and me that she always gave good weight – and she did.

Goldhanger had two pubs, an old church with hand-pumped organ and, opposite the village store, the water pump. We often saw older lads drawing water and assumed their homes lacked any supply. There was a two-classroom, two-teacher primary school which one of my brothers, my sister and I attended; she and I only briefly because we were already secondary age. I recall doing gas mask drill in the playground, but as yet, there was no sign of war. Indeed, several families had already returned home, unable to cope

The VE Day party in Hope Road, Benfleet reflected celebrations held in towns and villages across Essex.

with the quiet, seemingly uneventful village life, and no doubt lulled by common talk of a "phoney war".

One day, our hostess announced with considerable assurance that she had it on good authority that the war would be over by Christmas! Father thought otherwise, and so after nine weeks, we moved across the village from Lavender Cottage to a rented bungalow. Furniture, including our piano, was sent down from the Woodford house. We were to remain in our new home for over two years while my father kept our proper home going and worked as a representative for Hovis Limited with a territory that covered some of London's East End.'

A CHANGE IN LIFESTYLE

'I was seven years old in 1939 living in Wood Green, North London, with my parents and younger sister. I attended White Hart Lane school. Evidence of war preparations was obvious as a barrage balloon unit was stationed adjacent to the school. Mother attended a local baby clinic with my sister and had already placed our names on the evacuation list for mothers with young children.

After returning from our August seaside holiday at Whitstable in Kent my parents were informed of the forthcoming evacuation. Mother was told to report to a certain road where London Transport double-decker buses waited. Fortunately, mothers with pre-school children joined the White Hart Lane pupils and teachers but our destination was not revealed to Father or our other relatives who had come to wave goodbye before going to build an air raid shelter in Grandmother's garden.

The buses drove through Epping Forest where low tree branches rattled against the roof. The boys said it was machine gun fire and I hid under the seat. We stopped for a mid morning break and were told that war had been declared.

Eventually we ended up in Halstead where we were billeted with a local family. I cannot remember a great deal about this time except the very poor cramped conditions, catching head lice and having Yorkshire pudding with gravy before the main course. We moved from this billet to another and with the help of this kind family we found our own cottage to rent. I must add that this cottage was empty because it had been condemned as unfit for habitation.

What a change in our life style. In London our house had indoor sanitation, a bathroom with a gas geyser, a gas copper for washing clothes and what was nice for me, we had an upstairs verandah. Now we were in a tiny cottage with a shared toilet at the end of the garden and to reach this we had to pass another cottage. Not much of a convenience, particularly in the blackout. There was only one cold water tap, no bathroom, no electricity upstairs, undulating brick floors, a coal cupboard under the stairs and the plaster on the walls had a forest of horsehair apparently growing out of it.

At first we shared this cottage with another family of evacuees but eventually we took over the whole cottage. I was intrigued by the two staircases and we were told that originally this tiny building had been two back-to-back dwellings. It is incredible to imagine two families living in such cramped conditions.

Various relatives joined us to escape the bombing of London but returned when the cottage was damaged by a parachute mine. Obviously they thought London was safer. My parents eventually gave up the London house and we lived in the cottage for another 14 years before it was finally demolished.'

HIGHDAYS & HOLIDAYS

WE MADE OUR OWN ENTERTAINMENT

There seemed to be talent and enthusiasm in even the smallest village which enabled us to make our own entertainment, from drama groups to whist drives. Sports were popular in most areas and then there were the cinemas to visit once a week, an exciting night out.

AN ABUNDANCE OF TALENT

'There was always an abundance of talent in and around the village of Woodham Ferrers. Mr Castle had a concert party, and the St Roger Folk under Mrs Gregory Nicholson often came to entertain. Most of the events would take place in the school, but the Smallholders Hall at South Woodham would be used if a large number of people were expected. When the buses started to run to Chelmsford in the 1920s we went to the silent films. A pianist would play the appropriate music for the action on the screen and this was part of the pleasure.

Most of all I remember the magic lantern evenings at the Congregational chapel schoolroom. I was "church" but always went along and marvelled at the pictures of foreign countries. Sometimes we would come home with black smuts on our faces when the lamp had smoked! We had a crystal set at home to receive broadcasts, then we had a wireless. This needed an accumulator and these needed charging each week and were collected and taken to the old mill at East Hanningfield. Father made a little wooden case with a leather handle for each one for easy carrying.'

THE INSTITUTE

'A few months before an ex-army hut, donated to the recently formed WI was erected at Great Horkesley, I was born next door, at Wistaria Cottage. My mother was a founder member, and being a pianist with a lovely voice was actively involved with WI and village entertainment, so that I have memories of the "Institute". as it was known, from my earliest days.

Being the only public building of any size, all indoor social activities took place there. I particularly remember the "drill" classes for children of all ages, the Scout suppers, concerts, wedding receptions and, of course, the highlights of village life in those days, magic lantern shows for the children, and whist drives and dances for the grown ups. It was on its stage that I gave my first recitation, and played a small part in a Mabel Constanduros play.

The hall was heated (somewhat unevenly, I seem to remember) by a tortoise stove at either end, and until electricity came to the village in the mid 1920s, it was lit, and water heated, by paraffin oil. To this day the smell of paraffin reminds me of the "Institute" and the taste of the tea.

A visit to the spidery outside "lavvy" at the back of the hall was an experience undertaken at night only in the direst need, and then only if "two or three could be gathered together"! The huge chestnut trees nearby which provided such a rich harvest of conkers in the autumn could moan and whine frighteningly on a windy winter's night, and cast eerie shadows on moonlit nights.'

DANCES AND SOCIETIES

'Entertainment locally at Laindon meant regular dances in one or other hall, perhaps the Memorial Hall (built after the First World War), the Crown Hotel or the church halls. Various societies met, such as the Laindon Operatic and Dramatic, the Laindon Players drama group, and church youth clubs. Occasionally in the early days there was a magic lantern show in St Mary's church hall at a penny a time, and then there was the cinema, built in the 1920s – sixpence for the front row.'

THE ILFORD OPERATIC AND DRAMATIC SOCIETY

'The Ilford Operatic and Dramatic Society was founded over 100 years ago as the Ilford Social Club by W.W. Jacobs, the author, who had a get-together with friends in the kitchen of a meeting house in Ilford – now long gone. My family were musicians, some professional, and were involved in the orchestra from its early days. My mother was the accompanist for rehearsals at the age of 15, before the First World War. The society was reformed and renamed after that war, and I was allowed to go to the dress rehearsals from a very early age, as this was considered part of my musical education!

At 13 I was promoted to programme seller, and the job was done in style at the Ilford town hall. Full evening dress and gloves in "front of house". At 15 I became a rehearsal pianist, and at 16 I was on the stage. Rehearsals were at a local school, and were taken seriously. We worked hard for months and the reputation of the society ensured pretty full houses always.

The end of the season was celebrated by a dinner and formal dance at the Liverpool Street Hotel. Again full evening dress and gloves for everybody, a formal reception, and dancing led by the President and his lady. This was elegant living, but the tickets for the occasion were only one guinea each, and everybody went up by train. Steam trains can't have been that clean, but I don't remember anyone suffering much.

Dressing up didn't have to cost much either. There was in Ilford one of a chain of "Guinea Shops", and we bought dresses there. I remember a pretty white net dress with a very full skirt for myself, and my mother in gold taffeta from the same shop.

They were not all town people involved in the presentation of plays. We lived in Chigwell in the early days after the First World War, and my parents (before my time) would gallantly set forth for at least a mile's walk down a muddy lane to catch a bus to Ilford.

PART OF VILLAGE LIFE

'Concerts were part of village life at Great Yeldham. Indeed, I suppose the seeds were sown in the home when visitors would always listen to our latest recitation, or laboriously played tune on the piano, usually rewarded by a coin. We looked forward to these occasions, particularly to one more affluent uncle who would produce a shilling, and even sometimes half-a-crown. Riches indeed.

For concerts, the village hall – in the case of Yeldham, the reading room – was always packed with an enthusiastic audience. Mainly the seats were wooden forms, no one seemed to mind. Everyone who could do anything, did it. We particularly liked a Mr Napier from Hedingham, who played tunes on a saw. Then there was usually a shadow play – "The Operation"' very common, various groups of people sang, children from the dancing class performed, usually there was a monologue, and I remember one pianist insisted on playing at each concert a very long, very boring classical piece.

One musical item which has always remained in my memory was a skit on *Rule Britannia* by a group of rather large, bossy ladies, and they sang with great gusto the chorus "Marr-i-ed to a mer-mi-ed at the bottom of the deep blue sea". Some wit remarked, "God help the mermaids.'

There were lots of whist drives too, both progressive and partner; these were held in village halls – not very well heated then. I can remember going to one and playing without taking off any outer garments (except gloves), and in fur-lined boots, and our breath condensed as we breathed. The interval cuppa was very welcome! Sometimes, a drive would be held in one of the big houses, then there really was a full attendance. Not only was it likely to be warmer, but it was a good opportunity for those who would not see the interior of the house any other way.

The village social was another event, held in the village hall, or the school if no hall; it was always well attended. We would often sit on the school desks pushed against the walls if necessary. There would be party games, individual and team games, a few dances, perhaps entertainment by some talented parishioners, and refreshments – probably all non-alcoholic, no one seemed to mind, and whatever could be rustled up to eat. There had to be an MC who would be responsible for getting everyone to join in, sometimes quite a task with the shy country lasses and lads. I wonder how many courtships were begun at these events. Everyone would dress up, and the girls perfumed themselves liberally with "Evening in Paris" or "Californian Poppy". At the beginning of the evening, all the girls would stand giggling and whispering on one side of the room, and the boys awkwardly on the other, and it took all the efforts of the MC to get them fraternising.'

COMMUNITY SPIRIT

'There was a great community spirit in Tiptree in the 1940s and when we moved there in 1940 I soon got to know people through the chapel. The church had a Guide troop and Scouts, while the chapel had a Boys' Brigade and a Girls' Brigade. The boys had a band which was a great attraction. It wasn't long before my father and the minister had started a guild which kept us all together at the different meetings we went to, and to the monthly social. Quite a few of the girls were asked if we would like to join the Tiptree Amateur Dramatic Society (or TADS for short) and the first play we were going to put on was *Dear Octopus*, which had a very large cast. I was thrilled, being about 15 at the time. Unfortunately the leading man was called up and it was all cancelled! We did finally do the play after the war with a different cast.'

FLANNELS AND HOPS

'When I lived at Barkingside I belonged to the church AYPA (Anglican Young People's Association). In the summer we had dances called "Flannels", in the winter the dances were "Hops" – all at sixpence. Unfortunately they had to end during the war when all the young men had been called up.'

CLUBS AND CRICKET

'As children in the 1950s we passed our evenings playing cards or board games and listening to the wireless. It was infuriating when the battery or accumulator was running out; our ears would be glued

Fancy dress parties at the Wickham St Paul Institute were always popular in the early 1950s.

as close as possible to the set so as not to miss the end of something exciting.

When we were eleven we could join the youth club in the village institute at Wickham St Paul. This building had corrugated tin sides and roof and was heated by a black coke stove which was not too good when it smoked from the wind! In the poky kitchen there was a stove for heating water. The toilet was a little hut outside. Sometimes on Saturdays they held social evenings or fancy dress parties for the village. The hall was packed and the wooden floor vibrated with the dancing and games. Music came from a wind-up gramophone and records. Later came works dances with rock and roll. We tried to dress in the period and bought all the latest records.

At weekends we watched our cricket team with my friend's mother making the teas from her house. On 5th November there would be a bonfire on the green. Someone would make the guy and we'd form a procession at one end of the village with the guy on the back of a truck. Our torches were tin cans tied to sticks and packed tight with straw. We'd march to the green and, when the fire was lit, the guy was hoisted to the top with a big cheer and fireworks would be let off. Afterwards we would have tea and baked potatoes from the fire. A man from the village used to organise outings to the pantomime in Colchester and trips to Clacton or Walton.'

AROUND THE CHURCH

'Village life at Fobbing, where I came to live in 1910, revolved around the church, St Michael and All Angels. During the week there was choir practice, a girls' club and Red Cross meetings, the latter being held at the rectory by the Rev Gardner. This gentleman also started the Fobbing and Corringham Women's Institute. There were social evenings held in the old schoolroom situated in the churchyard – the church organist supplied the music and plays were also organised. There was a social evening for the elderly at Christmas. We played tennis on the Fobbing marshes and the men played cricket. Whist drives were great social events. Fobbing then had a village pond on which we would skate in the winter.'

THE EPPING FORESTERS CRICKET CLUB

'The Epping Foresters Cricket Club was formed shortly after the war. My father was captain and I used to score for the team at weekends. We travelled mostly by car, and would play village teams far and wide in Essex: Potter Street, Matching Green, Debden, North Weald. At Matching Green there was a lovely old pub facing the pitch,and as soon as opening time came round the cry would go, "They're up" and every outfielder would quickly have a pint beside him on the grass. The team members were drawn from all walks of life, and there was a great spirit in the club. The Foresters' ground was made by the members, after negotiations with the Epping Forest Conservators, from an area of swampy tussocky land; this was cleared and turfed and eventually turned into a fine playing surface. At first they changed in a tent, but later it was possible with the help and participation of all the members with their different skills, to make a pavilion. Here we had to shelter when the rain was too heavy, until one of the players would decide that it was "fairing up", and the game would resume.'

SPORTING LIFE

'When a piece of glebe land was offered to Great Bardfield as a tennis court by the parish council, we teenagers were delighted. With the assistance of District Nurse Wilding, who lived here in a tiny cottage, we got the plot in order, cutting grass, wiring in and marking out. Thus the Bardfield Tennis Club was formed, and it wasn't long before we were arranging matches with Thaxted, Finchingfield and other clubs. What a pleasure this sport was, every evening after I had done my homework and helped to pick the soft fruit!

Before the last war and after, when Mr Letts owned Little Bardfield

Punting on the river was great relaxation for these girls from Great Bardfield.

Hall, a local cricket team played on the Hall meadow. With Egerton Letts as captain, the men and lads were very accomplished. Football and hockey were played too, but on any meadow available as there was no pitch. The worst possible "pitch" for the combined Bardfield and Finchingfield hockey players was in the "halfway" meadow along the Finchingfield road. A mixed team of lads and girls contended with molehills and cowpats. We children knocked up a few runs at cricket in Piper's meadow. There had been cows there too. Sometimes we played rounders there, or in the road as there was hardly any traffic.'

'Traditional country sports have played a major part in Boxted life. Boxted Hall and Rivers Hall were important shooting estates and Lt Col Guy Blewitt was master of the Essex and Suffolk foxhounds for a number of years between the wars. Several of the local gentry followed the hounds and all this sporting activity provided a lot of permanent and part time jobs in stable and kennel.

Boxted has always managed to run well supported cricket and football clubs. The older men and some women went to the pub of an evening and played darts, dominoes and shove ha'penny. The cinemas in Colchester, particularly on a Saturday evening, were a strong draw for the young. By and large people entertained themselves instead of expecting someone else to do it for them.'

'The cricket team at Great Canfield excelled under the guidance of the Rev Maryon Wilson in the 1920s, and football matches against High Roding and other local villages regularly took place on the park, opposite Fitzjohns. Girl Guides and a darts team were also organised by the Reverend, as well as swimming in the lake at the bottom of Fitzjohns Road. A visit to the cinema meant travelling to Dunmow, but whist drives were held in the church hall and cribbage and dominoes were often played.'

'Every Easter Monday the Essex Farmers Hunt held their point-to-point at Stow Maries, on the site of the First World War aerodrome. This later went to Beeleigh Abbey and is now held at Marks Tey.'

WINTER SPORTS CHINGFORD STYLE

'Looking back, we seemed to have more snow when I was a child. The great occupation on snowy weekends was tobogganing. Although Pole Hill was known as the highest point in Essex, those who were really old hands knew that Yardley Hill, beyond Pole Hill, was far superior for tobogganing. It was steeper and did not have a fence or road at the bottom. The snow soon became packed down into a good icy toboggan run. There was a ditch at the bottom with a bridge and if you steered carefully you could cross the bridge, or if you were really lucky (or was it skilful?) you could hit the ditch just right and jump it. The most likely result of this strategy was to end up in a tangle of arms and legs in the ditch. As I was only twelve in the long snowy winter of 1947 I did not realise that this must have been a most desirable situation for many of the young people taking part in the "Winter Sports". Ah, the innocence of youth in the 1940s!'

GOING TO THE CINEMA

'Seventy years ago my family moved to the Dagenham council estate near the old Dagenham station. The estate expanded rapidly and was joined by a private estate built to accommodate families moving to Essex because of the Ford factory. An elegant cinema, the Princess, went up, much superior to the old Grange at Chequers Corner. In those days one saw a first rate stage show in addition to the films. The manager in evening dress, the uniformed doorman and a smart restaurant were all part of this leisure activity enjoyed by almost everyone.'

'In the 1930s we went to the circus, pantomimes and variety shows at the Walthamstow Palace. From the 1940s there were lots of cinemas: the Carlton, Gaumont, Savoy, King's Hall, Plaza, and the

Granada where Reginald Dixon himself came up out of the stage playing the organ before the performance. From the 1950s there were Saturday morning pictures for children at some cinemas.'

'The bus took us to Maldon on Saturday afternoons in the 1930s to visit the shops and picture house, which was later replaced by the Embassy, a very imposing building after the old one. It had a Wurlitzer organ which rose from the floor amid coloured lights. There was a very good restaurant above for a special treat of tea if we could afford it. It cost one shilling and threepence to go to the pictures. Later Colchester became our nearest town and weekly shopping included a visit to the cinema, where often a stage show was included.'

'There was a dance hall on Canvey Island in the 1930s, and a children's cinema for twopence where we had to sing *Onward Christian Soldiers* before the film started. We had "Lassie" type films and serials to keep us going for the next instalment. Our main local cinema had an organist and stage shows all for sixpence. The local theatre was a music hall where we as a family went to the pantomime on Boxing Day.'

FIRST RADIOS AND TV

'My Dad's first wireless was with the "cat's whisker". You had to tread quietly across the room otherwise the cat's whisker jumped off and the sound went. You daren't make a noise while the radio was on.'

'Short cine films were our entertainment on special occasions – Felix the Cat and the Ink Spots shown on a rickety screen indoors, until my uncle made a cat's whisker wireless. We children were entrusted with exchanging the "dead" accumulator battery for a new one at a shop in Chadwell Heath on Sundays, but were told "not to run" as it was the Sabbath! Later we enjoyed listening to the bands and *Henry Hall's Guest Night*, sitting by a roaring fire with our Mickey Mouse comics.'

'Accumulators always loomed large in our life – the charging of. Horrible things, they had to be kept upright at all times so the acid didn't spill on our clothes or person. They came in all shapes and sizes and they stood on the cross beams of my father's garage at Great Yeldham, wires leading from each to the other right back to the battery charger. We children soon learned to test them for customers, for as soon as it was ready, each one had to be changed for an "empty". Very few people could afford to have enough so that they could use their wireless all week, so on Monday and Tuesday there was an influx, all to be charged, for picking up on pay day, usually Saturday, and so the owner could listen to the football results, *In Town Tonight* and *Music Hall* on Saturday, and *Monday Night at Eight*, plus news bulletins. *Henry Hall's Guest Night* was another favourite. Charging prices varied from twopence to fourpence, and then had to go up gradually until the largest were eightpence. Some people had special carriers which made life easier, they had to be treated with such care. It was a major disaster when the plates would no longer hold the charge – with money so short, a replacement had to be saved for.'

'We were the first in our road at Romford to have a television in the 1950s. For some time everyone crowded in to watch. If the room was full people stood outside and looked through the window.'

HOLIDAY TIME

Who needed foreign parts when they could have the wonderful Essex seaside resorts. Holidays were few and far between for many families between the wars, but we made the most of those we had. And of course there was the other side – the memories of those who worked hard to make those holidays such a pleasure.

I WAS THE LANDLADY'S DAUGHTER

'The charge was sixpence, old pennies of course. For that, a boy would take your luggage, stack it on the trolley he'd nailed together out of old planks and wheel it to your destination at Sea View or Beach Villa. Those boys who gathered outside the station at Clacton on Sea every Saturday morning throughout the summer in the 1950s did a roaring trade. None of our visitors had cars. By the time they'd rattled down from Liverpool Street, squashed in a crowded compartment, they were only too pleased to have someone else take over the bags.

Holiday luggage was solid stuff in those days: no airline weight limits then. Your 1950s holidaymakers, sitting at last on bulging cases, had packed everything they could think of, with the seriousness of an Arctic explorer. When you were leaving home for a whole fortnight, every contingency must be foreseen.

"Visitors" we called them, sometimes guests, or holidaymakers, never tourists. They did not tour. Their modest holiday adventure was repeated year after year, always in the same format, sometimes even in the same town, the same house.

Dull enough by today's globe-trotting standards it may have been, but those visitors were the town's life, and from May to September it was wholly given over to them. Some houses opened for Easter; the big hotels had a Christmas trade, so did some of the guest houses. We never did. Oh yes, and "guest house" if you please, never "boarding house".

Such niceties were important, much cherished by the landladies who, through their all-important membership of the Hotel and Guest House Association, effectively ran what was – long before anyone thought of liberating us – a woman's town. Many of the landladies were widows. They found an at-home job more pleasant than going out to work. Forty years ago, a married woman did not expect, did not want, to work outside the home. Where there were husbands, they were seldom seen. It is not improbable that they slept in the garden shed.

That is no reflection on their wives. When the town was really full, around the all-important, uniquely profitable August Bank Holiday, families would let their own quarters and take to any available outbuilding. I would have a camp bed in the dining room among the chair legs, aware of the tables I'd just laid for breakfast, and listening to my mother chatting to the guests as they came back from their evening's entertainment. Not too late back. Doors were locked at eleven. I don't know what happened to late-comers. Indeed, I can't remember anyone having the nerve to *be* a late-comer.

It was a pleasant dining room, with French windows that could be opened onto a mini-terrace and rambler roses. Every Sunday morning, once I'd rung a handbell and the visitors had taken their places, I would appear and ask, "Porridge or cornflakes?" The visitor's answer determined his breakfast for the rest of his stay. Alterations did not happen. No one ever had the courage to "do an Oliver" and ask for a change. The rest of the meal did vary, by the day.

The first advice my mother had been given when she first considered the holiday trade was, "You must keep a good table." So, I suppose, she did – but it was the same table. Her menu, once established, was repeated exactly throughout the ten years. Presumably the guests liked it that way. Certainly many of them became our regulars – and that landlady was an anxious woman who had not received the first of next summer's bookings along with the Christmas cards from appreciative clients. And unless she could, by the first week in January, talk of her bookings she lost face with her peer group.

Through the winter the town lay dormant. The first spring sunshine brought the smell of paint, the sound of hammering. Repairs and redecoration were under way. There was a pleasant sense of communal effort. We were a community then. And single-minded. From May to September nothing would matter but the guests.

I could walk through our routine now, and it didn't differ much from that of other houses. I greeted each new intake with that "Porridge or cornflakes". Porridge in August – and there were always some takers. The cooked breakfast was expected and essential. Dinner – never lunch – was at one; high tea at six. Unimaginative English cooking was served – everywhere. The mere hint of a foreign dish would have emptied our dining rooms. We'd never heard of pizza, paella or pasta – apart of course from macaroni for puddings and spaghetti in tins.

The day began when I rang that little handbell, just before nine, while my mother hovered over the plates on the trolley which I would presently wheel to the dining room. The process was repeated at dinner and tea. I never stopped wishing we had a gong instead of that little bell. One is a great snob in one's teens – and a gong suggested hotels!

I can't remember just what we charged for this ample, if unexciting diet and the bleak accommodation that went with it. I do remember a great perturbation among the landladies when it was suggested that they might raise that charge, for an adult for a week, to £10. "Would the visitors stand for it?" They did. The charge would never include morning tea, left modestly outside your door, nor the evening coffee, which was such a nuisance to do and did keep you up so late.

Once a meal was over, guests scurried to their rooms, gathered up their morning's requirements and went out. Quickly. No one was allowed in the house between meals. That enforced exodus of the visitors, everywhere repeated, has become a standard joke, together with the rest of the rules. But those rules, fewer than the comedians would have us believe, were necessary and reasonable enough. Maybe some of the women were a little dragonish, but most of them were women alone and the house was their sole livelihood. The landlady's reputation and the condition of the furniture were both to be safeguarded.

All the same, we were guilty of persuading our guests out into the rain. One of my most persistent memories is of the holidaymakers, hunched in their raincoats, the children grizzling, the daring bikini never unpacked, prowling miserably in search of pleasure. You will know the town's advertising slogan: "Champagne air, rainfall rare".

Poetic licence, that was. But there were entertainments, ranging from the penny in the slot arcades to the shows. Those we had to see, so that we could tell our gullible clients, "Oh yes, just as good as last year, better really." We got free tickets for displaying the theatre posters. We advertised the summer rep too and, when old enough, I would spend my evening off there with a friend.

The school and guest house timetables dovetailed neatly; we needed little outside help. I think we normally had someone to do the heavier cleaning, and the washing up – though I seem to have done a remarkable amount of that myself. I was home well before tea time, and on Saturdays . . . well, that was room-cleaning, bed-changing day. That could be interesting. So often one would find, trustingly hidden beneath the mattress, the wallet. That would contain the precise amount of money needed to pay our bill. It was hidden, not for safety, but so that the money would not accidentally be spent in the excitement of the holiday.

That hidden money was safe enough, even though none of the bedrooms had keys and the front door was open all day long. No one locked their doors in summer; you could walk into any house, any room. It really was another world, another time.

Holiday expenses included, usually, a tip for me. I very soon learned how to position my curved palm so that a coin – sometimes a note! – could be pressed into it without embarrassment.

We were easily embarrassed in those days. No one had yet coined that useful word "loo". The "err-um", the "er . . . toilet?" or "bathroom" would be asked for in hushed tones. Our one bathroom, I'm sorry to say, contained the one toilet. The bath itself was seldom, if ever, requested. (Well, they'd all been in the sea . . ?)

The hectic Saturday morning also meant buying the "fancy pastries" that, along with the big roast, were a feature of Sundays. No one ever asked about a church or services.

The absence of a car did not trouble our clients. They had the coach trips, and some older visitors would still speak of "charrerbangs". (It was only years later that I discovered the actual charabanc!) The evening Mystery Tour invariably ended at the same country pub. During the day – need you ask? – they went to the Constable Country. We all had Dedham-and-Flatford carved on our hearts like Calais.

It was a surprisingly uneventful life. We had trouble, once, from two outrageously ill-behaved small boys; a girl was brought back nearly hysterical from jellyfish stings (they really can be serious); and an elderly gentleman removed himself to hospital with, he thought, a "dicky ticker". When I visited him there that evening, at the end of a busy day, he was sitting up right as ninepence, looking a good deal better than I felt!

Otherwise, well . . . It was a short season and September had to come. (No pupil was ever more pleased than I to be back for the autumn term – and a rest!) The landladies, happy, they would say, to have the town to themselves again, would settle down to their whist drives and go for walks along the front, always wearing a uniform of fur coat, headscarf and boots. They enjoyed the winter, and so did I. I've never lost my taste for the winter sea, or to be honest for the sea at any time. Certainly I'm never happy too far away from it.

The trade has gone now, the houses become old people's homes or sheltering discharged hospital patients. It's fashionable to make fun of the British Seaside Holiday, and perhaps those bleakly furnished, always unheated rooms were poor enough offerings for our visitors' one holiday of the year. But they had no Continental comparisons to make and somehow managed to enjoy themselves. Alongside that memory of holidaymakers in the rain I can set the picture of the beach by the pier, flower-bright with lazing people, playing children. Sometimes the sun shone, sometimes it all came right and then it really was just as your grandmother remembers it – happy!'

BY TRAIN TO THE SEA

'In 1905, for a day out at the seaside, the train fare from Colchester to Clacton was one shilling and threepence, children sevenpence halfpenny. On arrival our family immediately dug a large hole in the sand so that Mother could look after all the belongings.'

A day out at Clacton in 1905.

'We went by steam train to Southend in the 1920s, and boarded with a family in a private house next to the Kursaal funfair. There was a whole road of entertainment. Onions were frying in the windows, and sausages, and there were stalls with crabs, and whelks and cockles in little white dishes. Another year we went to Thorpe Bay, and another time to Shoeburyness, where we went cockling.'

A PLOT AT JAYWICK SANDS

'In the early 1930s my parents responded to an offer at the Ideal Home Exhibition and bought a plot of land at Jaywick Sands. This was to be a development of wooden chalets built to provide a weekend seaside holiday base, mainly for families living in the eastern suburbs of London. The whole estate was called "Brooklands", the name of a famous motor racing track before the war. Each of the roads was named after a make of car. Our chalet was in Bentley Avenue, but this did not mean it was grander than any of the others! It consisted of a living room, two double bedrooms, a "bunk" room (two bunks on each side, with a space in the centre, rather like a ship's cabin) and a kitchen. Steps outside led to an open balcony at first floor level. The only service laid on was electricity. Water was collected from a standpipe halfway down the road. An Elsan closet was situated at the bottom of the garden and because the chalets were only occupied intermittently a large "C" (for collect) was displayed outside when this service was required. The children were kept indoors – or sent to the beach when this "collection" took place.

The whole estate was built on the sea-ward side of the seawall, so occasionally after a high tide the whole area would be flooded and for this reason the chalets were built high on pillars. It was very exciting for me, a four year old, to wake up and find we were surrounded by water!

Every Friday evening in the summer we would pack up the car (a Bean, with mica windows and a canvas roof which leaked in the rain) with provisions and drive, at no more than 30 mph, from our home in Ilford through Ingatestone, Witham and Kelvedon to our second home. Even in those days Chelmsford and Colchester had by-passes. I always hoped that the level crossing gates at Alresford would be down so that I would get an ice cream, a twopenny brickette, from the "Wallsie" who used to ply his trade there. Bank holidays and summer holidays were spent there too. We had a wonderful carefree time. No sophisticated entertainment, just the beach and trips out into the countryside for picnics – and the weather was always fine.'

HOLIDAYS AT FRINTON ON SEA

'In 1945 the influence of the war years was still very strong at Frinton. It was possible to reach the beach only by a limited number of routes cleared through the barbed wire and, so I was told, land mines of the coastal defences. As far as I can remember, the beach huts had not yet returned in that first year, but by 1946 they were back in place. The routine of carrying down all the goodies for afternoon tea in the hut formed an important part of beach holidays, as no doubt it still does. We swam, built sand castles and elaborate sand villages for the sea to destroy and played French cricket. A regular sight from the beach were the brown sails of the beautiful Thames barges which were still carrying goods commercially up and down the east coast in the late 1940s.

There were still many American servicemen in the area and, aged nine years, I was roped in to help dispense tea and cakes in a church hall somewhere – very grown-up and glamorous it felt! Food rationing continued into the 1950s, so we had to take our ration books with us. We stayed with Mrs Oswald in a lovely flat over the International Stores and she cooked for us. On one occasion, my father picked some field mushrooms which he planned to have for a special breakfast. They disappeared into a frying pan with a week's ration of butter, but after cooking them, Ossie said, "I wouldn't touch them myself". After much discussion, discretion prevailed and into the bin they went, only for us to see identical fungi on sale in the grocer's. On a happier note, I had my first tastes of asparagus and sweetcorn during these holidays.'

MEMORIES OF LEIGH ON SEA

'I spent my childhood at Leigh on Sea. On the beach at Chalkwell there was a wooden structure which provided cover for a small stage where Uncle Sam and his Minstrels performed daily. Deckchairs were set out on the sand and the children sat on the beach. Halfway through the show, youngsters were invited on to the stage to perform. One day I took my courage in both hands and sang *Give yourself a pat on the back*. The winners were chosen by a show of hands and to my delight I came second. I remember getting a ball which never did bounce! Occasionally when there was a very high tide the theatre was awash – no shows on those days.'

PICNICS ON CANVEY ISLAND

'Among happy memories of my childhood when I lived at Leigh on Sea, I recall many occasions when my parents and I with two or three friends went to picnic on Canvey Island, before and during the 1920s.

In those days no bridge connected the island with the mainland of Essex at Benfleet. Instead, a man with a rowing boat would ferry passengers across when the tide was in, charging only a few pence. When the tide was out, one could cross the muddy creek by stepping stones.

If we had not too many things to carry, we would walk from Leigh Cliffs along the fields by way of Hadleigh castle to Benfleet. We knew there was a long walk ahead of us across the island if we intended to go to Shell Beach.

We liked to visit the village of Canvey where there were small round cottages built by the Dutch when they occupied the island after defeating our navy in the Thames in the 17th century. There was also an ancient well, with words from St John's Gospel carved into a stone wall round it.

Shell Beach lived up to its name – there were only shells and pebbles, no sand, but we bathed from there, modestly draping our bodies with large towels as we changed into what we called our "bathing costumes". My father used the conventional "University" bathing suit. My mother's and mine had nearly knee-length legs with short skirts. The voluminous skirts and long sleeves of pre-First World War days had long gone out of fashion.

We usually had ham and tongue sandwiches for this picnic lunch, with salad and fruit in season. Any plates or cups that we used we washed up in the sea afterwards. Tea or coffee or other drinks could be obtained from the one hotel nearby – Kynoch's Hotel.

A few bungalows had been built by 1921, and some of them took boarders. There was also a small camping site in one of the fields and in that year we hired a bell tent for a month, and also put up a small tent of our own. The weather changed from what had been an exceptionally hot dry summer to blustering rain, and after a gale split our own tent into three pieces one night, we returned home. Other campers collected winkles from the sea-covered rocks and boiled and ate them, apparently with no ill effects, but my mother could not be persuaded to allow us to do the same!'

ROYAL OCCASIONS

Jubilees and coronations were celebrated with enthusiasm all over Essex, and there were other royal occasions too – such as the visit by Queen Mary in 1938.

JUBILEE AND CORONATION IN THE 1930s

'The Jubilee in 1935 and then George VI's Coronation in 1937 brought an all-village event at Great Yeldham, and a large marquee erected on the recreation ground. There was a procession from the Oak Tree to the "rec" of all the folk in fancy dress. I was a crinoline lady on one of these occasions – crinoline ladies were thought very glamorous at the time, they appeared embroidered on many chair backs, cushions and tablecloths. All the children received a mug, and there was tea for them all, with jellies, which were only made then on special occasions. I remember getting very excited.'

Coronation celebrations in Western Street, Stratford in 1937.

'Jubilee and Coronation days were celebrated by the whole of Danbury village in a field opposite the Palace in Danbury Park. There was tea and sports and every schoolchild received a mug.

On Coronation Day it was wet, so the sports were postponed until the Saturday. My sister Mary and I went. It was about two and a half miles to walk. Knowing there was going to be a pig to try and catch for the ladies, our Dad said to Mary, "Don't forget to bring that pig home." She said, "I will Dad, and I'll call it Sally." She did catch it and called it Sally although it was a boy. Luckily my dad kept pigs so he had some food for it. After it was fattened up it went to market and made £2 5s. A good price in those days.'

GREAT DAYS IN RAMSDEN

'In May 1935 the country celebrated the Jubilee of George V. It was a great day in Ramsden. A May Queen (Elsie Pimborough) had been chosen and was crowned, attended by two little girls of whom I was one. The village was decorated, with a prize for the best house decoration in Church Road, and for the side roads; we decorated the end where it joined Church Road. We spent weeks preparing. Dad went off to committee meetings, my sisters sewed their fancy dress, we practised our May Queen crowning, and Mrs Sexton trained the other children in maypole dancing. It seems to me now that all the village came out in fancy dress for a long procession from the Fox and Hounds to Crays Hill school. I think the field opposite the school was used for the crowning, and sports events, but what made it really special was that a Mr Watson who lived on the hill by the river, and worked for a film company, filmed the whole day's events. Some weeks later we all went down to a hall behind the Castle in Wickford to see the resulting film. What a community spirit there was that day – and how we shrieked in recognition of everyone.

The Coronation in May 1937 of George VI was celebrated with equal enthusiasm. But it poured with rain all day and my only memories are of sugar sandwiches (bread and butter with sugar between the slices), and the colours in my Dad's jester outfit running so that his vest and pants stayed red one side and yellow the other until they wore out!'

QUEEN MARY AT BRIGHTLINGSEA

'I was a pupil at Brightlingsea senior school when Queen Mary visited the town on 13th June 1938. We lined the road to cheer her as she passed on her way to a civic reception. This included a visit to the quayside where she was shown some oysters, which she promptly prodded with her parasol! We lived at Thorrington on the

Queen Mary poking oysters with her parasol at Brightlingsea in 1938.

one road out of Brightlingsea, and my seven year old sister, home from the junior school in the village, waited on the side of the road for the Queen's car to come by. She was wearing some poppies, and as the car passed it slowed down and Queen Mary, with a nod of her head and a wave, acknowledged my sister's greeting. My sister never forgot getting a royal wave and the family weren't allowed to forget it either.'

CORONATION DAY 1953

'On Coronation Day those shops in Walton on the Naze which had television (not only the ones who sold them) put them in the window so that everyone could watch the proceedings. In the evening the town had its own procession, and on the Saturday we all had street parties.'

'The 2nd June 1953 will long stay in my memory, not least because it was the day our present Queen was crowned, but in particular because I was in hospital at the time recovering from an appendix operation.

Ten days before the great day, at the age of nine years, I had been

The 1953 Coronation brought more street parties, this one in Churchfield Road, Walton on the Naze.

taken into hospital with suspected appendicitis. In those days doctors were reluctant to diagnose appendicitis in children, so I spent over 24 hours before I had the operation. As a result I also had peritonitis and on my being taken to the operating theatre my parents were told to be ready for any news!

Rush Green Hospital in Romford was the only hospital in the district with a bed available. It was a very small cottage hospital and all the wards were in separate small buildings. On the great day many of the children had been sent home to enjoy the celebrations, but for those too ill to go out many plans were set in place on the ward.

Most families did not have television, but one of the children's fathers had access to a TV set that he would loan to the ward. All morning the excitement built up and come the appointed time all beds and chairs were circled round the TV. In those days televisions were not at all reliable and sure enough after about ten minutes from the start of the programme the screen went blank. A repair man was called, without success, and you can imagine the disappointment.

A special show had been laid on in the afternoon. I can recall many of the acts being children and from my bed I was absolutely enthralled. Tea with ice cream and other treats finished the day. (I believe another parent donated the ice cream.) All children were presented with gifts. I was lucky enough to receive a commemorative mug.

As I said at the beginning, I shall never forget the 2nd June as the day I missed the Coronation, but I was lucky to be taken to the cinema some weeks later to see the film version, which I loved.'

'I remember attending with my father, who worked in Whitehall. I slept on a camp bed in one of the offices, and we had covered seats outside the Abbey, where we heard the ceremony and saw the guests arriving in their coaches and on horseback, in the rain. Of course I remember Queen Salote of Tonga with her grey wavy hair, beaming and waving undaunted, and sitting opposite her the small ruler of another state; we thought he was probably her dinner. We sang the hymns and cheered with all the rest, and watched the film of the whole thing later.

In the meantime my mother, who had given me the ticket which she should have used, was running the Epping celebrations in the rain. There had been a considerable amount of preparation for the day, with committees deliberating and arranging food, transport, entertainment and competitions. The main event was a historical pageant, a procession of ancient and modern vehicles given and lent by local landowners and personalities, who sent their coaches and coachmen, landaus, traps, large cars and small bicycles. These were occupied and ridden by such people as Queen Elizabeth I and Sir Walter Raleigh! Afterwards there were refreshments and a fair for everyone's entertainment.'

CELEBRATIONS THROUGH THE YEAR

We looked forward to annual pleasures, some of which still survive though others have now long gone, such as Empire Day, celebrated on 24th May each year and known by every child in Essex since it promised a half day off school! Local fairs and flower shows were times of great enjoyment for the whole local community.

VILLAGE DAYS FOR THE CHILDREN

'On Ascension Day we all went to church at Danbury and had a service, taking flowers and eggs to be sent to Chelmsford Hospital, and the rest of the day was a holiday. On Empire Day 24th May, the young ones at school painted Union Jacks and the older ones wrote essays, for which we won prizes. Sports Day was in June in Major Hitchcock's field where the Mission is now. In July there was a fair and flower show in a field in Capons Lane, when we had another half day off school.

On Remembrance Day, 11th November, we walked down to the cenotaph, taking flowers if we wished, for a short service and the two minutes' silence, when everything in the village stopped.

At Christmas each school class produced a play which was held in the village hall for the parents.'

EMPIRE DAY

'We really looked forward to Empire Day when all activities centred around the village green at Writtle. All being well, we would be wearing our new ankle socks and sandals. Being on the plump side, I dreaded the sports and would try to hide in the crowd. On one occasion I recall our headmistress finding me to take part in the wheelbarrow race. My wheelbarrow was a very hefty lad so I had a double handicap! In the evening there was a competition for the older school lads, and others, to test their skills at walking across the greasy pole positioned over the village pond. This was very exciting and entertaining.

One of the activities on this day was for a number of us from Writtle council girls' school to sing a few well rehearsed songs, and for this we stood at the front of the boys' school at the top of the green. One of the songs was *Sweet lass of Richmond Hill*.'

CHELMSFORD CARNIVAL

'One of the popular events before the Second World War was the Summer Carnival held in Chelmsford. There was a procession which started in Rectory Lane and went right round the town. The procession was led by John Bull (Mr Fewell, I remember) riding a large horse. There were military bands, decorated cycles, prams and folk on horseback with hundreds of grown ups and children in every kind of costume, many collecting from the large crowds who lined the streets.

The apprentices from Hoffmanns, Cromptons and Marconi vied with each other for the best decorated lorries, *always* involving the throwing of water, flour etc, not only at each other but at the bystanders. The Scouts, Guides, and every organisation you can think of hired lorries, and their entries were imaginative and really attractive. All were encouraging the spectators to give their pennies. The trade part of the parade included all the firms in the town entering their lorries and carts, all beautifully cleaned and shining. The parade ended up in the "rec" (Centre Park) where the prizes were given out.

During the evening there were stalls and entertainment – a funfair and of course a firework display. There was a procession of decorated boats on the river after dark and little glass jars with candles floating in the water. As far as I can remember the money collected went to the Chelmsford and Essex Hospital.'

FLOWERS AND FAIRS

'Purleigh Flower Show was a field day for us children in the early part of the century. We all helped our parents to pick, clean and arrange fruit and vegetables. It was shown in a big tent and great excitement was felt in our family when our father got six first and four second prizes for his entries, and my mother got a first for her cooking apples. I remember once my brother, much to the disgust of us girls, got a first for his wild flower arrangement!

A fair was held just outside the Bell. Mr and Mrs Canham came from Maldon and erected a coconut shy, swingboats, a roundabout, and a stall on which Mr Canham sold home-made rock in raspberry, lemon and clove flavours, and also a delicious gingerbread.'

'In the early years of the century, Bardfield was noted for the horse fair held in Brook Street in June every year. It was called Bardfield Fair and ponies were even brought from Dartmoor. There were stalls with shellfish and other edibles down the unkerbed street, and a fair with roundabouts and swings in a meadow. This was traditionally the time of year to bake the first gooseberry pie of the season and to kill the backyard pig.'

THE LOCAL FLOWER SHOW

'Up and until 1939 our local flower show at Buckhurst Hill was held in marquees on a field loaned by Mr Charles Linder, whose son Leslie deciphered Beatrix Potter's diaries. This was a highlight in those days, being held on a Wednesday, early closing day. All the local tradespeople took part in various ways, when businesses were all family run. Children had the afternoon off school and took part in races and a variety of competitions. They were encouraged to collect and name wild flowers, which in those days were abundant. These were taken to the show site en route to school in the morning. This gained a child a free entry ticket, also anticipation of a prize when the awards were given. Boys made model gardens about twelve inches square. All liked to include a pond using a handbag or compact mirror.

A fair was always part of the event and I well remember the gypsy caravans with their shining brass and dainty lace curtains at the windows. With childhood curiosity I longed to see inside one but alas the doors were always closed, their owners busy earning their living.

For several years my late father in law won first prize for the best kept cottage garden, the runner up being the local policeman who was also a keen competitor. The smell of sweet peas takes me back to the floral displays of long ago. Towards the end of the day the produce was put up for auction, this being conducted by Mr Ambrose the local auctioneer. The money raised from this event was given to the Forest Hospital. The grand finale to the show was a spectacular firework display, so looked forward to and much enjoyed. On our way to school the next morning we would meet the gypsy children going to the shops for provisions before the fair moved off. We were blessed in those days to be able to roam at will in safety and took our freedom for granted. With the flower show of today being held in a hall the old excitement has gone.'

'The annual flower show at Great Yeldham was a most important event; there were open classes (those for people who had gardeners), cottagers' classes, domestic classes, and of course children's classes, usually collections of wild flowers, a miniature garden or a picture. The huge marquee would be crammed with a wonderful display of flowers, fruit, vegetables, eggs, jams and cakes. Everyone was very jealous of their own recipe for success. Teas and sideshows, and wonderful! a fair with roundabouts, swinging boats and coconut shy. Woe betide the father who was unable to knock off

Entrants in the Abridge carnival in 1946 – still relying on horse power!

a coconut. Also, in conjunction with the flower show, there was a tennis tournament. The big houses each had a grass court, the gardeners very anxious to produce a surface superior to everyone else. There were always a lot of entries, so a group would play on each court, American tournament it was called, where all in that group played each other, then semi-finals were played on chosen courts, and finally the final. It always seemed to be really dark when this finished. My father played, but I don't think he ever won. John Plat and Thora Tanner were usually champions, a very popular couple. These tennis tournaments were played throughout the summer in many villages, but now there are very few private courts, and flower shows don't have other attractions encompassing the whole village.'

'The annual flower show was always a big day at Broomfield in the 1920s, when nearly all the village took part, from babies to oldest residents, who were only too proud to show their vegetables and flowers and hopefully win a prize. Schoolchildren competed for the most number of wild flowers, or an arrangement. Races were organised, again for young and old, plus other sideshows.

Once a year the circus would come to town and it was the one morning we would be up early to watch the elephants go by, coming along the road from Braintree. Their keepers would have bags ready to accept stale bread for them to have a breakfast when they arrived at the King's Head meadow in Chelmsford where they were to perform that night.'

CHRISTMAS PAST

Even when we had very little, Christmas was a special time when families got together and the cares of everyday life could be forgotten for a while.

HAPPY FAMILY TIMES

'I was born in Epping in 1904 and came from a very large family – 15 children in all, so with our parents we made quite a houseful. Father was a farm worker, well respected and appreciated by his employers but very poorly paid. Mother was a wonderful lady, a friend and helper to everyone and the kind of homemaker who could make a meal out of very little. We didn't have luxury foods, but ate well and had nutritious and varied meals.

Our parents disciplined us with love and talked to us about our mistakes rather than slapping us, so that we all respected them and tried so hard to please them both. There was a real feeling of "togetherness" and I think that this was the solid foundation on which we all based our lives. When boyfriends and girlfriends came along our home was bursting at the seams. One Christmas there were so many of us that all the floor space was taken and we were sitting in pairs on the stairs! Mother played the accordion and sang and we all loved to gather round her and sing carols together.

The preparation time for Christmas was very exciting. We didn't buy decorations and couldn't afford a Christmas tree so we made our own festive streamers in the form of coloured paper chains, which we stuck together with flour-paste. There was always a competitive spirit as to who could make the longest chain in the shortest time – it was such fun. After we had finished making the paper chains we strung them around the room and placed berried holly behind pictures and mirrors. Now we were ready to celebrate Christmas! We all hung up a stocking on the lovely brass bedsteads on Christmas Eve. We were so excited next morning when we found our stockings bulging with gifts of an orange, apple and some sweets. The only time we received anything else was one year when an elder sister made us dolls from wooden spoons and dressed them with a handkerchief – what a thrill that was.

The food was very special although we didn't have turkey or chicken. Usually we had a piece of pork with all the trimmings and home-grown vegetables. There were always home-made puddings, and Father's wine. Tea time was a party-like meal with boiled bacon, cake, fruit and jelly – what a day! Christmas Day was always looked upon as a family day, but if 25th December fell on Sunday we would celebrate the next day, for Sunday was always a quiet day – Christmas or not! The neighbours always visited on Boxing Day and we had great fun playing darts, dominoes, snakes and ladders and ludo.

Bing Crosby's record of *White Christmas* takes me back in time to the snowy Christmases we usually had. Despite the snowy conditions, carol singers from the church and local brass bands – of which my brothers were members – toured the area. We attended Epping Congregational church which was normally full on Sundays and never missed the Christmas services.

Father's employers rented ten cottages for the farm workers from Mr Wise (known as the lord of the manor). He was very kind to the children and always invited the "under 14s" to a party at the manor house – Copped Hall, Epping. How we looked forward to this and especially the ride in the horse-drawn carriage which took us there. We could hardly contain our excitement as we entered the large room and saw the huge Christmas tree with all the parcels placed around it – no child was overlooked. After a lovely tea, we were taken home by carriage.

Times change and things are so different today. People have more money to spend at Christmas but I feel certain that no money can buy the kind of happiness and love that we shared.'

RABBIT PIE

'At Christmas time Granny would make a huge rabbit pie as a treat for all the family at Christmas morning breakfast. Being so large it had to be taken, with any other similar sized item, to the local baker's at Writtle for baking in his oven.'

TRAINS IN THE WINDOW

'I loved Christmas time when we had the shop at Walton on the Naze. We were the agents for Hornby trains and we set up a train in our main window and when the children came out of school we always had a crowd round the window watching it. This was very useful for mothers at Christmas, as while the children were busy watching the train go round, they were able to come inside and see about presents without the children knowing. If I thought one of them might follow their mother into the shop, I used to stop the train and make it go backwards or on to a branch line, so that they soon got fascinated and stayed outside.'

A CHRISTMAS CARD VILLAGE

'The snow fell gently making a soft carpet which glistened in the lamplight. This is the picture remembered of Aveley village at Christmastide over 60 years ago – when it always snowed at Christmas!

We were a self-contained community in those days when practically everything needed could be obtained in the village, which was always a hive of industry. A couple of grocery stores, a dairy, Mr Brown the baker, with bread baked on the premises., Mr Blows the butcher, Woolleys paper shop, which was a tiny establishment next door to the boot and shoe repair shop with its bow-fronted window, Mr Reader the taxi man, a drapery shop, dress shop, shoe shop and Johnny Clark's garage where we obtained our wireless accumulators for one shilling. We had the same "drinking houses" as we have now, and a number of sweet shops – Mrs Plumridge for one, and Sedgwicks, a cottage shop in one of the houses fronting the High Street. There was a market gardener and greengrocer who also boasted fish and chips twice weekly and home-made ice cream in the summer as well as flowers and poultry, the post office within Blewitt's shop at Ship Lane corner, and Barclays Bank (complete with aspidistras) next to Mrs Plumridge's shop – it was her front room which was leased by Barclays. We even had an abattoir, a wheelwright and a farrier and, as you can imagine, several farms surrounding the village.

All the lighting was by oil lamp or gas light so the picture was of quite a Christmas card village at the festive season, and with all these businesses the village was certainly very busy at this time of year. Home deliveries were made by trades-bike after orders had been taken by the various shops – no queueing or waiting at the checkout at Tesco's, and the shops were "open all hours"!

A complete Christmas grocery order for a family would cost around twelve shillings and a huge leg of lamb was no more than two shillings and sixpence. How about a box of Cadbury's chocs for sixpence?

For my family, being business people, this was an extremely busy time. Normally it was a trip to market three times a week, but at Christmas time it was up at 4 am and market every day. My grandfather went by horse and cart – either Prince, Kit or Tom at the helm, but my father had evolved to an old Model-T Ford with solid tyres.

On Christmas Day the whole family would gather together for Christmas tea and games. There were quite a number of us – aunts, uncles and cousins together with grandparents, friends and neighbours, and of course there was always a visit from Santa.

Boxing Day was spent at my maternal grandparents' cottage home and as people arrived and entered by the front door, everyone was eased backwards and finished up in the scullery or halfway up the stairs which led off from the kitchen. There was a present from Granny for all who arrived, be it a handkerchief or a tablet of Lux toilet soap. No one was left out and the table was always laden with a buffet for us all to enjoy.

The church choir always came around the village singing carols, and there were no girls then in the choir – all lads and men, about 36 of them. The Aveley Band have always honoured us with their Christmas music, the same all those years ago as it is now, the only difference being that then the whole band consisted of Aveley bandsmen.'

COAL FOR LUCK

'We lived at Brentwood in the 1930s and the children around us never had many toys. At Christmas they hung up their socks, and would find inside a piece of coal for luck, an orange, an apple, sweets, and maybe a ball or a skipping rope, but we were all happy with what we got. Mum did her best for Christmas dinner, with chicken or rabbit, and a pudding boiled in the copper the clothes were washed in.'

BOXING DAY FERRETING

'Some men at Great Bardfield kept ferrets in the backyard, in a wired wooden cage. Boxing Day was always "keeping the tradition", and going forth with a "four ten" gun, nets and the ferrets to catch a rabbit or two – and perhaps an illicit pheasant! A certain rector was known to shoot pheasants (previously enticed with grain) from his study window.'

Index

List of Contributing Institutes

Contributions have been received from the following Essex Women's Institutes:

Aldham, Althorne, Arkesden, Aveley, Barnston, Bassett, Belchamp St Paul & District, Berechurch, Billericay, Bishops Hall Park, Blackmore, Black Notley, Boreham, Boxted, Broomfield, Buckhurst Hill, Bulphan, Burnham on Crouch, Canvey Island, Castle Hedingham, Chadwell, Chigwell, Chingford, Colchester Centre, Cranham Engayne, Danbury, Doddinghurst, Dolphin, Dovercourt, Earls Colne, Eastons & Tilty, Engains, Epping, Erdelega, Eves Corner, Fobbing & Corringham, Friars Grove, Frietuna, Frinton on Sea, Gosfield, Great Bentley, Great Hallingbury, Great & Little Sampford, Great Totham, Great Warley, Greenstead Green, Gunfleet, Hall Green, Harlow, Harold Wood, Hatfield Peverel, Hawkwell, Henny & Middleton, High Roding & Great Canfield, Home Farm, Homestead, Hutton, Kelvedon, Kingston, Kirby le Soken, Lambourne, Langdon Hills, Langham, Langley, Layer de la Haye, Little Baddow, Littlebury Green, Little Walden, Little Warley & Childerditch, Loughton, Loughton Valley, Maldon Centre, The Maplesteads, Marks Tey, Mayland, Moreton & District, Navestock, Nelmes, North Weald, Orchard Springs, Orsett, Paglesham, Paycockes, Purleigh, Ramsdale, Ramsden Bellhouse, Rayleigh, Rayne, Ridgewell, Rosebay, Roxwell, Sandon, Sewardstone, Shalford, Sheering, Shenfield & Hutton Morning, Shenfield, Shoebury Village, Sible Hedingham, South Benfleet, South Minster, Springfield Afternoon, Stambridge, Stansted Afternoon, Stisted, Stock, Stondon Massey, Strood, Theydon Bois, Thundersley Village, Tollesbury, Upminster & Cranham, Walton on the Naze, Wendens Ambo, White Notley & Faulkbourne, Wickham Bishops & Great Totham, Wickham St Paul, Twinstead & Gestingthorpe, Widford, Willingale, Witham, Woodham Ferrers, Woodford Green, Writtle Afternoon.